The Birth of a Jungle

The Birth of a Jungle

Animality in Progressive-Era U.S. Literature and Culture

MICHAEL LUNDBLAD

OXFORD
UNIVERSITY PRESS

OXFORD
UNIVERSITY PRESS

Oxford University Press is a department of the University of Oxford.
It furthers the University's objective of excellence in research, scholarship,
and education by publishing worldwide.

Oxford   New York
Auckland   Cape Town   Dar es Salaam   Hong Kong   Karachi
Kuala Lumpur   Madrid   Melbourne   Mexico City   Nairobi
New Delhi   Shanghai   Taipei   Toronto

With offices in
Argentina   Austria   Brazil   Chile   Czech Republic   France   Greece
Guatemala   Hungary   Italy   Japan   Poland   Portugal   Singapore
South Korea   Switzerland   Thailand   Turkey   Ukraine   Vietnam

Oxford is a registered trademark of Oxford University Press
in the UK and certain other countries.

Published in the United States of America by
Oxford University Press
198 Madison Avenue, New York, NY 10016

Library of Congress Cataloging-in-Publication Data
Lundblad, Michael.
The birth of a jungle : animality in progressive-era U.S. literature and culture / Michael Lundblad.
p. cm.
Includes bibliographical references.
ISBN 978-0-19-991757-0
1. Animals in literature.   2. Human-animal relationships in literature.   3. American literature—
20th century—History and criticism.   I. Title.
PS228.A54L87   2013
810.9'362—dc23
2012019591

For Lizzie

Contents

Acknowledgments

I COULD NOT have developed and completed this book without the help and support of dozens of colleagues, friends, and family who continue to sustain me both personally and professionally. It is an honor and a pleasure to acknowledge some of these people, even if the list cannot be comprehensive. This project has witnessed a lot: the birth of my daughter, Harper; the illness and death of my wife, Lizzie; the companionship and death of my dog, Cooper; the illness and death of my nephew Jackson; the model of progressive living by my mother, Karen, and her partner, Lucy; and the reaffirming love of my new wife, Sonya. I am so grateful to everyone who has empowered me to keep striving with this work.

This book began as a dissertation at the University of Virginia, with an irreplaceable and inspiring committee: Eric Lott, Jennifer Wicke, Steve Cushman, and Carl Trindle. I am particularly thankful for the sage advice and steadfast support of Jennifer Wicke and Eric Lott for more than a decade. I am also grateful to other faculty members past and present at UVA, including Jim and Marcia Childress, Mark Edmundson, Elizabeth Fowler, Susan Fraiman, Jenny Geddes, Eleanor Kaufman, Chuck Mathewes, Erik Middelfort, David Morris, Teju Olaniyan, Ben and Maruta Ray, Marlon Ross, Marion Rust, Scott Saul, and Chip Tucker. Many thanks to fellow graduate students who became good friends: Sarah Hagelin, Justin Gifford, Andrea Stevens, Jolie Sheffer, Jayme Schwartzberg, Paul Gaffney, Michael Lewis, Willis Jenkins, and Rebekah Menning, as well as our environmental reading group: Melissa White, Bart Welling, Ann Dickinson, Maria Windell, and Sean Borton. Crucial financial support at UVA came from a Sara Shallenberger Brown Fellowship in Environmental Literature, a Graduate School of Arts and Sciences Dissertation Year Fellowship, the Seven Society, the Thomas J. Griffis Prize, and funding from the English department to participate twice in the Dartmouth American Studies Institute.

I would like to acknowledge the support of several institutions that enabled me to develop these ideas in a variety of ways, including Syracuse University, where I spent a year as a Postdoctoral Faculty Fellow in the Humanities, and the University of Nevada, Reno, where I earned an M.A. in Literature and Environment. I am grateful for the help and inspiration of Cheryll Glotfelty, Mike Branch, Ann Ronald, and Scott Slovic. At Colorado State University, I have been fortunate to have the support of Liberal Arts Dean Ann Gill, current and past chairs of the English department, Louann Reid and Bruce Ronda, as well as my colleagues in the department and across the university, including Dan Beachy-Quick, Leif Sorensen, Temple Grandin, Bernie Rollin, and Jane Shaw.

For financial support, I would like to thank Colorado State University for several Professional Development Program grants, the STINT Foundation in Sweden, the Centre for Gender Research at Uppsala University, and the Taiwanese Ministry of Education.

Colleagues at these and other institutions have provided much appreciated support and advice: Frida Beckman, Tora Holmberg, Jacob Bull, David Redmalm, Lisa Käll, Ann-Sofie Lönngren, Danuta Fjellestad, Robin Chen-hsing Tsai, Sun-chieh Liang, and Lisa Ying-wen Yu. Other valued colleagues and friends who have provided important encouragement and feedback include Rachel Adams, Don Pease, Colleen Boggs, Anne-Lise François, Laurie Shannon, Cary Wolfe, Elizabeth Dillon, Brett Mizelle, Jonathan Auerbach, Chuck Bergman, Dana Seitler, Matthew Calarco, Tina Gianquitto, Harold Fromm, Susan McHugh, Leo Marx, and Bill Kittredge.

I would particularly like to thank Neel Ahuja, Marlon Ross, and Marianne DeKoven for their thoughtful and constructive readings of earlier drafts of these chapters, along with anonymous readers for Oxford University Press. I am also indebted to Matt Bradley, who is a fantastic and thorough research assistant, and Brendan O'Neill and all of the staff at Oxford University Press for their guidance and assistance.

Many thanks to friends and family who have supported me and made it more fun along the way: Dan and Kristy Beachy-Quick, Dan Virgilio and Allison Wilder, Mindy and Ted O'Connor, Sarah Hagelin, Tara Troy, Kristen McElhiney, Jenn Broder, Paul and Nancy Margie, everyone associated with The MetaCancer Foundation, Merry and Ed Prostic, Seth and Lisa Prostic, Laura Prostic, Bunni and Paul Copaken, Bob and Lis Lundblad, Lucy McIver, and Karen Lundblad, whose life has been an inspiration for this project from the very beginning.

Finally, I want to thank my wife, Sonya, for her incomparable love; my dog, Cooper, for giving me a daily source of both critical reflection and much needed affection; and my daughter, Harper, for giving me the most important reason in the world to keep striving. I love you more than air.

* * *

Part of the Introduction was previously published as "From Animal to Animality Studies," *PMLA* 124.2 (2009): 496–502. Reprinted by permission of the Modern Language Association.

An earlier version of chapter 1 was previously published as "Epistemology of the Jungle: Progressive-Era Sexuality and the Nature of the Beast," *American Literature* 81.4 (2009): 747–73. Copyright, 2009, Duke University Press. All rights reserved. Reprinted by permission of the present publisher, Duke University Press.

An earlier version of chapter 5 was previously published as "Archaeology of a Humane Society: Animality, Savagery, Blackness," *Species Matters: Humane Advocacy and Cultural Theory*, ed. Marianne DeKoven and Michael Lundblad (New York: Columbia UP, 2012), 75–102. Copyright © 2012, Columbia University Press. Reprinted with permission of the publisher.

Figure 2, "Ready for Roosevelt" by Louis M. Glackens, is reprinted from *Puck*, 2 Oct. 1907, with permission of the Theodore Roosevelt Collection, Harvard College Library. Ms Am 1895 (253), Houghton Library, Harvard University.

Figure 6 is reprinted with the permission of the artist, Neal Adams.

The Birth of a Jungle

Introduction

The Nature of the Beast in U.S. Culture

IT'S A JUNGLE out there, supposedly: from Wall Street to the inner city; from animal instincts for (heterosexual) sex to national drives to be the fittest or most civilized nation on the planet. According to the "law of the jungle," the behavior of wild animals can be equated with natural human instincts not only for competition and reproduction but also for violence and exploitation. Titles of books about the U.S. marketplace illustrate this logic, such as *Monkey Business: Swinging Through the Wall Street Jungle*; *The Ape in the Corner Office: Understanding the Workplace Beast in All of Us*; and even labor histories such as *Unionizing the Jungles: Labor and Community in the Twentieth-Century Meatpacking Industry*.[1] The translation of animal instincts into human animality is what enables Sigmund Freud to declare in *Civilization and Its Discontents* (1930) that "Man is a wolf to man."[2] According to Freud, men are "creatures among whose instinctual endowments is to be reckoned a powerful share of aggressiveness. As a result, their neighbor is for them not only a potential helper or sexual object, but also someone who tempts them to satisfy their aggressiveness on him, to exploit his capacity for work without compensation, to use him sexually without his consent, to seize his possessions, to humiliate him, to cause him pain, to torture and to kill him."[3] Despite Freud's patriarchal pronouns (which lead to the perhaps surprising formulation of a man tempted to "use" his male neighbor sexually), the construction of a human being as a wolf in this sense resonates with what I identify in this book as the *discourse of the jungle* in the United States. Historically, this discourse is relatively new, from my perspective, but it has had a tremendous impact on the way a wide range of human behaviors have been explained or justified, particularly since the turn of the twentieth century. My general project in this book is to explore the historical emergence of the jungle as a discourse in the United States, including various cultural texts that resist it, in order to argue that this discourse is more recent, complicated, and significant than current scholarship tends to suggest.

The discourse of the jungle revolves around questions related to the figure of "the animal": constructing the nature of "the beast" in terms of both "real" animals and the human being as a Darwinist-Freudian animal. It produces new constructions of animality as "naturally" violent in the name of survival, and heterosexual in the name of reproduction. While the discourse of the jungle is thus derived from the work of Darwin and Freud, as well as from evolutionary theory in general, it can be distinguished from some of the ambiguities and complexities in Darwin's own work. But it is not solidified in U.S. culture until more recently than we might otherwise think. How far back do we need to go, then, to locate the birth of this discourse? We could start with William Jennings Bryan's objections to "monkey" ancestors in the Scopes trial of 1925, or go back to D. W. Griffith's *The Birth of a Nation* in 1915, with its racist construction of the mythic black male rapist as a savage beast. World War I and the Spanish-American War were simultaneously justified and condemned within the logic of "survival of the fittest" among nations, while many literary naturalists at the turn of the century were preoccupied with the implications of evolution. European influences would certainly include Charles Darwin's *The Descent of Man* (1871) and *On the Origin of Species* (1859), but there are even earlier formulations that might also seem important, such as Tennyson's "Nature, red in tooth and claw," from "In Memoriam A.H.H." (1850), or further back to Hobbes's characterization of human life as "nasty, brutish, and short" in *Leviathan* (1651). We might wonder if all these formulations (and others going back as far as the ancient Greeks) could be linked to current thinking about what we might call "the beast within," or the human as an animal.

With a commitment to historical and cultural specificity, though, I find it problematic to connect all these formulations together in any simple way, even if influences and reactions can be traced productively. I believe we can uncover a history of *animality* without assuming that even the same word "animal" signifies the same figure or trope at different historical and cultural moments. Laurie Shannon has argued recently, for example, that our current abstract nominalization of "the animal" does not exist until the Cartesian construction of it; prior to Descartes, Shakespeare uses the word "animal" only eight times in all his work, even though he uses a range of other terms in reference to specific kinds of animals.[4] From my perspective, to take another example, the invocation of *homo homini lupus* (man is a wolf to man) in Hobbes need not necessarily be identical with Freud's invocation of it nearly three hundred years later.[5] In this book I am primarily interested in what can be characterized as an explosion of literary and cultural texts focused on animality within a narrow time period, between 1894 and 1914, in the United States. During those two decades leading up to World War I, we find widely popular and influential works of fiction constructing jungle discourse, such as, most prominently, Upton Sinclair's *The Jungle* (1906), Rudyard Kipling's *The Jungle Book* (1894), *The Second Jungle Book* (1895), and *Just So Stories* (1902), and Henry James's "The Beast in the Jungle" (1903). Many of the first usages of phrases incorporating the word "jungle" in the English language are credited to Kipling in these texts. We also find works traditionally associated with literary naturalism focused on various "species" of animals or animal metaphors, such as Frank Norris's *The Octopus* (1901) and *Vandover and the Brute* (1914), and Jack London's *The Call of the Wild* (1903), *The Sea-Wolf* (1904), and *White Fang* (1906). Other texts at the turn of the century are invested in constructions of animality as well, such as Charles Chesnutt's *The Conjure Woman* (1899) and *The Marrow of Tradition* (1901); Thomas Dixon's "Reconstruction Trilogy": *The Leopard's Spots* (1902), *The Clansman* (1903), which became the basis of Griffith's *The Birth of a Nation*, and *The Traitor* (1907); James Weldon Johnson's *The Autobiography of an Ex-Colored Man* (1912); Kate Chopin's *The Awakening* (1899); Charlotte Perkins Gilman's *Herland* (1915); and Edgar Rice Burroughs's *Tarzan of the Apes* (1914).[6] Examples of the "wild animal story" also proliferate during these two decades, including many of London's most famous works, as well as Ernest Thompson Seton's wildly popular *Wild Animals I Have Known* (1898), William J. Long's *School of the Woods* (1902), and Charles Alexander Eastman's *Red Hunters and the Animal People* (1904). This proliferation of texts negotiating constructions of animality at the turn of the twentieth century presumably could be explained simply as evidence that Darwinian thinking had achieved hegemony in the United States, forty to fifty years after his major works were published. But all these texts do not easily fit into such an explanation. In fact, as this book will explore, many of them offer striking alternatives to a Darwinian understanding of animality.

The Progressive Animal

Why, then, do representations of the jungle proliferate just over a century ago? The intervention of Freud, within the context of the new fields of psychology

and sociology, is crucial, I believe, along with Progressive-Era efforts to understand and regulate exploitative behaviors of various kinds. In the discourse of
the jungle, the behavior of "real" animals comes to represent "natural" human
instincts, particularly in terms of violence and heterosexuality. A major shift
occurs once the desire to have sex or to exploit one's neighbor is less likely
to be seen as a lustful, evil, or devilish impulse within a Protestant Christian
framework, and more likely to be seen as a natural instinct within the human
animal. Conversely, an "unnatural" desire, such as a homosexual one, could be
condemned for threatening Darwinian reproduction rather than a Christian
god's will. Darwin's *On the Origin of Species by Means of Natural Selection; or,
The Preservation of Favoured Races in the Struggle for Life* was first published
in 1859, and the sequel, *The Descent of Man, and Selection in Relation to Sex*,
followed in 1871. But the key confluence, in my view, was when Freudian psychoanalysis traveled to U.S. shores and translated Darwinist constructions of
"real" animals into "animal instincts" within the human psyche.[7] The early work
of Freud, such as *The Interpretation of Dreams* (1900), *The Psychopathology of
Everyday Life* (1901), and *Three Essays on the Theory of Sexuality* (1905), crys-
tallized these constructions of human animality for European and American
psychologists, such as Richard von Krafft-Ebing, Havelock Ellis, G. Stanley
Hall, and William James.

Freud's visit to the United States in 1909 brought him into contact with
James and Hall, and his Clark University lectures indicated how his formulation of psychoanalysis was built, at least in part, on the naturalization
of animal instincts.[8] Freud insists that to break down the ill effects of "civilized" repression, for example, "we ought not to go so far as to fully neglect
the animal part of our nature."[9] In his 1917 paper, "A Difficulty in the Path
of Psycho-analysis," he reveals his premise that the instincts of the human
mind are derived from "hunger and love, as being the representatives of the
instincts which aim respectively at the preservation of the individual and at
the reproduction of the species."[10] Freud famously identifies Darwin as dealing the "biological blow" to human narcissism: "Man is not a being different
from animals or superior to them; he himself is of animal descent, being more
closely related to some species and more distantly to others."[11] A human being's
animal instincts thus become essential for understanding human behavior.
The third and final blow to human narcissism, according to Freud, is the psychoanalytic discovery that the human mind cannot always control or even be
aware of its unconscious instincts, including those that can be explained by its
"animal descent."[12] This Darwinist-Freudian framework soon associates animality with the supposedly essential, biological instincts for heterosexuality

in the name of reproduction and for violence in the name of survival. Kill or be killed, in other words, and produce as many offspring as you can. The animal within you, just like the animal in the wild, is naturally hardwired for survival in the jungle, even if the human part of you is defined by the capacity for restraining—or repressing—those animal instincts, or so the logic goes.[13]

The central claim of this book, though, is that texts from the turn of the century that are often thought to epitomize this kind of logic also include varied forms of *resistance* to the Darwinist-Freudian jungle, particularly as they explore alternative formulations of human violence and sexuality. Critical attention to what *else* animality might signify during that period can reveal alternatives to the growing hegemony of the jungle. While Darwinist-Freudian constructions of animality historically have justified atrocities related to eugenics, imperialist conquest, and widespread abuses of nonhuman animals, for example, the alternative constructions of animality explored in this book suggest different possibilities, even though they are not necessarily always better. At the turn of the century, the discourse of the jungle was much more unsettled, complex, and inconsistent than current critical interpretations tend to suggest. Chapters of this book thus focus on different formulations, such as desire and pleasure that would not lead to propagation, in Henry James's "The Beast in the Jungle" and Jack London's *The Call of the Wild*; corporate exploitation that is more monstrous than animalized, in Upton Sinclair's *The Jungle* and Frank Norris's *The Octopus*; and distorted evolutionary hierarchies that place animality above blackness, in Edgar Rice Burroughs's *Tarzan of the Apes* and William James's antilynching and antivivisection advocacy. These texts, juxtaposed with the contemporaneous work of figures such as Freud, Herbert Spencer, Andrew Carnegie, Theodore Roosevelt, Ida B. Wells, W. E. B. Du Bois, and William Jennings Bryan, point toward a historical moment in which constructions of animality—both human and nonhuman—seem rather different from what we might expect today.

Consider Topsy, for example: a circus elephant publicly electrocuted in front of a large crowd at Coney Island in 1903; should animals (and the working-class immigrants they sometimes symbolized) be punished as agents responsible for their own actions? Or, Ota Benga: an African man publicly displayed in the Monkey House of the Bronx Zoo in 1906; could animals be claimed as closer to white men within evolutionary discourse, making "savages" somehow "lower" than animals? This book explores these issues in relation to other historical questions as well: Why does growing pressure to treat animals more "humanely" coincide with an explosion of lynchings at the end of the nineteenth century? What is the relationship between new constructions of animality and the invention of "the homosexual," along with the corporation newly defined as a "person," at that same historical moment? Exploring these questions reveals how cultural events and texts both produce and resist the discourse of the jungle in complicated ways. Together, they illustrate how new constructions of what it means to be human, as well as animal, become broadly significant in U.S. culture at the turn of the twentieth century. These constructions of animality become mutually constitutive, for example, with new ways of thinking about human races, classes, genders, and sexualities, in various intersecting formulations.

How to Do the History of Animality

New ways of thinking about animality were not necessarily reducible to whether one believed in evolution, natural selection, or social Darwinism, although these discourses were certainly relevant at the turn of the century. The key reference point in the discourse of the jungle was the construction of what was "natural" for "the animal," whether in the wild or within the human, even if one generally argued that the human part of the human was far more significant than the beast within. The history of animality in relation to jungle discourse can thus be distinguished in part from related histories of evolution and Darwinism, pointing toward the jungle as a broader and more influential discourse that continues to be deployed even today. Since scientific consensus (as well as earlier debates) about evolution and Darwinism can be traced back to the mid-nineteenth century, most scholarly studies assume that the turn of the twentieth century can be characterized by the pervasiveness of belief in some form of evolution. In *Evolution: The History of an Idea* (2003), Peter J. Bowler argues, "By 1875 the majority of educated people in Europe and America had accepted evolution."[14] Among scientists, according to Ronald L. Numbers in *Darwinism Comes to America* (1999), by the end of the 1870s, "scientific opposition in North America had diminished to a whisper."[15] Numbers suggests that by the end of the nineteenth century, liberal Protestants, Catholics, and Jews had all found ways to accommodate evolution.[16] In *Darwin in America: The Intellectual Response, 1865–1912* (1976), Cynthia Eagle Russett argues, "By 1898 Darwinism had largely ceased to be considered an alien cancer on the body of American intellectual life. It had been scrutinized, sifted for useful ideas and methods, and incorporated in one way or another into the general stock of most academic disciplines."[17]

Most historians of evolution and Darwinism distinguish between these two terms, noting that Darwinism was equated with natural selection as the primary means of evolution. Scientists might believe in evolution, for example, but disagree that natural selection was the primary driver of the process. As Edward J. Larson indicates in *Summer for the Gods: The Scopes Trial and America's Continuing Debate over Science and Religion* (1997), the turn of the twentieth century was called the "eclipse of Darwinism" by Julian Huxley, T. H. Huxley's grandson, not because scientists no longer believed in evolution but because there were many competing theories that were opposed to Darwin's theory of natural selection.[18] Bert Bender's *Evolution and "the Sex Problem": American Narratives during the Eclipse of Darwinism* (2004) goes to great lengths to distinguish between the work of Darwin and, for example, that of Joseph Le Conte, Henri Bergson, Peter Kropotkin, and Ernst Haeckel, as well as key psychological texts, such as Geddes and Thomson's *The Evolution of Sex* (1889), Joseph T. Cunningham's *Sexual Dimorphism in the Animal Kingdom* (1900), and Havelock Ellis's *Studies in the Psychology of Sex* (1897–1910). Bender's claim is that "the sex problem," from Darwin's theory of sexual selection, is central to American literature, both before and after literary naturalism, arguing that "a broad range of American writers explored sexual *reality* in the context of evolutionary thought."[19] A major difference between my and Bender's view of "reality" is this supposedly self-evident truth of evolutionary discourse.[20] Bender is right to point out how Ellis focuses on the centrality of sex, though, in 1897: "We want to know what is naturally lawful under the various chances that befall man, not as the born child of sin, but as a naturally social animal."[21] But Bender has no comment on the shift thus registered from Christian to Darwinian language: a shift that is central to the discourse of the jungle, from my perspective.

Jungle discourse is more preoccupied with implications of what it might mean to be an animal (whether human or nonhuman) than with scientific debates over various evolutionary theories, and it is far from settled at the turn of the century. Bender's approach is to determine, in a sense, how Darwinian various writers might have been at that moment; "whether or not a particular novelist drew on one of the specifically anti-Darwinian theories, such as Le Conte's, Bergson's, or Kropotkin's, all the novels treated here *begin* with Darwin."[22] From Bender's perspective, Jack London would thus be "one of American literature's most perceptive and devoted Darwinians" and the "chief American writer of these years to resist the eclipse of Darwinism."[23] But how should we respond, for example, to the erotic fireworks that often light up the wild when London's human characters interact with dogs and wolves, in texts such as *The Call of the Wild* (1903) and *White Fang* (1906)? London characterizes the love between the dog Buck and his human partner, John Thornton, in *The Call of the Wild* as: "Love, genuine passionate love.... love that was feverish and burning, that was adoration, that was madness."[24] In *White Fang*, the half-wolf of the title experiences a love for Weedon Scott that "manifested itself to [White Fang] as a void in his being—a hungry, aching, yearning void that clamored to be filled. It was a pain and an unrest; and it received easement only by the touch of the new god's presence."[25] Whether we read these nonhuman characters as "real" animals or "men in furs," in Mark Seltzer's memorable phrase, how can we reconcile these erotic feelings with instincts driven by Darwinian reproduction?[26] Jack London might have thought of himself as a Darwinian, but his texts reflect and produce broader cultural anxieties and alternatives in relation to sexuality, for example, whether he is conscious of them or not.

There might be general agreement among historians that evolution—as a process explaining the development of both human and nonhuman animals—was considered a fact at the turn of the century, at least among scientists, educated people, and liberal theologians. But belief in evolution did not necessarily translate into a belief in social Darwinism. According to Richard Hofstadter's classic study, *Social Darwinism in American Thought* (1944), the *critics* of social Darwinism, such as Lester Ward and pragmatists such as William James, succeeded in debunking the dominant logic of social Darwinist thinking at the turn of the twentieth century. In the last three decades of the nineteenth century, Hofstadter identifies social Darwinism with a conservative resistance to reform based upon the individual struggle to survive: "The most popular catchwords of Darwinism, 'struggle for existence' and 'survival of the fittest,' when applied to the life of man in society, suggested that nature would provide that the best competitors in a competitive situation would win, and that this process would lead to continuing improvement."[27] As Larson notes in *Summer for the Gods*, "Many Americans associated Darwinian natural selection, as it applied to people, with a survival-of-the-fittest mentality that justified laissez-faire capitalism, imperialism, and militarism,"[28] particularly as this logic was articulated by Herbert Spencer. The other aspect of social Darwinism used to resist reform, according to Hofstadter, was the "glacially" slow pace of change within the evolutionary narrative: "the idea of development over aeons brought new force to another familiar idea in conservative political theory, the conception that all sound development must be slow and unhurried. Society could be envisaged as an organism (or as an entity something like an organism), which could change only at the glacial pace at which new species are produced in nature."[29]

Hofstadter reads the Progressive Era as a shift toward a reform-minded rejection of social Darwinism, even though imperialism and racism are justified in the first few decades of the century within the logic of races and nations struggling to survive. Reformers might then point toward examples of collectivism in nature to refute the argument that selfish individualism is "natural." According to Hofstadter, World War I represents the turning point (and terminal point) of social Darwinist thinking, putting an end to biological justifications of warfare and violence: "These dogmas were employed with success until the outbreak of the First World War. Then, ironically, the 'Anglo-Saxon' peoples were swept by a revulsion from international violence. They now turned about and with one voice accused the enemy of being the sole advocate of 'racial' aggression and militarism" (203). Acknowledging the hypocrisy of such an accusation, Hofstadter still argues that "As a conscious philosophy, social Darwinism had largely disappeared in America by the end of the war" (203). His conclusion echoes William James, who, as Hofstadter notes, claimed that "the idea that mind ministers to survival alone cannot explain the full range of higher cultural activities which have no survival value" (131). There is more to the human, to put it in different terms, than animal instincts. Hofstadter himself argues that "the life of man in society, while it is incidentally a biological fact, has characteristics that are not reducible to biology and must be explained in the distinctive terms of a cultural analysis" (204). Whether we agree with Hofstadter and James or not, we can see how their logic implies that the supposedly *animal* side of life (which is concerned with survival and can be reduced to biology) can still be explained in Darwinist-Freudian terms. Constructions of animality at the turn of the twentieth century, then, can be seen as moving toward the discourse of the jungle, which persists, in my view, long past World War I.

Hofstadter's analysis has been criticized by later historians of social Darwinism, but these critics also reveal the limitations of focusing exclusively on this discourse. Perhaps most prominently, Robert C. Bannister's *Social Darwinism: Science and Myth in Anglo-American Social Thought* (1979) attacks Hofstadter's claims about the extent of Darwin's influence at the end of the nineteenth century. Bannister sees social Darwinism as a caricatured (and often unfair) blanket term used only against beliefs one doesn't like: "social Darwinism is singular in that virtually no one adopted it as a badge of honor. A social Darwinist, to oversimplify the case, was something nobody wanted to be."[30] According to Bannister, the label of social Darwinist should only be applied to one "who embroidered his (and, far less frequently, her) message with the phrases *natural selection, the struggle for existence,* or *the survival of the fittest*, or who otherwise invoked the authority of Charles Darwin or the *Origin of Species* in discussing social policy" (xii). From this perspective, "References to 'nature,' 'natural,' or even the 'social organism,' in the absence of tell-tale Darwinian phrases, do not count either" (xii). While this approach might bring greater precision to the phrase "social Darwinism," it does little to help our understanding of why the broader label or accusation—echoing Hofstadter's broader usage of the phrase—persists past World War I, up through debates over sociobiology in the 1970s and 1980s, as Bannister himself acknowledges (xii). A narrower history of social Darwinism, in other words, is less useful than pursuing a history of animality within jungle discourse, including shifting constructions of the animal at the turn of the twentieth century.

Another framework that is useful for understanding animality at that historical moment is one that has been explored in provocative ways by Dana Seitler in *Atavistic Tendencies: The Culture of Science in American Modernity* (2008). Covering many of the same works that I explore in this book, Seitler's general project is to explore atavism—"a theory of biological reversion emerging out of modern science"[31]—as not only a biological category and a theoretical concept but also a "historical category that emerged to (re)produce and negotiate social anxieties over the status of the human being" (10). Focused primarily upon constructions of modern subjectivity, Seitler's claim is that "Modernity is an atavism. Its advent in Western culture led to and was given shape by political, social, and aesthetic developments that can be characterized by a recursive temporal subjectivity" (1).[32]

I believe we need more specificity, though, when exploring what "the animal" signifies at the turn of the twentieth century. This is not to say that atavism is not a productive discourse at that moment—to the contrary, I find Seitler's work compelling, insightful, and complementary to my own in this book. But, as Seitler notes, atavism is "not much in use in our everyday vocabulary" (1), even if it was more common at the turn of the twentieth century. Further, Seitler suggests that "when we think of the past, we don't tend to think of the figure of the animal" (13). In the discourse of the jungle, though, which I would argue to be more pervasive than atavism both a century ago and today, the past is the history of human beings acting out—or restraining—their animal instincts. The figure of the animal, then, is always present. And while there is a risk—and sometimes a desire—that the animal will be unleashed within the human being, narratives of degeneration or regression do not always best represent the ways that certain groups of people have been historically animalized; rather than returning to an animal state from the human, or cycling back and forth from one to the other, some groups of people have been denied ever achieving humanity in an evolutionary sense. The construction of the animal, in other words, can be very different in relation to various human groups, from "savage" Africans to "civilized" white Americans, from working-class immigrants to middle-class muckrakers and reformers, to name just a few groups highlighted in this book.

Animal Studies, Posthumanism, and Animality Studies

The history of animality, from my perspective, can be focused productively on its cultural significance in relation to human oppression, violence, and exploitation. But it needs to pay attention to various ways of thinking about "real" animals as well, including the ways that various kinds of animals have been treated historically by various human groups. While my methodology is not driven primarily by an explicit form of advocacy for animals, it approaches "the question of the animal," as Jacques Derrida has recently put it, with a different kind of advocacy in mind.[33] Biological explanations of behavior—supposedly driven by instincts for reproduction and survival—are constructed by the discourse of the jungle for both human and nonhuman animals. My hope is that revealing the constructed nature of this discourse for humans (rather than reinforcing an essentialist evolutionary "reality") might also help us to see it as a constructed discourse for "real" animals as well, whose lives are more complex than many biological explanations suggest.[34] One of the purposes of this book, in other words, is to explore alternatives to thinking about *either* human or nonhuman animals as "beasts" in the Darwinist-Freudian discourse of the jungle. Most people would presumably object to constructing or treating various human groups as "animals," but we also need to pay critical attention to problematic histories of animalizing *animals*, in which they are seen as driven essentially, if not exclusively, by instincts for violence and heterosexuality. This kind of motivation can still be seen as a form of advocacy, but it suggests a different approach when compared with much of the work that is being called animal studies in the academy today.

Animal studies has been strongly influenced by the recent work of Jacques Derrida, Donna Haraway, and Cary Wolfe, among many others, often with a focus on how difficult it has become to maintain easy distinctions between "the human" and "the animal." With incredibly rich and complex inquiries into the question of the animal, much of this work has prompted fundamental reconsiderations of nonhuman and human difference, otherness, and subjectivity. But the phrase "animal studies" strikes me as too limiting, too easily mistaken for a unified call for universal advocacy for nonhuman animals.[35] I believe a distinction should be made between critical attention to how we think about "real" animals and various forms of advocacy that emphasize treating nonhuman animals better or that prioritize identifying whether texts and practices succeed or fail in modeling ethical treatment of animals. Animal studies can be associated even further with that kind of advocacy, with work explicitly concerned about the living conditions of nonhuman animals. Despite the fact that animal studies up to this point has been seen as a more expansive term, including work that sometimes focuses more on human cultural politics than on nonhuman animal advocacy, I believe it would be useful to narrow the category now, even when considering how to categorize various examples of scholarly work that might previously have been identified as animal studies.

Conversely, "animality studies" can be a term to describe work that does not prioritize advocacy for various nonhuman animals, even though it shares an interest in how we think about "real" animals. Animality studies can prioritize questions of human cultural politics, then, in relation to how we have thought about human and nonhuman animality at various historical and cultural moments. In retrospect, the earlier work of Donna Haraway in *Primate Visions: Gender, Race, and Nature in the World of Modern Science* (1989), for example, can be categorized as closer to animality studies, while her more recent work, such as *When Species Meet* (2008), can be aligned more explicitly with animal studies, as I am defining it. Increased attention to the history of animality and related discourses from the perspective of animality studies can lead to new insights (and a different form of theoretical advocacy) in fields such as the history of sexuality, critical race studies, and American studies more broadly, with an eye toward antihomophobic, antiracist, and antisexist cultural politics, for example. To the extent that this kind of methodology resists engaging with explicit concern for nonhuman animals, it could be seen as "speciesist." But I believe there should be space for new critical work that might have different priorities, without an imperative to claim the advocacy for nonhuman animals that runs through much of the recent work in animal studies.

In *When Species Meet*, Haraway illustrates this concern for animals by drawing attention to the "actual wolves" that she finds absent in Gilles Deleuze and Félix Guattari's well-known critique of Freud's Wolf Man.[36] In their book *A Thousand Plateaus* (1987), Haraway finds instead a "call-of-the-wild version of a wolf pack" and "scorn for all that is mundane and ordinary and the profound absence of curiosity about or respect for and with *actual animals.*"[37] Derrida's "The Animal That Therefore I Am (More to Follow)" is similarly taken to task because "actual animals" are ultimately "oddly missing." Although Derrida writes "at length about a cat, his small female cat, in a particular bathroom on a real morning actually looking at him," he does not "seriously consider an alternative form of engagement" with that cat.[38] Derrida shares a kind of outrage with Haraway, though, when he focuses on "the annihilation of certain species" that is "occurring through the organization and exploitation of an artificial, infernal, virtually interminable survival."[39] In *Animal Rites: American Culture, the Discourse of Species, and Posthumanist Theory* (2003), Wolfe echoes this feeling when he suggests that in a hundred years we will most likely "look back on our current mechanized and systematized practices of factory farming, product testing, and much else that undeniably involves animal exploitation and suffering…with much the same horror and disbelief with which we now regard slavery or the genocide of the Second World War."[40] Wolfe is also clear that he has "no intention in this book of providing a 'foundation' on which we might justify more humane, less exploitative treatment of nonhuman animals," arguing instead that "the ethical and philosophical urgency of confronting the institution of speciesism and crafting a posthumanist theory of the subject *has nothing to do with whether you like animals*. We all, human and nonhuman alike, have a stake in the discourse and institution of speciesism…" (190, 7). But his "posthumanist ethical pluralism" also draws particular attention to the "overwhelmingly direct and disproportionate effects" that the institution of speciesism has on animals (7).

In his recent book, *What Is Posthumanism?* (2010), Wolfe brings together the question of the animal from Derrida with the significance of systems theory from Niklas Luhmann, but his formulation of posthumanism can be distinguished from animality studies as I am proposing it. While Wolfe makes clear once again that he is not interested in formulating universal principles in relation to the treatment of animals, he suggests that a posthumanist approach to thinking about nonhuman animals must be the most important or most profound form of advocacy to be done. The emphasis in *What Is Posthumanism?* is whether a given text or thinker is posthumanist enough, particularly in terms of whether there is a humanist formulation that limits subjectivity to the human. This kind of methodology strikes me as a brilliant and important application of Derrida and Luhmann to a wide range of contexts, but it also seems limited in terms of its stance toward historicized cultural studies and the political stakes most often inherent in that kind of work. According to Wolfe, Luhmann's second-order systems theory provides an "extraordinarily rigorous and detailed account of the fundamental dynamics and complexities of meaning that subtend the reproduction and interpenetration of psychic and social systems," as well as "the additional step of linking those dynamics to their biological, social, and historical conditions of emergence and transformation..."[41] While Derrida "has not been especially interested in articulating the relationship between the theoretical complexities of those dynamics and the historical and sociological conditions of their emergence..." (9), it becomes clear that Wolfe believes this position to be a "principled refusal on Derrida's part," rather than a failure (9). Thus evoking a very old debate between Derrida and Foucault, Wolfe concludes that "the empiricism on which any historicism depends and tacitly trades is rendered permanently problematic" (28). In a note later in the book, Wolfe makes the contrast more explicit: "from Derrida's vantage, Foucault's historicism, although it focuses on the production of the subject by external agencies, is not sufficiently aware of the production and nontransparency of his *own* discourse" (318n87). Wolfe clearly aligns himself with Derrida's stance, even though he makes very brief gestures at times to sketch Luhmann's thinking on "the relationship between the theoretical complexities of those dynamics and the historical and sociological conditions of their emergence..." (9). But I do not believe these gestures go far enough in terms of historicized cultural studies.

For Wolfe, Luhmann can give us a "theoretical vocabulary" for analyzing social systems, including nonhuman animals, while also suggesting a better way to understand Foucault's "blind spot." Art, for example, is "like any other autopoietic system" that "finds itself in an environment that is always already more complex than itself; and all systems...attempt to adapt to this complexity by filtering it in terms of their own, self-referential codes, which are based on a fundamental distinction by means of which they carry out their operations. The point of the system is to reproduce itself, but no system can deal with everything, or even many things, all at once—hence the need for a code of selectivity" (220–21). This means that "the environment is not an ontological category but a functional one," since it is "always the outside of a specific inside" (222). This way of thinking about a system can explain a wide variety of entities, from architectural design to the legal system, for example, in which "the distinction between the two sides legal/illegal is instantiated (or 'reentered,' to use Luhmann's terminology) on only one side of the distinction, namely, the legal" (222). But a system's "constitutive distinction" actually represents a "blind spot" that cannot be observed from within the system. As Wolfe points out, that "blind spot" can be "observed from the vantage of *another* system—it can, and that is what we are doing right now—but that second-order observation will itself be based on its *own* blind spot, thus for-mally reproducing a 'blindness' that is (formally) the same but (contingently) not the same as that of the first-order system" (223).

Wolfe's posthumanism therefore shies away from the kind of discourse analysis that animality studies might want to pursue, even if that kind of blind spot could be seen as less crucial, ultimately, in relation to the need for historicized cultural studies. Animality studies need not necessarily be dis-tinguished, then, from Wolfe's move to observe texts "from the vantage of *another* system" (223). One of the primary differences I see between animality studies and Wolfe's posthumanism, though, is the prioritization of politics (in animality studies) over philosophy, of historicized cultural studies over an emphasis on aesthetic form, with animality studies focusing more on discourse analysis within the framework of theoretical advocacy against a wide range of exploitative practices, even if it cannot proceed with that analysis from a transcendent observational position. But animality studies can certainly be seen as posthumanist in the sense of resisting universalist prescriptions and challenging essentialist constructions of "the human" and "the animal," par-ticularly in relation to specific historical and cultural contexts.[42]

The work of Donna Haraway can generally be seen as ranging from animal to animality studies, sometimes even within the same work, such as including an emphasis on situated histories that are not necessarily always focused on the treatment of nonhuman animals. In the opening pages of *When Species Meet*, for example, Haraway analyzes a digital picture of what appears to be a dog but is actually composed of a "burned-out redwood stump covered with redwood needles, mosses, ferns, lichens—and even a little California bay lau-rel seedling for a docked tail."[43] The central questions that she explores and clarifies throughout her book can be asked in relation to this creature, just as they can be asked in relation to "real" dogs: "Whom and what do we touch when we touch this dog? How does this touch make us more worldly, in alli-ance with all the beings who work and play for an alter-globalization that can endure more than one season?"[44] To respond to this dog, we must pay attention to intertwined histories: "Visually and tactilly, I am in the pres-ence of the intersectional race-, sex-, age-, class-, and region-differentiated sys-tems of labor that made...[this] dog live."[45] Representations of animality can thus point toward complex human histories, without necessarily prescribing how various human beings should treat various nonhuman beings, globally or locally.

Haraway's approach in this example resonates more closely with my own work in this book, in which I offer an animality studies approach

to a specific construction of animality at the turn of the twentieth century. I ask questions like Haraway's in relation to representations of both
nonhuman animals and humans as animals at that historical and cultural
moment. Most of the representations I explore are fictional, but there are
also "real" animals and people here too: from jackrabbits slaughtered *en
masse* in California to African Americans lynched throughout the South
(and elsewhere in the United States); from laboratory animals vivisected
in the name of "science" to union workers killed in the name of economic
"progress"; from histories of inhumane treatment to homophobic persecu-
tion in the context of the Wilde trials. Rather than focusing on whether
or not various movements succeeded in their resistance to these oppressive
contexts, or whether these contexts should be seen as equivalent, this book
focuses more on discursive resistance, on examples of texts that offer alternative constructions of what it means to be "human" or "animal" in relation to the growing hegemony of the Darwinist-Freudian jungle. Implicit
in this interest in alternative constructions, then, are antiracist, antisexist,
antihomophobic, and antioppressive motivations, among others, in both
human and nonhuman contexts.

Animality studies in this sense presumably becomes more relevant to
cultural studies in general, while animal studies, conversely, runs the risk of
reinforcing universalist prescriptions about how to treat or interact with all
nonhuman animals. But the spectrum running from animal studies to animality studies produces a unified insistence that critical attention to discourses
of animality is increasingly necessary, provocative, and even crucial within
literary and cultural studies today. There is more work to be done in animality studies, though, and this book is intended to lead that charge. In general
terms, we need further explorations of how constructions of the animal have
shifted historically in relation to the human, and how discourses of human
and nonhuman animality have produced various identity categories within
the human.[46]

The Nature of Naturalism

An animality studies approach to the discourse of the jungle at the turn of
the twentieth century reveals a more complex engagement with the question of the animal and constructions of the human than we might otherwise
assume. This book explores that complexity in dialogue with a range of current critical conversations, from histories of evolution and atavism, to animal and animality studies, to American studies more broadly. But studies of

literary naturalism are another important context for examining many of the primary texts in this book. Arguing for more subtlety and nuance in studies of naturalism is not necessarily new, but assumptions about the stability and consistency of what it means to be an animal within a naturalist text tend to remain in place. In *Women, Compulsion, Modernity: The Moment of American Naturalism* (2004), for example, Jennifer Fleissner argues that naturalism does not depict an equivalence between humans and animals but rather the intertwining of "the natural" and "the social" in the human, without necessarily privileging either one: "What is crucial to grasp here is the sense of the natural and the social as intertwined yet still distinct, thus calling for ongoing theorization of their interconnection; this is a very different thing from, for example, the social Darwinist view that the social world turns out to be simply equivalent to, a mirror of, an already grasped natural world of predator and prey."[47] But this approach, from my perspective, suggests a glossing over of the complexity of "the animal" within naturalism, even if it is constructed as part of a compulsive dialectic within "the human."

This kind of approach echoes, to a certain extent, part of Walter Benn Michaels's influential argument in *The Gold Standard and the Logic of Naturalism* (1987). Responding to earlier formulations of naturalism as choosing the "beastly" or animal side over the human side, Michaels argues instead for a logic that relies upon the "antithetical relation" between the two: "this doesn't mean that the naturalist writer is someone who has chosen the beastly side of these dichotomies (the side literary history ordinarily associates with naturalism) or even that he [*sic*] is someone who has chosen with any consistency either side. The consistency—indeed the identity—of naturalism resides in the logics and in their antithetical relation to one another, not necessarily in any individual, any text, or even any single sentence."[48] Yet even within this formulation, the connotations of "the beastly" are assumed to be stable and consistent at the turn of the century. In addition, as Fleissner notes, Michaels "swiftly became something of a poster boy for the shortcomings of the new-historicist criticism" with this book, mostly because it was actually not "historical enough."[49] New historicism like Michaels's was "deemed too eager to reduce history's actual complexity and unevenness of development to a single totalizing 'logic'—a *formal* structure, capable only of repeating the same set of patterns over and over again."[50] But there is a thread in studies of literary naturalism, I believe, running from Michaels to Fleissner, that continues to overlook the complexities of what it means to be an animal, the "natural" side of the human, in texts that both produce and resist the discourse of the jungle at the turn of the century.[51]

Michaels's work on the nature of representation at that historical moment, though, is useful for pointing toward new ways of exploring questions of animality that have thus far been overlooked. Michaels connects historical debates about the nature of money—whether paper money can represent "real" money in the form of gold or silver, for example—with both a literary text like Norris's *McTeague* and a political cartoon by Thomas Nast (figure 1).[52] In this cartoon, reprinted in David A. Wells's *Robinson Crusoe's Money* (1896), there is a piece of paper, meant to represent money, with the words "This is money" printed on it. In *McTeague*, as Michaels points out, the eponymous character is banned from being a dentist because he does not have a diploma: "McTeague can't practice dentistry, he can't *be* a dentist, unless he has the diploma, the piece of paper on his wall that says, 'This is a dentist,' like the piece of paper drawn by Nast that says, 'This is money.'"[53] Michaels works toward "an account of representation that ultimately identifies the possibility of money with the possibility of being a person…" (177), drawing parallels between constructions of what is supposedly "real" and what is only representation: precious metal as opposed

Figure 1 "Milk-Tickets for Babies, in Place of Milk" by Thomas Nast. From David A. Wells, *Robinson Crusoe's Money* (1896).

to paper money, paint as opposed to picture (as in *trompe l'oeil* paintings of paper money), and, ultimately (drawing upon the work of Joseph Le Conte in *Evolution* [1892] and William James in *The Principles of Psychology* [1890]), the physical brain of the human being as opposed to the ephemeral nature of the human mind, in which the ability to represent becomes the marker of the human, as opposed to the animal (160–74). Writing in general, according to Michaels, "marks the potential discrepancy between material and identity, the discrepancy that makes money, painting, and, ultimately, persons possible" (169–70). But Michaels's analysis of "persons" at the turn of the century suggests that everyone agrees what an *animal*—and therefore a human—is at that historical moment. In fact, there are multiple ways of claiming human/animal difference, beyond the ability to represent, even though naturalist (and other) representations of animality are often the most productive sites for negotiating constructions of difference.

Debates over what should be seen as "real" are volatile at the turn of the century, not only in terms of the gold standard, but also in terms of representing animals. In addition to a piece of paper saying, "This is money," Nast's cartoon presents another saying, "This is a cow, by the act of the artist." The representation of the cow, like money, is satirized as a "fake." But what is the nature of a cow at the turn of the century? Do cows possess the ability to suffer and feel pain? The new movement advocating for the "humane" treatment of domesticated animals at the end of the nineteenth century can also be seen as saying, "This is a cow"—one that deserves better treatment—in ways that others might see as a "fake" representation.[54] In terms of "wild" animals, stories by widely popular writers were quite literally accused of representing "fake" animals (see figure 2).[55]

Nature Fakers and the Animalization of Race

In what came to be known as the Nature Fakers controversy, writers such as Ernest Thompson Seton, William J. Long, Charles G. D. Roberts, and even Jack London were satirized, essentially, for their attempts to represent animality, to claim, "This is an animal" in their texts. A cartoon by Louis M. Glackens (figure 2) suggests the ridicule to which these writers were subjected, including sharp critiques by President Roosevelt himself. But it is also true that these writers were selling a tremendous number of books, tapping into a demand for different constructions of animality. Seton's *Wild Animals I Have Known* (1898), for example, "went through sixteen printings in its first four years alone," while the books of Long were "widely used in school classrooms

Figure 2 "Ready for Roosevelt" by Louis M. Glackens. From *Puck*, 2 October 1907. Reprinted with permission by the Theodore Roosevelt Collection, Harvard College Library. Ms Am 1895 (253), Houghton Library, Harvard University.

during the first decades of the twentieth century."[56] The Nature Fakers controversy illustrates the extent to which constructions of animality were in flux in the popular imagination, as well as the power of written texts to shape that imagination. But the stories and related articles in national magazines also illustrate the ways that constructions of animality were deeply intertwined with seemingly unrelated contexts, such as U.S. race relations and imperialist agendas at the turn of the century.

Why, then, was the president of the United States, Teddy (Bear) Roosevelt, so concerned about what he considered to be inaccurate natural history in these popular wild animal stories?[57] On the surface, Roosevelt is upset with any text that does not represent animals as instinctual, Darwinian creatures, fighting to survive in the wild, and therefore fair game for hunters like himself wanting to "bag" them. The primary target of Roosevelt (and John Burroughs, who initiated the attack), is Reverend William J. Long, who articulates a very different view of animality. In his "Preface" to *Northern Trails* (1905), for example, Long objects to the reduction of animal life to instinct: "To cover our own blindness and lack of observation we often make a mystery and hocus-pocus of animal life by using the word *instinct* to cover it all...".[58] While he calls the motivations of an animal "more simple and natural" than a human's, he argues that human life can be a model for understanding an animal's life: "a life, not an automaton, with its own joys and fears, its own problems, and its own intelligence; and the only conceivable way for me to understand it is to put myself for a moment in its place and lay upon it the measure of the only life of which I have any direct knowledge or understanding, which is my own."[59] Equating his stories with trails for the reader to follow, Long argues that the reader "will find at the end of every trail a real animal, as true to life as I am able to see and describe it after many years of watching in the wilderness."[60] But Long's claim that "This is an animal," as depicted in his various stories, is vehemently disputed by Roosevelt and Burroughs. This disagreement can thus serve as a brief introductory example of contested constructions of animality and their cultural implications at the turn of the century.

The controversy begins in March 1903, in an article in the *Atlantic Monthly* titled "Real and Sham Natural History," when Burroughs argues that "it is the real demand for an article that leads to its counterfeit, otherwise the counterfeit would stand a poor show."[61] While Burroughs attacks Ernest Thompson Seton and Charles G. D. Roberts as well, his primary target is Long, particularly for stories that he considers to be preposterous. Burroughs objects to Long's notion of "schooling" among wild animals, for example, in which crows teach their young how to fly (136) and kingfishers teach their young how to fish by bringing minnows to a shallow pool (141). Burroughs also objects to other species that can supposedly do amazing things, such as partridges counting and noticing missing members of the flock (141), and an eagle committing suicide (140). According to Burroughs, "The young of all the wild creatures do instinctively what their parents do and did. They do not have to be taught; they are taught by nature from the start" (137). Furthermore, "What Mr. Long and Mr. Thompson Seton read as parental obedience is simply obedience to instinct, and of course in this direction alone safety lies, and there is no departure from it..." (138).

Burroughs's attack leads to a slew of rebuttals from many of the writers involved, often along with affidavits from various witnesses, all published in major national magazines and newspapers, such as *North American Review*, *Century Magazine*, *Science*, *New York Times Review of Books*, *Everybody's Magazine*, *Collier's*, and the *New York Times*.[62] Long becomes the most visible and passionate defender of the truth of his stories, arguing against blanket statements about instinct, for example, that would classify all animals together. In "The Modern School of Nature-Study and Its Critics," he argues that "animals of the same class are still individuals...they are different every one, and have different habits...they are not more alike than men and women of the same class..."[63] Roosevelt eventually enters the fray in a June 1907 interview with Edward B. Clark in *Everybody's Magazine*, insisting that "Men who have visited the haunts of the wild beasts, who have seen them, and have learned at least something of their ways, resent such gross falsifying of nature's records."[64] Roosevelt's argument is that these misrepresentations are teaching incorrect information to gullible schoolboys.[65] But in a subsequent piece titled "I Propose to Smoke Roosevelt Out," Long attacks Roosevelt as a hunter blinded to the true nature of animality: "The bloody endings over which you gloat bring little 'self-satisfaction' to a thoughtful man who has seen the last look in the eyes of a stricken deer, and who remembers that even this small life has its mystery, like our own."[66]

Roosevelt's interest in this debate over the nature of animality can be mapped onto his investment in the discourse of the jungle, in which "higher animals"—such as nonhuman primates—could be equated with "lower humans," both within the United States, in terms of African Americans and Native Americans, and abroad, at sites of U.S. imperialism, such as Cuba, the Philippines, and Panama. At home, T.R. joined writers such as Charlotte Perkins Gilman in worrying about "race suicide," in which the birth of white babies would be outpaced by the birth of nonwhite babies. Abroad, T.R.'s "big stick" policies could be derailed by a logic like Long's that might find "mystery" in every "small life," rather than the individuals of other countries—and the countries themselves—characterized as animals fighting to survive in the jungle.[67] In "The Strenuous Life" (1899), Roosevelt argues, "We cannot avoid the responsibilities that confront us in Hawaii, Porto [*sic*] Rico, and the Philippines....If we stand idly by, if we seek merely swollen, slothful ease and ignoble peace, if we shrink from the hard contests where men must win at hazard of their lives and at the risk of all they hold dear, then the bolder and stronger peoples will pass us by, and will win for themselves the domination of the world."[68] Even more bluntly, John Barrett, former minister to Siam, argues in an article titled "The Problem of the Philippines" in the *North American Review* (1898), "The rule of survival of the fittest applies to nations as well as to the animal kingdom. It is a cruel, relentless principle being exercised in a cruel, relentless competition of mighty forces; and these will trample over us without sympathy or remorse unless we are trained to endure and strong enough to stand the pace."[69]

The way readers of the Nature Fakers think about animals, then, both reflects and produces broader ways of thinking about other questions of difference among *humans*, as well as between humans and animals, at the turn of the century. Roosevelt and others consumed by the Nature Fakers are invested in policing boundaries not only between "real" and "fake" animals, between "fact" and "fiction," but also between white and nonwhite humans, among other identity categories. In an article titled "'Nature Fakers,'" Roosevelt is explicit in his denigration of Native Americans, for example, claiming that they "live in a world of mysticism, and they often ascribe super-natural traits to the animals they know, just as the men of the Middle Ages, with almost the same childlike faith, credited the marvels told of the uni-corn, the basilisk, the roc, and the cockatrice."[70]

While Jack London refrains from entering into the controversy until September 1908, he exhibits a similarly racist logic, though directed in his case against the "lower humans" of "the tropics"[71] and Tahiti (209), considered to be representative of the "adult savage" in general (209–10). London's article for *Collier's*, titled "The Other Animals," is a defense against being called a "faker" along with Long and others, claiming that he actually knows more about evolution than Roosevelt and Burroughs. He insists that his stories are in fact about "real" animals and that his work is "in line with the facts of evolution"; that he has "hewed them to the mark set by scientific research" (199–200). London goes to great lengths to prove that animals can, in fact, reason in at least rudimentary ways, con-trary to his understanding of the position represented by Burroughs and Roosevelt. But he is also quite clear about the racial hierarchy underlying his evolutionary thinking, in which "the adult savage," for example, can be fooled into thinking that a voice on a telephone must be coming from a man in an adjoining room (209). Whiteness is clearly at the top of the hierarchy, while black "savages" are not so different from "higher animals." London ultimately claims that "We who are so very human are very ani-mal" (210), but his belief in evolutionary theory also both reflects and pro-duces a broader cultural imperative to justify racial boundaries between white and black human beings.[72]

The Nature Fakers controversy illustrates how racial hierarchies can construct and be constructed by representations of animality, particularly within the discourse of the jungle. London's work is explored in more detail in chapter 2 of this book, in the way that it simultaneously, although per-haps unconsciously, constructs and resists the Darwinist-Freudian jungle. Most of the texts explored in this book fit that description, revealing how the discourse of the jungle is produced primarily by white male writers who reach wide audiences. This book does not therefore emphasize, on the one hand, texts written by women or people from more diverse racial and ethnic backgrounds, or, on the other hand, texts that engage less centrally with—or actively challenge—the discourse of the jungle. There is certainly more work to be done, then, on texts that fit these latter categories in relation to the history of animality at the turn of the century, even if they are beyond the scope of this book.

Charlotte Perkins Gilman's novella *Herland* (1915), for example, is perhaps surprising in the extent to which it does *not* emphasize jungle discourse. Gilman's description of an all-female utopia, hidden from the rest of the world, engages with her well-documented (and racist) thinking about evolution and eugenics in general, which has been explored productively in numerous scholarly studies.[73] But Gilman makes it clear that Herland is located in a cultivated and civilized "forest," high up and secluded in the mountains, rather than down with the "savages" of an unnamed tropical jungle below; these "savages" are mentioned only in passing and are never seen. Herland is not populated by Darwinist-Freudian animals, and the women have no "animal instincts" for sex or sexual pleasure, supposedly. They have figured out how to reproduce without men, through parthenogenesis, and all come from the same founding mother and the same national obsession with motherhood, although the children are raised collectively. Even with three male explorers who stumble upon this region and might be perceived, in some ways, as Darwinist-Freudian animals, the novella relies less upon the jungle and more upon metaphors such as the anthill or the beehive to debate what might be "natural," including in relation to sexual desire. Despite a construction of "savages" that resonates with Jack London's work, then, *Herland* offers a different formulation of animality, outside the discourse of the jungle that is the emphasis of this book.[74] But the lack of female writers in the present study does not mean that gender is not a significant aspect of the book, since gender is frequently one of many intersectional categories explored in various texts.

Birth of a Jungle

The debate over "fake" representations of human and nonhuman animals in the Nature Fakers controversy illustrates both the growing hegemony of the Darwinist-Freudian jungle and resistance to it. In a broad range of texts—from literary naturalism and beyond—questions about what it means to be an animal or a human are fiercely contested, even as the jungle is simultaneously produced. Roosevelt acknowledges that answers to those questions (and even the questions themselves) have changed since the Middle Ages, when there were "quaint little books on beasts...in which the unicorn and the basilisk appear as real creatures," and "there was no hard-and-fast line drawn between fact and fiction even in ordinary history; and until much later there was not even an effort to draw it in natural history."[75]

Such distinctions call to mind Foucault's reference in *The Order of Things: An Archaeology of the Human Sciences* (1966 in French) to a passage from Borges's "The Analytical Language of John Wilkins." Quoting a "certain Chinese encyclopaedia," Borges presents us with an entirely different way of thinking about animals, since they can be "divided into" the following:

(a) belonging to the Emperor, (b) embalmed, (c) tame, (d) sucking pigs, (e) sirens, (f) fabulous, (g) stray dogs, (h) included in the present classification, (i) frenzied, (j) innumerable, (k) drawn with a very fine camelhair brush, (l) *et cetera*, (m) having just broken the water pitcher, (n) that from a long way off look like flies.[76]

Foucault's laughter while reading this passage becomes the inspiration for his entire study of how radically different the ordering of knowledge—in this case about animals—can be at different historical and cultural conjunctures: "In the wonderment of this taxonomy, the thing we apprehend in one great leap, the thing that, by means of the fable, is demonstrated as the exotic charm of another system of thought, is the limitation of our own, the stark impossibility of thinking *that*."[77] Foucault's argument is that a fundamental rift can separate "the order of things" from one historical period to the next, and that everything changed in Western thought around 1800. I believe that Foucault's stroke is too broad, that his work is of relatively limited use when applied directly to U.S. cultural texts, and that he doesn't consider a paradigm shift in thinking about animality around 1900, at least in the United States. But the spirit of his efforts to track different epistemologies is a significant influence on my own work in this book.

I believe that an "incitement to discourse" can be located at the turn of the century, in other words, that reveals how constructions of animality shift in U.S. literature and culture. It is important to point out, however, that I am not attempting to suggest a new way of thinking about what is exceptional or exemplary in terms of "*the* American mind" in the myth and symbol tradition of early American studies.[78] But I do mean to suggest that the historical and cultural conjuncture of the United States at the turn of the century is essential for understanding why the discourse of the jungle moves toward hegemony, at least among those in power.

* * *

Each chapter in this book weaves together intersectional explorations of various human and nonhuman categories—such as race, class, gender, sexuality, species, and environment—rather than aligning each chapter exclusively with a single category. But the first part of this book, "Epistemology of the Jungle," generally focuses on the sexual history of "the beast" in two chapters: "Progressive-Era Sexuality and the Nature of the Beast in Henry James"[79] and "Between Species: Queering the Wolf in Jack London." In this part, I argue that it is no coincidence that the discourse of the jungle is constructed at the same historical moment as the invention of "the homosexual" as a distinct human sexual identity. Bringing together the work of theorists and historians such as Eve Sedgwick, Michel Foucault, and George Chauncey, I illustrate how attention to the discourse of the jungle unsettles influential readings of Henry James's "The Beast in the Jungle" (1903), Jack London's *The Call of the Wild* (1903) and *The Sea-Wolf* (1904), and Freud's case study of the Wolf Man (1918). Many theorists continue to reinforce a construction of the beast or animality in general as inherently heterosexual, despite recent work by Chauncey, for example, that has uncovered queer human males self-identified as "wolves" at the turn of the century. Recent work of animal behaviorists also documents extensive examples of "homosexual" behavior among nonhuman animals. James and London register formulations of queer desire within what would otherwise seem to be straightforward social Darwinist logic, illustrating alternative ways of thinking about "the beast" and interspecies pleasure that would otherwise be inconceivable in the discourse of the jungle.

In the second part of this book, "Survival of the Fittest Market," two chapters focus on new ways of thinking about the marketplace as a jungle: "The Octopus and the Corporation: Monstrous Animality in Norris, Spencer, and Carnegie" and "The Working-Class Beast: Frank Norris and Upton Sinclair." These chapters explore how corporate exploitation could still be condemned as *monstrous*, rather than "natural," even though constructions of the marketplace were moving toward jungle discourse. Building upon the work of critics such as Walter Benn Michaels, Jennifer Fleissner, and Mark Seltzer, I argue that working-class laborers were the first to be animalized, while middle-class reformers and even wealthy robber barons could still be seen within a Protestant Christian framework, rather than the Darwinist-Freudian jungle.

Herbert Spencer's influence on Andrew Carnegie's *The Gospel of Wealth* (1900) reveals how a robber baron's ethic could contain residual Christian elements, as well as emergent jungle discourse. Texts such as Frank Norris's *The Octopus* (1901) and Upton Sinclair's *The Jungle* (1906) simultaneously naturalize and resist this new discourse. The seemingly unrelated public electrocution of a circus elephant at Coney Island is also shown to be a signifier of animalized class warfare. Despite Progressive-Era reforms, "survival of the fittest" rhetoric eventually justifies class difference for the first time at the site of the animal, including the distance between middle-class reformers and animalized working-class immigrants.

The third part of this book, "The Evolution of Race," explores the problematic relationship between animality and U.S. race relations in two chapters: "Archaeology of a Humane Society: Animality, Savagery, Blackness"[80] and "Black Savage, White Animal: *Tarzan's* American Jungle." While engaging the work of critics and theorists such as Jacqueline Goldsby, Gail Bederman, and Marianna Torgovnick, I highlight the significance of the "humane" movement for both animals and criminals in relation to shifting constructions of black and white identities. At the end of the nineteenth century, I argue, a new logic of humane reform contributes to a rewriting of black male identity as more "savage" than "animal." At a moment when black men are attempting to distance themselves from racist constructions of their animality, humane reform works to contrast whiteness with the "savagery" of blackness, in an attempt to link a Darwinist-Freudian "savage" who delights in torture with a black man supposedly delighting in the rape of a white woman. Texts such as Edgar Rice Burroughs's *Tarzan of the Apes* (1914) and William James's work on both antilynching and antivivisection advocacy reveal how white men could claim the capacity for humane behavior—in relation to either real animals or "savage" others—as a marker of racial difference. As a result, animality is essentially "elevated" over blackness, enabling white men to torture and vivisect black men, thus treating them *worse* than animals at the turn of the century.

The epilogue focuses on the reception of William Jennings Bryan's anti-evolution arguments in the Scopes "Monkey Trial" of 1925, in contrast with his reputation as a progressive reformer at the turn of the century. Bryan's objection to being characterized as an animal with "monkey" ancestors in the Scopes trial reveals both the racist subtext of jungle discourse and the hegemony of that discourse by 1925. Ridiculed by writers such as H. L. Mencken, Joseph Wood Krutch, and W. E. B. Du Bois, Bryan's resistance to evolutionary theory is mocked in a way that signals a fracture between progressivism of various kinds and Christian fundamentalism: a fracture that was not nearly as evident at the turn of the century but that resonates today within debates over intelligent design, sociobiology, and evolutionary psychology. Underlying these debates, though, is a common affirmation of a Darwinist-Freudian construction of "the animal" within the human, even if various critics object to an oversimplification or reduction of "the human" to "the animal."

Ultimately, this book illustrates how literary and cultural representations of animality are both more complex and more central to constructions of U.S. identities than previously imagined. An animality studies approach to the turn of the century reveals not only new ways of thinking about familiar texts but also new ways of illustrating the significance of the question of the animal in relation to fields such as the history of sexuality, studies of literary naturalism, and critical race studies within American literary and cultural studies. This book reveals how the figure of the animal evolved in U.S. culture at the turn of the century, particularly through the birth of the jungle: a discourse that continues to enable enduring justifications of homophobia, economic exploitation, and racism in the United States and beyond.

PART ONE

Epistemology of the Jungle

Progressive-Era Sexuality and the Nature of the Beast in Henry James

IN *EPISTEMOLOGY OF THE CLOSET* (1990), Eve Kosofsky Sedgwick argues that the discourse of sexuality as we know it today was first constructed at the end of the nineteenth century through a shift in attention from sexual acts to sexual identities: a shift "from viewing same-sex sexuality as a matter of prohibited and isolated genital *acts* (acts to which, in that view, anyone might be liable who did not have their appetites in general under close control) to viewing it as a function of stable definitions of *identity* (so that one's personality structure might mark one as *a homosexual*, even, perhaps, in the absence of any genital activity at all)."[1] Sedgwick's work builds upon Michel Foucault's famous declaration in *The History of Sexuality, Volume 1: An Introduction* (1978) that the "species" of the homosexual was born at the end of the nineteenth century.[2] Her primary focus, though, is on the effects rather than the origins of this paradigm shift: "*Epistemology of the Closet* does not have an explanation to offer for this sudden, radical condensation of sexual categories; instead of speculating on its causes, the book explores its unpredictably varied and acute implications and consequences."[3] This condensation signals for Sedgwick one of the "most crucial sites for the contestation of meaning in twentieth-century Western culture," which is "the historical specificity of homosocial/homosexual definition, notably but not exclusively male, from around the turn of the century."[4] My purpose in this chapter is to explore the relationship between this discourse of sexuality and an intimately related but currently overlooked discourse related to animality at the same historical moment. Sedgwick and others working on the history of sexuality in U.S. literary and cultural studies often elide what this book identifies as "the jungle," a discourse that suggests some of the reasons why sexuality and animality shift at roughly the same time. Tracing the genealogy of the jungle can lead to new possibilities for understanding the "species" of the homosexual in relation to shifting constructions of animality in U.S. cultural and literary texts at the turn of the twentieth century.

Foucault's use of the term "species" to describe the new construction of the homosexual might seem appropriate, for some, in the sense that human and nonhuman animals do not voluntarily sign up for species membership; they are born into a species as defined by biologists. While the precise definition of "species" has long been debated among biologists, the profound influence of Charles Darwin since the end of the nineteenth century has ensured that reproductive capability remains an essential element for defining species boundaries.[5] Members of the same species are supposedly hardwired to desire sexual intercourse with the opposite sex in order to produce offspring of the same species. This becomes one of two key animal instincts naturalized by the discourse of the jungle at the end of the nineteenth century: heterosexuality in the name of reproduction. The other instinct naturalized in this way is violence in the name of survival. Further Darwinian implications within the discourse of human sexuality are not fully explored in Foucault's *Introduction*. In fact, constructions of nonhuman species play almost no role in his study of the discourse of sexuality. Following Foucault, queer theory today has been slow to explore the significance of the animal.[6]

Foucault's identification of the homosexual as a new species evokes a biological realm of animals fighting not only to survive but also to reproduce, where homosexuality would be "unnatural" because of its threat to species propagation. Deploying the term "species" as a description of the homosexual thus links normative human sexuality with animality. In contrast to Foucault, though, my aim is to explore a different framework, an "epistemology of the jungle," that has intertwined the history of sexuality with the history of animality at least since the confluence of Darwin and Sigmund Freud at the turn of the twentieth century. My primary concern in this chapter is the naturalization of heterosexuality that is produced by the discourse of the jungle, the genealogy of which I trace through Darwin, Rudyard Kipling, Freud, and the proliferation of American literary texts deploying representations of "the jungle" and "the animal" at the turn of the century. Together, these texts contribute to the hegemonic shift in constructions of both homosexuality and animality in the United States. On the cusp of this new formulation, though, there are alternative ways of thinking about the relationship between animality and sexuality: representations that seem to reinforce but actually resist the Darwinist-Freudian "jungle," despite reigning critical interpretations by

Sedgwick and others. After suggesting alternative constructions of "the wolf" in particular, I offer a new reading of Henry James's 1903 story "The Beast in the Jungle" in light of sexual histories of "the beast" that are crucial but often overlooked in studies of U.S. literature and culture.

Welcome to the Jungle

Survival of the fittest. Kill or be killed. Fight for your mate and pass on your genes.[7] Violent and sexual instincts, essential to the discourse of the jungle, continue to structure an imaginary "law of the jungle" in U.S. culture which assumes that both human and nonhuman animals are "naturally" inclined toward heterosexuality and violence. James seems to evoke this construction with his descriptions of the "Beast" in "The Beast in the Jungle": "Something or other lay in wait for him, amid the twists and the turns of the months and the years, like a crouching Beast in the Jungle. It signified little whether the crouching Beast were destined to slay him or to be slain. The definite point was the inevitable spring of the creature..."[8] This construction of the Beast might seem to be the product of a Darwinian shift at the end of the nineteenth century, in which both human and nonhuman "beasts" are defined by violent instincts for survival. Within this logic, human beings become just another animal species, rather than divine creations within a Protestant Christian framework. The shift from natural theology to natural selection dethrones human history. "Natural selection," as Gillian Beer points out, "is a pithy rejoinder to 'natural theology.' Instead of an initiating godhead, Darwin suggests, diversification and selection have generated the history of the present world.... In the world he proposed there was no crucial explanatory function for God, nor indeed was there any special place assigned to the human in his argument."[9] The human being, in other words, "was neither paradigm nor sovereign."[10] Darwinism's main contribution to the construction of "the jungle" is what amounts to self-interest: instinctual behavior that strives to perpetuate itself through "survival of the fittest" (a phrase coined by Herbert Spencer, though often attributed to Darwin). *On the Origin of Species*, written in 1859, tentatively defines an instinctive action as that "which we ourselves should require experience to enable us to perform, when performed by an animal, more especially by a very young one, without any experience, and when performed by many individuals in the same way, without their knowing for what purpose it is performed."[11] Despite the perhaps surprising implications for human performativity in this passage, the key point is that instinctual actions in nonhuman animals are performed with no self-consciousness.

It does not matter, Darwin later argues, whether instincts are "endowed" or "created"; more important, they are "small consequences of one general law, leading to the advancement of all organic beings, namely, multiply, vary, let the strongest live and the weakest die."[11] Such formulations are subsequently appropriated in a variety of ways to construct social Darwinism among human beings, often in ways that run contrary to Darwin's own work.[12] It is not until the intervention of Freud, though, that instinct is explicitly linked with human sexuality in a broader cultural sense. But the connection with propagation in Darwin would seem to make such a move almost inevitable. Darwin himself is quite willing to extrapolate into the human in *The Descent of Man,* from 1871, generalizing that "Sexual Selection depends on the success of certain individuals over others of the same sex, in relation to the propagation of the species; whilst Natural Selection depends on the success of both sexes, at all ages, in relation to the general conditions of life."[14] Roger Lancaster summarizes the implication: "everything in Darwin's text on sexual selection converges to make reproduction the privileged, unique, and sole aim of sex."[15]

In *Three Essays on the Theory of Sexuality* (1905), Freud writes, "The fact of the existence of sexual needs in human beings and animals is expressed in biology by the assumption of a 'sexual instinct,' on the analogy of the instinct of nutrition, that is of hunger. Everyday language possesses no counterpart to the word 'hunger,' but science makes use of the word 'libido' for that purpose."[16] David Halperin notes that the "conception of the sexual instinct as an autonomous human function without an organ appears for the first time in the nineteenth century, and without it the currently prevailing, heavily psychologized model of sexual subjectivity…is inconceivable."[17] Freud's model of sexual subjectivity is built upon a construction of animal instincts that begins with Darwin but is not solidified until the turn of the century when the discourse of the jungle links "real" animals with "the animal within" the human being.

But the naturalization of heterosexuality in this discourse is somewhat ambiguous in Freud. As Henry Abelove has argued, Freud felt that "homosexuality is no advantage. That it is also no illness. That it should be neither prosecuted as a crime nor regarded as a disgrace. That no homosexual need be treated psychoanalytically unless he also, and quite incidentally, happened to be neurotic."[18] But some of Freud's colleagues and many, if not most, analysts in the United States "tended to view homosexuality with disapproval and have actually wanted to get rid of it altogether."[19] I think it is fair to argue, though, that Freud's conception of "normal" sexuality—even if that term only refers to a reduced tendency toward neuroses—is taken directly from a Darwinian for-mulation of the instinct to propagate one's species, observable supposedly in animals and applicable supposedly to human beings. Homosexual tendencies might be universal, but the "normal sexual aim" for Freud is still heterosexual genital intercourse and the transmission of semen. Perversions, while not nec-essarily negative, are "sexual activities which either (a) extend, in an anatomi-cal sense, beyond the regions of the body that are designed for sexual union, or (b) linger over the intermediate relations to the sexual object which should normally be traversed rapidly on the path towards the final sexual aim."[20] But the sexual instinct in Freud, even when it is not explicitly heterosexual, is not necessarily conscious. Just like the animal, supposedly, it acts not according to reason but because of its biologically coded "nature."

Psychoanalytic studies, along with other literary and cultural texts, not only contribute to the new discourse of the jungle but also reflect the imperial-ist history that brings Western Europeans and Americans into contact with the geographic jungles of India, Africa, and other parts of the world. This colonial context needs to be sketched here as well in order to reveal how the birth of the jungle eventually produces new constructions of sexuality in the United States. The *Oxford English Dictionary* indicates that the word "jungle" comes from the Hindi and Marathi word *jangal*, meaning "desert," "waste," "forest"; as well as from the Sanskrit *jangala*, meaning "dry," "dry ground," or "desert." Its first appearance in English is in 1776, with its meaning already shifted toward what might be more recognizable today: "Land overgrown with underwood, long grass, or tangled vegetation; also, the luxuriant and often almost impenetrable growth of vegetation covering such a tract."[21] Brought into English as a result of an imperialist presence in India, "jungle" is intimately related to the larger rise of Western imperialism around the world, particularly in the nineteenth century. Western powers such as Britain and France went from controlling 35 percent of the earth's surface in 1800 to, by 1914, "a grand total of roughly 85 percent of the earth as colonies, protectorates, dependencies, dominions, and commonwealths."[22] A significant proliferation of terms incorporating "jungle" emerges, according to the *OED*, at the end of the nineteenth century, including "jungle-bush," "jungle-tale," "jungle-people," "jungle-clad," "jungle-trudging," and so on. Kipling's *The Jungle Book* and *The Second Jungle Book* register or coin many of these usages, and his stories include some of the most recogniz-able and popular accounts of the Indian jungle in the English language.[23] The legacies of imperialism are represented in Kipling as well, in stories such as "The Undertakers," from *The Second Jungle Book*, which sets up the 1857 Indian "Mutiny" as a backdrop for a crocodile who eagerly eats up the corpses that float down the river to him: first the bodies of the English, then whole villages of Indian bodies in retribution.[24]

The continuing evolution of the word "jungle" has led to its negative and often racist connotations over the past century, including "jungle bunny," "jungle fever," and "jungle market," but it has also specifically expanded into urban applications, such as "asphalt jungle" and "concrete jungle." As Candace Slater points out, "jungle" is often contrasted today with "wilderness," a signifier that has gained increasingly positive connotations in American culture: "Although travelers may lose their way in either a wilderness or a jungle, the latter is distinguished less by the vast solitude that makes it a fitting stage for either contemplation or heroic action than by its disordered and disorienting growth."[25] Racist constructions of "growth" might thus include concentrations of racial minorities in urban spaces. But Kipling's constructions of the jungle are more varied than this recent condensation of meanings. Included in *The Jungle Books* are locations from around the world that are outside of Mowgli's Indian jungle, many of which we might be inclined to label more generally as "the wild," or more specifically in terms of geographic location: the frozen Arctic, the rugged Himalayas, the vast sea. Kipling's connections with the United States are many: he married an American, Caroline Balestier, in 1892; he wrote *The Jungle Books* in Vermont while living there from 1892 to 1896;[26] and his famous poem "The White Man's Burden," published in February 1899, performed a significant role in debates over U.S. imperialism in the Philippines. Animated film versions of *The Jungle Books* continue to proliferate in the United States. Kipling's contributions to a meaning of "the jungle" as, according to the *OED*, "the dwelling-place of wild beasts" and later "a place where the 'law of the jungle' prevails" continue to impact American culture, even though his texts are actually more complex than is often assumed. At the moment of the birth of the jungle, in other words, there are still alternative ways of thinking about animality that might seem rather surprising to us today.

Kipling's animals are simultaneously *born* knowing "Jungle Law" (as opposed to Mowgli, a human being who must learn it from wolves) and *raised* to internalize its strict rules—which regulate behavior and appropriate social roles according to a rigid hierarchy—whether within a single species or throughout "the animal kingdom." Kipling's Jungle Law is not, in other words, the Disneyfied "bare/bear necessities" of happy-go-lucky Baloo; nor is it the harsh, survival-of-the-fittest, every-beast-for-himself (or his family/ pack/species) formulation that evolves from Darwin through Spencer and Jack London. Some of Kipling's jungle stories draw upon these narratives, but the principal command of the Law for Kipling is presented as obedience to hierarchy: knowing one's place in the social order. In "The Law of the Jungle," for example, a poem from *The Second Jungle Book*, we find the following conclusion: "*Now these are the Laws of the Jungle, and many and mighty are they; / But the head and the hoof of the Law and the haunch and the hump is—Obey!*"[27] There is an immense range of laws, though, "hundreds and hundreds" that are referenced by this poem, including guidelines for such virtues as cleanliness, moderation, self-reliance, and the proper way to perform gender roles. For the wolf pack, if there is ever a doubt, the default is whatever the "Head Wolf" says: "In all that the Law leaveth open, the word of your Head Wolf is Law."[28]

Outside the Mowgli stories we can find interesting tales such as "Servants of the Queen" (in the first *Jungle Book*) to illustrate the broader politics of this hierarchical view, which will have significant implications for my reading of sexuality in "The Beast in the Jungle" later in this chapter. In many of Kipling's stories, animals become transparent allegories for proper (human) native subjects who submit willingly to the crown. As Edward Said points out in *Culture and Imperialism*, "Historically this has always been how European imperialism made itself palatable to itself, for what could be better for its self-image than native subjects who express assent to the outsider's knowledge and power, implicitly accepting European judgment on the undeveloped, backward, or degenerate nature of their own society?"[29] In "Servants of the Queen," we are given an explicit contrast between Indian creatures (human and nonhuman) and Afghani "savage men and savage horses from somewhere at the back of Central Asia."[30] Fortunately for the reader, the first-person narrator can speak "beast-language—not wild-beast language, but camp-beast language of course" so that he can translate the conversations of rank-and-file mules, camels, and horses, all about to be displayed for the Viceroy of India (153). Whatever complaints or prejudices they may have, they all snap into line for the procession simply because "An order was given, and they obeyed" (166). The native officer subsequently explains to the "old grizzled, long-haired Central Asian chief" that animals obey orders too: "'They obey, as the men do. Mule, horse, elephant, or bullock, he obeys his driver, and the driver his sergeant, and the sergeant his lieutenant, and the lieutenant his captain, and the captain his major, and the major his colonel, and the colonel his brigadier commanding three regiments, and the brigadier the general, who obeys the Viceroy, who is the servant of the Empress. Thus it is done'" (166–67). The conclusion to the story is that Afghanistan, where the chief says, "we obey only our own wills," is therefore justifiably subjugated: "your Amir whom you do not obey must [therefore] come here and take orders from our Viceroy" (167). Kipling's "beasts," whether human or nonhuman, thus serve as the means for narrating the proper role of the native subject. Even if the human being is nothing more than another animal species, obedience within the hierarchy of imperialism remains a central aspect of the Law of the Jungle.

Kipling's emphasis on obedience seems to run counter to current prevailing assumptions about jungle law, or at least about what it might mean to think of a human male as a wolf, or among wolves, like the character Mowgli. While *The Jungle Books* contribute to the birth of the jungle as we typically imagine it today, Kipling's texts also illustrate that this discourse was still open to alternatives at the turn of the century. The relationship between the nature of the beast and new discourses of sexuality was similarly more complex than we might otherwise imagine. Strikingly different constructions of the wolf in particular at that moment indicate that the Darwinist-Freudian formulation of animality had yet to achieve hegemony.

Wolf Species

What would it mean to think of a wolf as "homosexual" in terms of either sexual acts or a stable sexual identity? Despite recent evidence of queer behavior among hundreds of animal species,[31] the discourse of the jungle tends to reinforce the idea that heterosexuality is more "natural" than homosexuality for most if not all animals, including human beings. Freud's comment in *Civilization and Its Discontents* (1930) that man is a wolf to man (*homo homini lupus*) is focused more on aggressiveness than sexuality, but his interpretation of the wolf in a broader sense, and in individual case studies, often explicitly associates animality with human heteronormativity. Freud's comment reads rather differently, though, in light of an alternative usage of the term "wolf" in the early decades of the twentieth century. In certain contexts, wolf was used to designate the role of the penetrator, rather than the penetrated, in queer anal sex. The *OED* registers this definition of the wolf as early as 1917: "orig. *U.S.*, a male homosexual seducer or one who adopts an active role with a partner." Eric Partridge identifies a slang definition of "wolf" in the United States as a "brutal, dominant pederast" from around 1900.[32] According to George Chauncey in *Gay New York: Gender, Urban Culture, and the Makings of the Gay Male World, 1890–1940* (1994), early twentieth-century American males identified as wolves "combined homosexual interest with a marked masculinity. None of them behaved effeminately or took feminine nicknames, and few played the 'woman's part' in sexual relations—and then only secretly."[33] There were different ways of defining the wolf as a species, in other words, that resisted a simplistic association between animality and heterosexuality, or the species of the homosexual as an essentialized human identity.

Chauncey's research complicates studies in the history of sexuality which suggest that the shift from acts to identity in defining homosexuality was universal in U.S. culture at the turn of the century.[34] Chauncey argues that the construction of "the homosexual" at the end of the nineteenth century in medical discourses had a more immediate impact on middle-class culture and elite discourses than on less privileged domains. Working-class culture in New York, for example, maintained discursive categories related to sexual acts and roles much longer before shifting to the homosexual/heterosexual binary: "'the modern homosexual,' whose preeminence is usually thought to have been established in the nineteenth century, did not dominate Western urban industrial culture until well into the twentieth century, at least in one of the world capitals of that culture" (27). Chauncey reveals that the culture of the early twentieth century "permitted men to engage in sexual relations with other men, often on a regular basis, without requiring them to regard themselves—or to be regarded by others—as gay" (65). But what is the logic, we need to ask, that allows these men to call themselves wolves?

The association of the wolf with the "active" or "man's part" of queer anal sex might suggest the trope of inversion, constructed in nineteenth-century medical and psychological discourses, as one way of explaining the logic at work here. As Sedgwick explains, inversion allows for "the preservation of an essential *heterosexuality* within desire itself."[35] What I am interested in, though, is the preservation of an essential heterosexuality within *animality* itself, a formulation that is elided in Chauncey's analysis. Chauncey focuses instead on the violent or predatory associations of animality, even as he argues, for example, that "their very appellation, *wolf*, evoked the image of the predatory man-about-town intent on seducing young women, and their masculine dominance over [male] punks was further emphasized by the fact that the latter were also referred to as *lambs* and *kids*."[36] Chauncey's analysis evokes Freud's conclusion that "man is a wolf to man," even as it suggests the "phallocentric presumption that a man's sexual satisfaction was more significant than the gender or character of the person who provided that satisfaction in definitions of sexual identity."[37] Chauncey's discussion of what the wolf signifies, though, still tends to reinforce an association between animality and heterosexuality that might not be warranted at the turn of the twentieth century, even as it resists the essentialism of a human homosexual identity.

Chauncey's assumptions about animality seem indebted, in this sense, to Freud, even if Chauncey's wolf seems to be rather different than the species found in Freud's famous analysis of the "Wolf Man." Freud's interpretation of the wolf in this case study, "From the History of an Infantile Neurosis" (published in 1918 in German and in 1925 in English), leads to predictable conclusions about the Oedipal complex, the fear of castration, and "natural" heterosexuality, rather than queer anal sex. But Freud's analysis, like Chauncey's, links animality with heterosexuality through the discourse of the jungle. Freud's evaluation of homosexuality and bestiality in the case of the Wolf Man illustrates his logic that anything other than heterosexuality must be a diversion from "normal" sexual development.

The basic problem for the Wolf Man, as Freud constructs it, is that he never moves beyond each stage of development, and he fails to see the connection between the wolves of his famous recurring dream and his own Oedipal desires. Freud summarizes the first problem in this way: "no position of the libido which had once been established was ever completely replaced by a later one. It was rather left in existence side by side with all the others, and this allowed him to maintain an incessant vacillation which proved to be incompatible with the acquisition of a stable character."[38] The link between the Wolf Man's dream about wolves and the primal scene of parental copulation leads to Freud's conclusion that the parents must have been having sex with "the man upright, and the woman bent down like an animal" (17:39).[39]

What is particularly interesting here is the implication that sex "like an animal" suggests how the "natural" heterosexuality of animals is the "natural" model of heterosexuality for humans. The human desire to have sex with another human being "from behind," though, is dangerous territory, supposedly, because of its resemblance to anal sex. A human male should be like the biological or "real" wolf, we might infer, but not in terms of sexual positions, since the penis could more easily slip or be inserted into the "wrong" orifice during sex "from behind." The wolf, on the one hand, would not seem to run this risk, since his animal nature supposedly precludes the possibility of homosexuality. Freud's Wolf Man, on the other hand, develops a subsequent preference for having sex "from behind" a woman that is presented as evidence for the link between "the anal-erotic disposition" and neurosis: "a sexual preference of this kind for the hind parts of the body is a general characteristic of people who are inclined to an obsessional neurosis" (17:41). But the root cause of the Wolf Man's problem, for Freud, must be Oedipal, and all the associations and implications of the wolves in the dream can be reduced to this complex. Freud argues, "It is always a strict law of dream interpretation that an explanation must be found for every detail" (17:42n1), even though his explanations sometimes seem rather convoluted. The wolves are white in the dream, for example, because his parents were wearing white underclothes in the primal scene. But stillness in the dream is explained as indicating its exact opposite, violent motion. And several wolves, ultimately, must be reduced to one.

In *A Thousand Plateaus: Capitalism and Schizophrenia*, Gilles Deleuze and Félix Guattari famously ridicule this kind of reductionism: "Who is Freud trying to fool? The wolves never had a chance to get away and save their pack: it was already decided from the very beginning that animals could serve only to represent coitus between parents, or, conversely, be represented by coitus between parents. Freud only knows the Oedipalized wolf or dog, the castrated-castrating daddy-wolf, the dog in the kennel, the analyst's bow-wow."[40] The point I want to stress here, though, is that regardless of Freud's psychoanalytic conclusions, his interpretation of the wolf as a "species" reinforces two broader assumptions about animality that are essential to the discourse of the jungle: first, animals are instinctually heterosexual; and second, representations of animals are legible signifiers of human sexuality. Both of these assumptions continue to frame current critical interpretations of Progressive-Era texts, including those literary and cultural texts that contribute to but also resist the discourse of the jungle at the turn of the century. In what follows I explore the significance of these assumptions through the example of James's story "The Beast in the Jungle" and conclude by exploring other possibilities available "between species" at this same historical moment.

The Nature of the Beast in James

Sedgwick's influential reading of "The Beast in the Jungle" in *Epistemology of the Closet* remains a foundational text in queer theory and the history of sexuality in American and European contexts. Despite her crucial antihomophobic analysis of the structure of the closet, her reading of "the Beast" *itself* in James overlooks the historical significance of the relationship between representations of animality and sexuality that I have been tracing in this chapter. Sedgwick's reading relies upon an unacknowledged Freudian construction of animality, resonating with Freud's interpretation of the 1909 "Rat Man" case study (formally titled "Notes upon a Case of Obsessional Neurosis"), as well as with histories of "jungle law" influenced by Kipling and Darwin. Sedgwick's "Beast" thus elides the possibilities suggested by Chauncey's wolf that can raise new questions about James's story and its relationship to the intertwined histories of sexuality and animality at the turn of the century.

Sedgwick's reading is presented in a chapter of *Epistemology of the Closet* titled "The Beast in the Closet" and a section titled "The Law of the Jungle." Acknowledging that the shifting signifier of the Beast can signify a whole range of signifieds, including metaphor itself, Sedgwick suggests that the Beast evokes both violence and a preoccupation with sex, however veiled. The Beast is linked with John Marcher's "secret," his feeling that something "rare and strange" will happen to him, even though this kind of event seems to be denied in the end of the story, when we are told, "he had been the man of his time, *the* man, to whom nothing on earth was to have happened."[41] But this "stylish and 'satisfyingly' Jamesian formal gesture" points to a heterosexual content at least initially—the idea that Marcher has missed an opportunity with May Bartram—and to a subsequent homosexual content in Sedgwick's formulation of the closet.[42] Sedgwick shows that the closet does not necessarily contain a "homosexual" man, but that Marcher lives his daily life as a man closeted by an "outer secret, the secret of having a secret" that necessitates the "playacting of heterosexuality" with Bartram (205–6).[43]

For Sedgwick, "The Law of the Jungle" thus relates primarily to heteronormativity. The internalized Beast becomes the agent of that Law, she argues, but there is no discussion of other contexts and constructions of "jungle law" at this historical moment. Kipling's emphasis on obedience to hierarchy, for example, resonates with Sedgwick's formulation of heteronormativity as the dominant logic to be obeyed, a logic at least suggested, if not insisted upon, by Freud as a path for avoiding neuroses. Sedgwick insists that the central metaphor of the Beast is in dialogue, if nothing else, with the construction of what she calls "male homosexual panic": "Because the paths of male entitlement, especially in the nineteenth century, required certain intense male bonds that were not readily distinguishable from the most reprobated bonds, an endemic and ineradicable state of what I am calling male homosexual panic became the normal condition of male heterosexual entitlement" (185). The key claim she makes in relation to understanding James's short story is that "to the extent that Marcher's secret has *a* content, that content is homosexual" (201). This conclusion runs contrary to an older tradition in James scholarship that Sedgwick identifies as having repressed the homosexual implications of the story, where the "net effect is the usual repressive one of elision and subsumption of supposedly embarrassing material" (197). To the extent that the figure of the Beast *itself*, then, has a content, it is primarily sexual in Sedgwick's reading, but its "species" remains to be seen.

What appear to be explanations of Marcher's fate shift throughout, including the sense that nothing will actually happen to him and the sense that Bartram knows but he doesn't, particularly after what seems to be a failed sexual overture on her part.[44] From her deathbed, Bartram offers what appears to be an explanation of Marcher's fate as the construction of the closet itself, an event that has already come and gone: "You've nothing to wait for more. It *has* come"; "your not being aware of it is the strangeness *in* the strangeness. It's the wonder *of* the wonder" (389). As a result, once Bartram dies, Marcher proceeds to think that the Jungle has been cleared and the Beast is gone, but he longs for its presence:

> poor Marcher waded through his beaten grass, where no life stirred, where no breath sounded, where no evil eye seemed to gleam from a possible lair, very much as if vaguely looking for the Beast and still more as if missing it.... stopping fitfully in places where the undergrowth of life struck him as closer, asked himself yearningly, wondered secretly and sorely, if it would have lurked here or there. (394)

Aside from this yearning, which could be mistaken for a description of a fitful desire for queer sex, Marcher's other preoccupation is seemingly fit for psychoanalysis: "the other question, that of his unidentified past, that of his having to see his fortune impenetrably muffled and masked" (395). This "lost stuff of consciousness," we are told, "became thus for him as a strayed or stolen child to an unappeasable father; he hunted it up and down very much as if he were knocking at doors and inquiring of the police" (395). After traveling in Asia for a year, disillusioned at the supposed romance of the East, he returns to Bartram's grave and reflects that "*there* were the facts of the past, there the truth of his life, there the backward reaches in which he could lose himself" (398), convinced for the moment that his past revolves around heterosexual desire, or so it might seem at this point.

Marcher's visit to Bartram's grave seems to confirm this heterosexual narrative, but his "ache" also suggests homosexual possibilities. It is linked first with blood: "his ache had only been smothered. It was strangely drugged, but it throbbed; at the touch it began to bleed. And the touch, in the event, was the face of a fellow mortal" (398–99). This face remains gender neutral at first, with such generic labels as "person," "figure," "visitor," and "neighbor," until the encounter takes on violent images. It then reveals "an expression like the cut of a blade. He felt it, that is, so deep down that he winced at the steady thrust" (399). Marcher's desire, after this assault, is initially to lie down on the grave before him, "treating it as a place prepared to receive his last sleep" (399). But he is subsequently inflamed with desire at the "shock of the face," the "kind of hunger in his look," the "scarred passion," the "something that profaned the air" (399–400). He is thus "roused, startled, shocked" into the question, "What had the man *had* to make him, by the loss of it, so bleed and yet live?" (400). The possibility of bleeding from an encounter and yet remaining alive indicates to Marcher, "as in letters of quick flame, something he had utterly, insanely missed, and what he had missed made these things a train of fire, made them mark themselves in an anguish of inward throbs" (400). But as quickly as this torch is inflamed, the heteronormative Law extinguishes it, and Marcher is returned to a logic that, as Sedgwick argues, internalizes the heteronormative. His "revelation" quickly returns to the figure of Bartram; she, we are told, "*she* was what he had missed" (401). Although the logic vacillates back to a sense that his fate is much more mundane—that he was "*the* man, to whom nothing on earth was to have happened" (401)—the epiphany appears to reveal the heterosexual tragedy: "The escape would have been to love her; then, *then* he would have lived" (401).

Ultimately Sedgwick wants to read the role of Bartram in this story as "far bleaker" than might otherwise be possible. On the one hand, if Bartram is seen as trying to liberate Marcher's heterosexual potential, with "success" only coming too late, then Marcher's "revelation" is tragic. On the other hand, "if what needs to be liberated is in the first place Marcher's potential for homosexual desire...the trajectory of the story must be seen as far bleaker."[45] According to this reading, Bartram has sensed from the beginning that Marcher has homosexual desires that might be allowed to surface, but his final "revelation" represents the internalization of heteronormative Law; he becomes his own enforcer. From the homoerotic possibilities of the man he encounters in the cemetery, to the conclusion that "*she* was what he had missed,"[46] to the submission to the Beast in the end, Sedgwick argues that Marcher moves "from being the suffering object of a Law or judgment...to being the embodiment of that Law."[47] Sedgwick's reading seems persuasive here, particularly in the context of Kipling's formulation of obedience in "The Law of the Jungle" (1895), but it relies on a Freudian construction of animality that might not be warranted in this story.

Sedgwick's Beast, in other words, is an instinctually violent animal (even if it is a part of human "nature") that enforces heteronormativity. Freud's case study of the "Rat Man" suggests a similar formulation and provides interesting parallels with Sedgwick's reading. For Freud's patient, the figure of the beast—in this case a rat—is associated most importantly with punishment as well. The trigger for an obsessive neurosis in the young soldier is a conversation with an officer who has read about a "specially horrible punishment used in the East": "a pot was turned upside down on his buttocks...some *rats* were put into it...and they...*bored their way in*..."[48] What is most interesting here, from my perspective, is an implication about the nature of the *rats*, rather than the anal eroticism of the human being, in terms of either the design or the desire for the "punishment." The rats, we assume, are simply trying to survive, willing to push forcefully through any potential hole to find freedom. There is no possibility, for example, of linking the rats themselves with queer constructions of animality. One of the goals for the rats in finding freedom and ensuring their survival, we assume, would be to have the opportunity to achieve "success" in terms of heterosexual reproduction within their own species. The rat's "animal instincts," then, are the instrument of punishment.

For the Rat Man, the figure of the rat is associated with a beast lurking around his father's grave, reminiscent perhaps of James's Beast in the cemetery. According to Freud, "Once when the patient was visiting his father's grave he had seen a big beast, which he had taken to be a rat, gliding along over the grave. He assumed that it had actually come out of his father's grave, and had just been having a meal off his corpse" (10:215). Freud's note argues that the beast was probably a weasel, but the figure of the rat, for the patient, contains a "series of symbolical meanings, to which...fresh ones were continually being added" (10:213), including money, disease, the penis, or the "dirty animal" itself. The "real" rat is "a dirty animal, feeding upon excrement and living in sewers" (and therefore linked, according to Freud, with female prostitution) (10:214). It has "sharp teeth with which it gnaws and bites." Significantly, though, rats are victimized when "they are cruelly persecuted and mercilessly put to death by man, as the patient had observed with horror" (10:215–16). Freud's primary interest is not in the bodies of rats, though, and his interpretation of this sympathy is to infer that his patient had been punished like the rats, if only figuratively, as a child: "he had often pitied the poor creatures. But he himself had been just such a nasty, dirty little wretch, who was apt to bite people when he was in a rage, and had been fearfully punished for doing so" (10:216). For Freud, the Rat Man, like the Wolf Man, must be thinking about himself when he thinks about animals, but he also must be thinking about human sexuality. Sedgwick's reading of Marcher follows suit, as we shall soon see.

Despite the initial range of possibilities, Freud reduces the figure of the rat back to a construction of "normal" sexuality, here presented as the drive for species propagation. The child identifies with the rat; rats signify children in general; and the father's desire for his son to have his own children eventually leads to the obsessional neurosis with "a lady" who is physically unable to have children. Freud is thus able to "fill out the ellipsis" of his patient's formulation, from: "*If I marry the lady, some misfortune will befall my father* (in the next world)," to the true logic of the neurosis: "If my father were alive, he would be as furious over my design of marrying the lady as he was in the scene in my childhood; so that I should fly into a rage with him once more and wish him every possible evil; and thanks to the omnipotence of my wishes these evils would be bound to come upon him." The obsession thus becomes formulated as the following: "Every time you copulate, even with a stranger, you will not be able to avoid the reflection that in your married life sexual intercourse can never bring you a child (on account of the lady's sterility). This will grieve you so much…" (10:226). Rats boring into his anus, then, or eating the corpse of his father, are imagined as forms of punishment for failing to satisfy the obligation to procreate.

The Beast in James's story could be read from a similar perspective in which Marcher punishes himself for failing to procreate with Bartram, on the one hand, or for attempting (consciously or unconsciously) to reveal his potential for homosexual desire, on the other hand. What is interesting about these formulations, along with Freud's, is the implication that putting an animal into someone's anus is the most appropriate way to punish resistance to "natural" human heterosexuality. What is also interesting is the assumption that a "beast" cannot be linked with queer human desire. Chauncey's study of the human "wolf" at this historical moment, though, offers at least one significant alternative to a series of assumptions central to Sedgwick's reading: the Beast must be internalized within Marcher; it must be essentially heterosexual; and it must be committed to keeping the closet intact.[49] In his first conversation with Bartram that recollects his initial revelation to her, Marcher describes the Beast: "It hasn't yet come. Only, you know, it isn't anything I'm to *do*, to achieve in the world, to be distinguished or admired for. I'm not such an ass as *that*. It would be much better, no doubt, if I were."[50] But what is the nature of this Beast? And what kind of "ass" is Marcher?

Sedgwick's conclusion about the ultimate return of the Beast stops short of naming Marcher's compulsions as desires. The structure of the closet is maintained, she argues, even in terms of Marcher's self-knowledge, by turning his back to the Beast in the "heterosexual, self-ignorant acting out" of a fantasy that re-creates "a double scenario of homosexual compulsion and heterosexual compulsion" (212). "To face the gaze of the Beast," or to face the grieving man, "would have been to dissolve the closet, to recreate its hypostatized compulsions as desires."[51] I want to push this logic one step further. Sedgwick's formulation assumes that Marcher's turning away represents the heteronormative force (the tragically internalized Law) that is maintained by the figure of the Beast. The sexuality of the Beast itself, in other words, is "natural," and Marcher's punishment by the heterosexual Beast would appear to keep the closet intact. But if the Beast itself represents something else—the penetrating active wolf, or the desire to be penetrated by that species of wolf, or queer desire in general—then Marcher's response, his recognition that turning his back will lead to death, can in fact be seen as a form of coming *out* of the closet, albeit in the form of a tragic and brutally depressing acknowledgment of Jungle Law. The operative logic from the imperialist project is obedience to hierarchy, translated here even into the case of queer desire that itself might be seen as "natural." As Marcher notes, the "strangeness" of the waited-for event will not seem strange to him at all, only to others: "I don't know of it as—when it does come—necessarily violent. I only think of it as natural and as of course, above all, unmistakable. I think of itself as *the* thing. *The* thing will of itself appear natural."[52] But the final "act" is of course violent and even, perhaps, fatal. In the final lines the Beast is Marcher's "hallucination," and its final leap is the one, we are told, "that was to settle him," so he "flung himself, on his face, on the tomb" (402). Unlike the grieving man, Marcher cannot possibly "so bleed and yet live" (400); he appears to have accepted his fate, the inevitable penetration of the Beast, and the subsequent fatal dissolving of his closet. The act, in other words, or the desire for the act, perhaps defines an identity that cannot live.

Between Species

The nature of "the beast" at the turn of the century is thus more complicated and more interesting than critics have often assumed. The discourse of the jungle, naturalized through Darwinist-Freudian animality, eventually gives birth to biological determinism as we know it today, including popular constructions of heteronormativity. The assumption is that animals must be driven essentially, if not exclusively, by heterosexual and violent instincts. Once "the human" is constructed as having "animal instincts" or "the animal within," questions about human sexuality are framed within an evolutionary epistemology that is fundamentally new, though still in transition, at the turn of the twentieth century. My goal here, though, is not to uncover the "true" nature of animality. Rather, I want to emphasize the need to historicize how we have constructed "the animal" differently at various historical and cultural moments, and I want to illustrate how discourses of animality and sexuality have been mutually constitutive in U.S. literature and culture.

In "The King's Ankus," from *The Second Jungle Book*, Kipling's representation of the relationship between a human being and a python—Mowgli and Kaa—can provide a final example of provocative alternative interactions between "species" at the turn of the century. After running his hand "down the diagonal checkerings of the immense back" of the python, Mowgli remarks, "The Turtle is harder-backed, but not so gay," while "The Frog, my name-bearer, is more gay, but not so hard. It is very beautiful to see."[53] In order to carry Kaa to his nightly bath, Mowgli stoops down, "laughing, to lift the middle section of Kaa's great body, just where the barrel was thickest," while "Kaa lay still, puffing with quiet amusement" (257). Their "regular evening game" includes "a wrestling match—a trial of eye and strength"; "a little rough handling"; while they "rock to and fro, head to head, each waiting for his chance, till the beautiful, statue-like group melted in a whirl of black-and-yellow coils and struggling legs and arms, to rise up again and again" (257). After "making feints with his head" and calling attention to his touching of Mowgli, Kaa's "lightning lunge" ends the game, and they both slip into the "snake's pet bathing-place," where they "lay still, soaking luxuriously in the cool water" (257–58). Mowgli's response to this ritual of tangled bodies is that life "is better in the Jungle," but Kaa wonders whether "the Jungle gives thee all that thou has ever desired, Little Brother?" (258). While Mowgli responds with aggressive posturing that links "desire" with wanting to test his strength and kill larger and larger animals, Kaa is insistent: "Thou hast no other desire?" (258). Our post-Freudian inclination might be to situate this question about desire within the epistemology of the jungle, within survival-of-the-fittest heteronormativity, or perhaps within a sentimentalized racial fantasy of the orientalized other. But the acts of Kaa and Mowgli here suggest more interesting constructions of desire—particularly between a man and a python—that go beyond the reproduction of a "species." There are alternative possibilities for such relationships, in other words, not only in Kipling's texts but also at the turn of the century in the United States.

2

Between Species

QUEERING THE WOLF IN JACK LONDON

FREUD'S DECLARATION IN *Civilization and Its Discontents* that man is a wolf to man (*homo homini lupus*) reads rather differently in the context of "The Beast in the Jungle" and alternative histories of what it means to be a "wolf." The deployment of the animal reference suggests both violence and sexuality, but the discourse of the jungle is still in the process of being solidified as a naturalization of *hetero*sexuality at the turn of the century. The work of Jack London, the most famous self-designated Wolf in America at this historical moment, also suggests a series of negotiations related to sexual acts and desires that both resist and reinforce the construction of the dominant discourse. His plots often include "real" wolves and "wolf-like" men who construct a space of sexual possibility, even as narrative structures are set up in an attempt to police what might be seen as transgressions. Critics may debate whether London's stories are ever really "about" those four-footed creatures that biological discourses categorize as wolves or dogs. Mark Seltzer's analysis of "men in furs," for example, points toward a trend among certain critics of literary naturalism of assuming that London's animals are merely disguised human beings.[1] But there are two central questions I want to explore in the work of Jack London that have yet to be fully examined and that connect his work to Freud and James. First, how does the homoerotic content of interactions between men in a novel like *The Sea-Wolf* (1904) draw upon, challenge, or construct the epistemology of "the jungle" I have been suggesting thus far? Second, why do readings of *The Call of the Wild* (1903) and *White Fang* (1906) tend to choose between either an emphasis on human sexual allegory dressed up as animal representation or an assertion of "realistic" animal stories devoid of interspecies sexuality?

As Jonathan Auerbach has pointed out, Jack London's "fascination with lycanthropy" played an important role not only in his fiction but also in his sense of himself. In *Male Call: Becoming Jack London* (1996), Auerbach notes that London was known for "signing letters to his wife Charmian and his intimate friend George Sterling 'Wolf,' naming his dream ranch home 'Wolf House,' and in 1904 soliciting the design of a wolf-head logo... that appeared on his library bookplates (his literary property) as a kind of personal authorial logo—a standardized, exclusive, and recognizable identity."[2] Just how recognizable the identity of the Wolf might be, and in which contexts, is a question I explore in this chapter. In London's own life, the possibility of homosexuality is suggested by a number of circumstances, including his relationship with Sterling. As Scott Derrick points out in "Making a Heterosexual Man: Gender, Sexuality, and Narrative in the Fiction of Jack London," "London referred to Sterling as 'Greek' and was called 'Wolf' in return"; in addition, at an earlier point in his life, "London may have engaged in a homosexual relationship while in prison for vagrancy."[3] Auerbach cites London's *The Road* (1907) to support the claim that London "confessed to being the 'meat' of a 'powerfully-muscled man'—'a brute-beast' whose eyes nevertheless revealed to the youth 'humor and laughter and kindliness.'"[4] Such an experience completes, in a sense, as Auerbach notes, a series of identities and occupations that George Chauncey has identified as typically linked with what might be called "wolf" sexualities at the turn of the century: the sailor, the hobo, and the prisoner. Auerbach matches these roles up with "a series of identities and episodes at the center of London's sexually formative years, 1893–94: his shipping out to sea at the age of seventeen, tramping with Kelly's Army of the Unemployed the following year, and subsequent jailing in the Erie County Penitentiary for vagrancy."[5]

Eric Partridge's slang dictionary suggests shifting definitions of words such as "wolf" and "jungle" at this time that correspond to constructions of sexuality: "wolf," as I have previously noted, is defined as a "brutal, dominant pederast" from around 1900, and subsequently as a "tramp pertinaciously and courageously riding trains illicitly" from around 1915.[6] In addition, "jungles" becomes a "vagrant's camp" from 1910, and "to jungle-up" is "to stay as a tramp at a jungles" from 1920.[7] The *OED* lists such a meaning for "jungle" as early as 1908, attributed to U.S. slang, with the later introduction of the verb form "to jungle up" defined as "to prepare a meal at a hoboes' camp; to form such a camp; to join forces with another person." The jungles of Jack London's life are thus interesting to consider, but I am reluctant to resort to biography as a methodology for analyzing his texts; I am interested instead, in the first part of this chapter, in the deployment of "the jungle" as a discourse constructed in a novel like *The Sea-Wolf* (1904). The abstract Beast becomes the more specific Wolf in this text, embodied most recognizably in the title character of Wolf Larsen. The "jungle" of transient, working-class sailors on board the *Ghost* can be seen as representing a space for alternative sexualities and constructions of masculinity. But it also draws upon and constructs Spencerian and Darwinian "survival of the fittest" discourses. From both registers, though, *The Sea-Wolf* can be seen as a text that is fully engaged with the narrowing of discursive categories related to sexuality, specifically through the site of "the animal," at the turn of the century.

On Board with The Sea-Wolf

When Humphrey Van Weyden, also known as "Hump," is rescued from a sinking ferry in San Francisco Bay by Wolf Larsen and the crew of the seal-hunting *Ghost*, it is clear that he has stepped into an animalized world. While this world might seem rather far removed from the jungles of James or Kipling, it is in fact closely tied to the legacies of imperialism in "the jungle" and the Darwinian suggestion that humans are also evolving animals. London's representation of seal hunting and the sea as a different kind of jungle echoes Kipling's settings in stories such as "The White Seal," from the first *Jungle Book* (1894), which is told from the perspective of a seal. The initial plot of *The Sea-Wolf* borrows from Kipling's *Captains Courageous* (1897), as well as Dana's *Two Years before the Mast* (1840) and Norris's *Moran of the Lady Letty* (1898). But London's supposed bildungsroman of a privileged figure who learns about life through the harsh world of the sea differs from other narratives in this genre in its focus on an adult man, in this case an effete literary critic, rather than an adolescent boy. Hump's first impression of Wolf indicates the kind of jungle we have entered by focusing on his animal-like strength:

> It was what might be termed a sinewy, knotty strength, of the kind we ascribe to lean and wiry men, but which, in him, because of his heavy build, partook more of the enlarged gorilla order.... It was a strength we are wont to associate with things primitive, with wild animals, and the creatures we imagine our tree-dwelling prototypes to have been—a strength savage, ferocious, alive in itself, the essence of life in that it is the potency of motion, the elemental stuff itself out of which the many forms of life have been molded...[8]

Wolf Larsen's philosophy, we soon learn, is a mishmash of Darwin, Spencer, and Nietzsche, and he is overly anxious to discuss his views with the intellectual Hump. Wolf repeats such declarations as, "life is a mess...like yeast, a ferment"; "The big eat the little that they may continue to move, the strong eat the weak that they may retain their strength. The lucky eat the most and move the longest, that is all" (520). The crew of the *Ghost*, according to Wolf, operates under the same laws, where "Might is right" and morality is meaningless (543). The profligacy of Nature, as well as human life, is designed to ensure propagation, on the one hand, and production, on the other, in this case the production of profits through the labor of the seal hunters. While Wolf points out that "In our loins are the possibilities of millions of lives" (534), his conclusion is that "life is valueless, except to itself" (538).

The links between instinct and sexuality suggested by this Spencerian construction of social Darwinism become much more interesting as the novel develops. But it is important to note that the site for negotiating such links is the figure of the beast in the jungle, drawing as it does from constructions of both evolution and sexuality. From Henry James's Beast to Jack London's Wolf, we have moved into an embodied individual character, but not necessarily a less ambiguous conception of sexuality. A description of Wolf illustrates the movement of "the jungle" into an individual human being: "The jungle and the wilderness lurked in the uplift and downput of his feet. He was cat-footed, and lithe, and strong, always strong. I likened him to some great tiger, a beast of prowess and prey. He looked it, and the piercing glitter that arose at times in his eyes was the same piercing glitter I had observed in the eyes of caged leopards and other preying creatures of the wild" (648). In a sense, though, Wolf is a leopard who has not yet changed his spots; figuratively speaking, the role of the wolf in terms of male-male sexualities might be seen as not yet policed discursively, and the difference between middle-class and working-class constructions of homosexuality that Chauncey makes clear is on display in this novel at this historical moment.

Critics often draw attention to the homoerotic interactions that develop between Hump and Wolf on board the *Ghost*, particularly in what is referred to as "the first half" of the novel, before the figure of Maud Brewster miraculously appears to rescue Hump from the threat of homosexuality.[9] The homoerotic gaze that "Hump"—slang for "sexual intercourse" from 1900, according to Eric Partridge[10]—levels toward Wolf is fairly obvious to most critics, illustrated in scenes such as Hump nursing Wolf after a fight with the crew: "I had never before seen him stripped, and the sight of his body quite took my breath away."[11] As Hump is "fascinated by the perfect lines of Wolf Larsen's figure," by the "terrible beauty of it," he reflects that Wolf Larsen is clearly

> the man-type, the masculine, and almost a god in his perfectness. As he moved about or raised his arms the great muscles leapt and moved under the satiny skin.... His body, thanks to his Scandinavian stock, was fair as the fairest woman's. I remember his putting his hand up to feel of the wound on his head, and my watching the biceps move like a living thing under its white sheath.
>
> ...I could not take my eyes from him. I stood motionless, a roll of antiseptic cotton in my hand unwinding and spilling itself down to the floor. (593–94)

This "spilling" results from the erotic tension of the scene, focused in part on muscles that leap and move as the embodiment of animality beneath the surface of Wolf's skin. After noticing Hump's gaze, Wolf flexes his muscles and commands him to "Feel them" (594). Hump finds them "hard as iron" but also "softly crawling and shaping about the hips, along the back, and across the shoulders" (594). The reward for such intimate contact is that Hump is promoted to "mate," after Wolf calls him a "handy man" (595). Hump thus completes a cycle of sorts from outsider to newly initiated mate, a position first made available by the death and burial of the previous mate, a man who "had gone on a debauch before leaving San Francisco, and then had the poor taste to die at the beginning of the voyage and leave Wolf Larsen short-handed" (496).

Intimate contact is not reserved solely for Hump and Wolf, though, on board the *Ghost*. The rest of the hunters, who are described as "some semi-human amphibious breed," sleep together in bunks in the forecastle that look "like the sleeping dens of animals in a menagerie" (513). Bodies in contact with other bodies sometimes result in intimacies, but also jealousies and often violence. The fight between Wolf and the crew-turned-mutineers (the same fight that leads to Hump nursing Wolf in the aftermath) is described in terms that might even sound like a gang rape of Wolf in the dark of the forecastle. The narrative follows "the impact of the blows—the soft crushing sound made by flesh striking forcibly against flesh. Then there was the crashing about of the entwined bodies, the labored breathing, the short quick gasps of sudden pain" (587). Out on deck, once the attack is repelled by Larsen, the comparison of bodies reveals a racial distinction between the "masculine" whiteness of Larsen and the "feminine" beauty of Oofty-Oofty, the "Kanakan" from the South Seas.[12] Oofty-Oofty may be "a beautiful creature, almost feminine in the pleasing lines of his figure" (590), but he cannot compare with Larsen, "the man-type," because his "lines...in so far as they pleased, that far had they been what I should call feminine" (593). This "ship of madmen and brutes" (550), of knifings, beatings, and brutality, thus reveals "the animality of man" (575) on display, in this case in what appears to be "a half-brute, half-human species, a race apart, wherein there is no such thing as sex" (583). But "sex" here, significantly, refers only to the goal of propagation. Without women on board, the *Ghost* is "a company of celibates, grinding harshly against one another and growing daily more calloused from the grinding"; "their masculinity, which in itself is of the brute, has been overdeveloped"; they seem to be "hatched out by the sun like turtle eggs, or receive life in some similar and sordid fashion" (582–83). And while Hump assumes that the lack of "womankind" is "unnatural and unhealthful" (582), he also later confesses; "though I had been surrounded by women all my days, my appreciation of them had been aesthetic and nothing more. I had actually, at times, considered myself outside the pale, a monkish fellow denied the eternal or the passing passions I saw and understood so well in others" (651). All of which would seem to call out for, according to the growing anxiety of the narrative, the figure of a woman to rescue these men from themselves on board the *Ghost*.

Roughly halfway through the novel, then, comes the appearance of Maud Brewster, accomplished poet and essayist, picked up by the *Ghost* from a shipwrecked mail steamer en route to Tokyo. Hump's first reaction is that she seems "like a being from another world" (620), and most critics have followed suit by confidently proclaiming a radical shift in the narrative at this moment, where the arrival of "woman" means the end of all homoerotic possibility. Jonathan Auerbach, for example, argues that Maud's entrance signals the narrative's "affirmation of normative heterosexuality" and "the end of all homoerotic contest," so that "we can all but hear a palpable, massive, sigh of relief,"[13] now that the "feminine" side of men has been "driven underground."[14] Scott Derrick's reading is subtler, with his claim that the second half of the novel reveals a "narrative rigidity...which engineers a containment of its own homoerotic impulses,"[15] but he still wants to argue that *The Sea-Wolf* "employs a narrative teleology aimed at the construction of heterosexual masculinity to repress and marginalize a finally unacceptable and disruptive homoeroticism."[16] Derrick's emphasis on narrative structures follows June Howard, who has argued that the radical shift that coincides with the arrival of Maud is the arrival of the sentimental love story.[17] From this perspective, Maud becomes the "real lady on the masculine 'brute-ship,'"[18] even though narrative tension remains as a result of "the uncomfortable, discontinuous coexistence of naturalism and sentiment in the text."[19] This tension, according to Howard, accounts for the narrative energy devoted to Wolf Larsen in the second half of the book, while other critics seem to equate the extent of the narrative's torture of Wolf Larsen with the extent to which the novel must go to police the homoerotic, to bury the return of the repressed. While I think many of these readings are useful for understanding *The Sea-Wolf,* I want to suggest several reasons for being less pessimistic about constructions of sexuality in the novel, even if the possibilities are often produced within problematic contexts. The ambiguous nature of the relationship between Hump and Maud, for example, is far less heteronormative than it might first appear. In addition, the text's ultimate relationship to "the jungle" and shifting discursive formations of sexuality is also more ambiguous than it might first appear, including the possibility that the "ghost" of "wolf" sexuality is not simply suppressed but also lamented by the logic of the text.

The relationship between Hump and Maud is certainly a form of containment of the sexual energy emanating from Hump's interactions with Wolf. And yet, as Derrick has pointed out, the figure of Maud cannot be reduced to generic "woman," as some critics have suggested. Derrick claims that Maud is drawn from both the New Woman of the turn of the century and the more conservative nineteenth-century conception of essential maternity or womanhood. Sam S. Baskett's conclusion about such constructions is that London is actually trying to illustrate "an ideal androgynous union" in which both Hump and Maud have an "identity that transcends conventional concepts of gender roles."[20] But, as Derrick points out, "androgyny, which implies a complementary blending of men and women into a wholeness tragically lost, tends to conceal the complexity of London's relation to questions of gender."[21] Jonathan Auerbach has noted that Baskett's argument relies on static conceptions of "masculine" and "feminine" in order to then combine them in the androgynous individual.[22] Derrick, though, ultimately wants to read Hump's desire for Maud through the structure of fetishism,[23] and therefore to suggest that transferring male characteristics to Maud can be seen as "the sublimation of a prohibited male homoeroticism by finding desired male characteristics in women, but this need makes heterosexual desire less identifiable and conventional."[24]

While I agree with the general argument that Derrick suggests, I have difficulty with his reliance on the homosexual/heterosexual binary to describe what might be "less identifiable and conventional" sexualities. Certainly Maud is cross-dressed on several occasions, and she takes on "male" roles when it comes to steering the lifeboat she takes with Hump to escape from

Wolf, or clubbing seals once they reach "Endeavor Island" and begin to live out a Robinson Crusoe–like existence. As Hump describes his growing "love" for her, it often happens that his most sentimental declarations are followed by actions or thoughts that undermine the sense that the heteronormative has so clearly won the battle for the shape of his desire. At one point, for example, Hump admits, "I was surprised, and joyfully, that she was so much the woman, and the display of each trait and mannerism that was characteristically feminine gave me keener joy.... She was woman, my kind, on my plane, and the delightful intimacy of kind, of man and woman, was possible, as well as the reverence and awe in which I knew I should always hold her."[25] But on the same page we find Hump dressing her up in men's clothing, presumably to keep her warm. He gives her a heavy man's shirt and then exchanges "the boy's cap she wore for a man's cap, large enough to cover her hair, and, when the flap was turned down, to completely cover her neck and ears. The effect," we are told, "was charming."[26]

As Marjorie Garber has shown in *Vested Interests: Cross-Dressing and Cultural Anxiety* (1992), transvestism can play a useful role in deconstructing binaries of gender and sexuality and revealing other cultural anxieties. Particularly useful here is Garber's resistance to the tendency to look *through* cross-dressing to what it says about either-or categories. Garber explores the erotics of the crossing itself, and, to apply her formulation here, we might try to look *at* the cross-dressed figure of Maud rather than through her to some sort of "essential" heterosexual desire. The potentially liberating form of a "third," what Garber calls "a mode of articulation, a way of describing a space of possibility,"[27] also points to the power of category crisis: "a failure of definitional distinction, a borderline that becomes permeable, that permits of border crossings from one (apparently distinct) category to another."[28] In short, Garber shows that the power of transvestism lies in its questioning of "the very notion of the 'original' and of stable identity," and that "*transvestism is a space of possibility structuring and confounding culture*: the disruptive element that intervenes, not just a category crisis of male and female, but the crisis of category itself."[29] Rather than overlooking Maud's transvestism as representative of the New Woman or the androgynous ideal, I want to leave open a space to call into question easy distinctions between Hump and Maud, between "man" and "woman," between performativity, in Judith Butler's sense, and the "essence" of one's gender or one's sexual object choice.

Another interesting scene to reconsider for its supposedly obvious and limiting constructions of heteronormativity is the often-cited passage that describes Hump and Maud "stepping the mast" of the disabled *Ghost*, which eventually washes up on the shore of their island with the now-disabled Wolf inside. Considerable narrative energy is spent describing the plan to first build a mechanism and then utilize its leverage to lift up the broken mast and place it back down in the hole on deck that has been built for it.[30] The project takes several months, lengthened in part by Wolf's dismantling of the work while they are asleep. But on the dramatic final day, Hump begins by swinging the mast over the hole, even though he misses it at first. The signifier shifts from "mast" to "the butt of the mast" as Hump goes below to wait for it and Maud takes over control. Eventually the term becomes just "butt" and an obvious reading begins to seem less likely: "Straight toward the square hole of the step the square butt descended; but as it descended it slowly twisted so that square would not fit into square."[31] After going back up on deck and making a further adjustment, Hump returns below, and we are told that "Slowly the butt descended the several intervening inches, at the same time slightly twisting again. Again Maud rectified the twist with the watch-tackle, and again she lowered away from the windlass. Square fitted into square. The mast was stepped."[32]

Traditional readings would see this scene as a triumph of the restored phallus: Maud helping Hump to be a "real man" with an erect "mast." But the triumph could also be seen from a different perspective, and that would be the successful "fitting" of the "butt" and the "square." Could this be an unconscious or even conscious trace of anal sex in the midst of what otherwise might seem to be clearly heteronormative?[33] We might think of a definition of "square-head" that Eric Partridge has identified as "A Swede" (from 1905), or also "in English more usually a German."[34] Wolf Larsen's fair "Scandinavian stock" comes to mind and offers the possibility of different "partners" involved in this scene (recalling, too, that Larsen is still below the deck in another part of the ship at this point). Immediately following Hump's declaration that "The eyes of both of us [meaning Maud], *I think*, were moist with the joy of success,"[35] Hump realizes that something is burning. "The Wolf is not yet dead" (758), we find out, and as both Hump and Maud descend into the fire below that Wolf has set, Maud becomes disoriented and lost. Hump resolves to feel "about among his blankets," and then we are told that "something hot fell on the back of my hand. It burned me, and I jerked my hand away" (759). What Wolf has done is to reach up "through the cracks in the bottom of the upper bunk" to set fire to them, or, perhaps, to ensure that the right "butt" has been enflamed (or inflamed) (759). It might also be possible to read this scene as evoking Hump's sublimated desire for anal sex with a cross-dressed Maud. Rather than arguing for any of these readings definitively, I merely want to suggest that alternatives outside the reductive homosexual/heterosexual binary are possible, even in those moments that seem to do so much police work.

To situate *The Sea-Wolf* in the context of shifting discursive possibilities at the turn of the century is not to suggest that it occupies a clear and consistent position between an emphasis on acts or identity. Two distinctions that George Chauncey has suggested need to be inserted into this discussion to complicate what might otherwise appear to be a universal, linear shift from one mode to another. First, as I have noted in the previous chapter, Chauncey has challenged the notion that elite medical discourses constructed "the homosexual" as a personality type that was then adopted by the culture as a whole. Chauncey points out that "the medical literature was more complex...and represented simply one of several powerful (and competing) sexual ideologies"; and, in addition, that "the invert and the normal man, the homosexual and the heterosexual, were not inventions of the elite but were popular discursive categories before they became elite discursive categories."[36] The second important distinction for Chauncey is thus revealed to be class, even if simple distinctions are still difficult to make: "The homosexual displaced the 'fairy' in *middle*-class culture several generations earlier than in *working*-class culture; but in each class culture each category persisted, standing in uneasy, contested, and disruptive relation to the other."[37] Such qualifications make it difficult to assert that *The Sea-Wolf* merely moves from one class formulation of sexuality to another, but they can help to draw attention to the class dynamics at play in the novel. Scott Derrick's reading of the novel misses these subtleties when he suggests that a "profound cultural paradox" is revealed when the homoerotic is linked with the bestial and with filth, rather than the "dandification and effeteness" of "the gay man as he emerges in late-nineteenth- and early twentieth-century culture."[38] Chauncey's work provides evidence that this is no "paradox" at all, unless one assumes that middle-class constructions are universal, and that sexual preferences can only be described from within the framework of either homosexuality or heterosexuality. For Derrick, Wolf can be seen as "ostensibly heterosexual" (126), even if his "desirable femininity" "renders him a dangerously seductive object even to a heterosexual man" (118). Such terminology could be seen as anachronistic when applied to Wolf, particularly when the rhetoric of "normality" would appear to be more appropriate for the time, a rhetoric I will return to at the end of this section.

Derrick makes a useful distinction between the clean, white body of Wolf and the racialized body of Oofty-Oofty, associated with the odors and filth of the forecastle, but I am not sure that the homoeroticism directed toward Wolf is thus contained. For Derrick, "London's narrative separates Larsen from the contagion of the erotic by demonizing the lower-class racial body as the real place of fluid, odor, and warmth, consequently effecting a sublimation of homoerotic energy into an apparently innocent, homosocial gaze" (121). In what sense, though, does the homosocial become more "innocent" than the homoerotic?[39] Jonathan Auerbach's discussion of class appears to be more useful when he argues that the narrative shift from Wolf to Maud can be seen as the rejection of working-class sexuality and the submission to middle-class constructions of heteronormativity that require the repression of anything that might be perceived as "homosexual." By "giving up his 'Wolf' for a woman," Auerbach thus argues, "London in effect turns his back on his working-class origins to affirm his allegiance to an emergent set of middle-class norms."[40] Auerbach reads Hump's misplaced identification-turned-desire for Wolf to be a distorted oedipal structure that is restored to normality once Maud appears. And Auerbach's reliance on biographical material for Jack London allows him to read this shift in class-constructed sexuality to be decisive not only for Hump but also for London himself.[41] But within the logic of the text, I am not convinced that such definitive claims are most useful for understanding the shifting dynamics of sexuality in the jungle of *The Sea-Wolf*.

One of the questions I ask throughout this book is about the nature of the beast in specific contexts, and I think there is more to be said not only about Wolf as the beast but also about Hump in his fascination, if not explicit desire, for Wolf that persists throughout the novel. Rather than looking at the "second half" of the text as simply the substitution of Maud for Wolf, with Wolf punished for his sexual sins with blinding headaches and ultimately complete bodily paralysis, I think it is important to note that only five out of thirty-nine chapters go by from the time Hump and Maud leave the *Ghost* to Wolf's appearance on Endeavor Island; he is still alive even after Hump and Maud have set sail in the remasted ship, and it is not until the penultimate page of the novel that he finally dies and is buried at sea. Certainly much of what is going on for these last several chapters can be seen as the return of the repressed for Hump, but I am less convinced than others that the ultimate repression is successful or even desired in the end. What is affirmed, I believe, is the sense that true masculinity must be in touch with the "primitive animal" buried within the "civilized man." From this perspective, *both* Hump and Wolf are too civilized because their masculinity is self-conscious: it is not truly instinctual. The amorality of the animal may be terrifying, but it can also be liberating if "morality" includes the need to reject all erotic energy between men.

The fact that Wolf's debilitation comes from within his brain, from the center of his intellect, is a fact that is too often overlooked. From Hump's perspective, it is puzzling "why such a magnificent animal as he should have headaches at all."[42] The attraction for Hump is "a man so purely primitive that he was of the type that came into the world before the development of the moral nature" (557). This "leopard" (662) is not so purely primitive, though, that he does not relish an intellectual explanation of the "instinctual" animal world he claims to inhabit, a world where his animal body is destined "to be fed upon, to be carrion, to yield up all the strength and movement of my muscles that it may become strength and movement in fin and scale and the guts of fishes" (538). Wolf's final resting place is in fact the sea, but his death comes not from some physical clash with another animal, human or nonhuman. Instead, as he explains to Hump toward the end, "Something's gone wrong with my brain. A cancer, a tumor, or something of that nature,—a thing that devours and destroys. It's attacking my nerve-centres, eating them up, bit by bit, cell by cell—from the pain" (753). To be shot by Hump would be fitting, "But to die this way—" (753) is a sentence that cannot be finished. Hump may be "impotent" in his inability to kill Wolf when he has the chance because of his sense of morality (720), but he still mourns the fact that Wolf has been reduced to "a woman" in his despair, looking "for all the world like a woman wringing her hands" rather than "Wolf Larsen, the fighter, the strong man, the indomitable one" (727–28). Watching this "magnificent animal" body be crippled, while the intellect remains intact until the end, is awful for Hump: "It was horrible. I was trembling all over, and I could feel the shivers running up and down my spine and the sweat standing out on my forehead. Surely there can be little in this world more awful than the spectacle of a strong man in the moment when he is utterly weak and broken" (728). Even though he is blinded and paralyzed with his tumor and a series of strokes, Wolf's presence will not allow Hump and Maud to believe that the power of his body has been destroyed: "we could not adjust ourselves to his condition. Our minds revolted. To us he was full of potentiality. We knew not what to expect of him next, what fearful thing, rising above the flesh, he might break out and do" (754). His final "disembodiment," then, is described in existential terms: "To that intelligence there could be no objective knowledge of a body. It knew no body. The very world was not. It knew only itself and the vastness and profundity of the quiet and the dark" (764). And while Maud is "surprised and shocked" at Hump's behavior during the burial at sea, Hump admits that "the spirit of something I had seen before was strong upon me, impelling me to give service to Wolf Larsen as Wolf Larsen had once given service to another man" (770), his previous "mate."

But what kind of "service" could Hump have in mind? Is it to live according to the "primitive" values that Wolf embodies? Certainly the narrative seems unforgiving of what is usually read as Wolf's attempted rape of Maud on board the *Ghost*, and the violence in the jungle of the ship is not valorized, except perhaps in the resultant sexual possibilities. The attempted narrative solution, it seems to me, is at first an appropriation of social Darwinism to construct masculinity as embracing "the primitive" in an overcivilized world. Morality no longer conflicts with "the animal" within "civilized" human beings if the "primitive animal" can engage in "survival of the fittest" struggles for the benefit of individual and species propagation. Heteronormative sexuality, then, *must* be right (the logic might go), not because of middle-class considerations but because of the "law of the jungle." Through this kind of rationalization Hump can find a way to legitimate his fascination with Wolf through the end. After clubbing seals with Maud, for example, he can exult in the thrill of the primitive and proclaim, "The youth of the race seemed burgeoning in me, over-civilized man that I was, and I lived for myself the old hunting days and forest nights of my remote and forgotten ancestry. I had much for which to thank Wolf Larsen, was my thought, as we went along the path between the jostling harems" (711), of seals, that is. The attraction of Maud, then, described at this point by Hump as "my woman, my mate," is the potential she holds for the perpetuation of "the race" as opposed to the "sleek young bulls" of the seal herd, "living out the loneliness of their bachelorhood" (712). At one point, when Wolf has appeared on the island and tries to strangle Hump, Maud shows up with a seal club, ready to fight for her man, and Hump is ecstatic once more: "Truly she was my woman, my mate-woman, fighting with me and for me as the mate of a caveman would have fought, all the primitive in her aroused, forgetful of her culture, hard under the softening civilization of the only life she had ever known" (750). Yet even a moment such as this is undermined by the subsequent "sober thought": "she was only a woman, crying her relief, now that the danger was past, in the arms of her protector or of one who had been endangered. Had I been father or brother, the situation would have been in no wise different" (751). And we are left with ambiguities once again. After sighting another ship on the penultimate page of the novel, Hump is not sure "whether to be glad or not," and Maud's final line is that the ship can now "rescue us from ourselves" (771). But none of the preceding examples suggest that what Hump and Maud really want to do is continue living "the primitive life" together on an "uncharted island." The

presence of a woman, while helpful for fending off the suggestion of homoerotic currents between men, would still be somehow not quite right.

What is most interesting in the case of *The Sea-Wolf*, from my perspective,
is the sense in which a discourse of animality can help to construct masculinity even within conceptions of sexual desire that would come to be seen
as "abnormal." The figure of the Wolf in this novel is *not* necessarily abnormal in his choice of sexual object; he is abnormal in his overcivilized intellect
that can rationalize human violence according to the principles of Spencerian
social Darwinism. As George Chauncey describes constructions of masculinity at this historical moment, "so long as the men abided by the conventions
of masculinity, they ran little risk of undermining their status as 'normal'
men."[43] What we would today call sexist constructions of homosexual activities would not have been recognizable at this time to some groups of men,
particularly in working-class gay culture: "The phallocentric presumption
that a man's sexual satisfaction was more significant than the gender or character of the person who provided that satisfaction allowed gay men to make
certain arguments in their approach to 'normal' men that would seem utterly
incredible in the absence of that presumption."[44] The intervention of Freud,
as Chauncey notes, is to shift the focus to object choice and ultimately to
sexual identity as determined by that object choice. Wolf Larsen seems to be
punished for his intellect, for thinking too much about his actions, rather
than acting instinctually as the embodiment of an animalized masculinity
that does not yet depend upon object choice. The space of possibility that is
being mourned, then, the "ghost" that remains so hauntingly appealing, could
be seen as the "true" call of the wolf: the vitality and exhilaration of a wider
range of sexualities between men, and the thrill of experience unfettered, supposedly, by "civilization."

Becoming-Wolf

Representations of man as a wolf are eventually evacuated of these alternative
sexualities in the discourse of the jungle. But there is a further question to be
explored here: Must representations of animals primarily signify sexual possibilities between members of the same species? Foucault's declaration that the
homosexual becomes a distinct species at the end of the nineteenth century
deploys the language that would seem to answer this question affirmatively, as
Freud's work certainly does. As heterosexuality becomes naturalized among
human beings in the discourse of the jungle, the possibility of deriving pleasure from interspecies contact becomes even more taboo as well. Kipling's

work suggests this possibility at the turn of the century, though, through several interactions between Mowgli and Kaa, the python, as I noted at the end of the previous chapter. My question for this cultural moment in general, then, is, what kinds of "desire" might be suggested by representations of interspecies eroticism? In the case of Mowgli and Kaa, is this a homosexual (human) invitation in disguise as animal representation? Conversely, does it indicate a desire for interspecies sexual pleasure? What other formulations of desire might be possible at this moment? Finally, from an animality studies perspective, how might interspecies pleasure relate to better ways of thinking about relationships between human and nonhuman animals?

Jack London's most famous novels raise these questions as well when men interact with "real" wolves or dogs in novels such as *The Call of the Wild* (1903) and *White Fang* (1906). Certainly one way to read these works is to look *through* such dog or half-wolf characters as Buck and White Fang and to see homoerotic energy directed toward them as a displacement of sexual desire between human males. Given the context I have laid out thus far, such readings would seem to offer similar possibilities for a wider range of male-male sexualities. *The Call of the Wild*, for example, as London's best-known novella, is eponymous in its "call" at the turn of the century, but its evocation of "the wild" might be rather different from what is usually associated with London. Enacting many of the same conflicting agendas I have laid out in *The Sea-Wolf*, this short novel provides similar spaces of sexual possibility within what might otherwise appear to be a rigid, survival-of-the-fittest ideology, particularly in the erotic energy that develops between Buck, the aristocratic dog-becoming-wolf, and John Thornton, his love-god.

After being brutalized by the incompetent trio of Hal, Charles, and Mercedes, Buck is saved by Thornton and grows to experience what is described as "Love, genuine passionate love....love that was feverish and burning, that was adoration, that was madness...[that] had taken John Thornton to arouse."[45] Thornton, we are told, "had a way of taking Buck's head roughly between his hands, and resting his own head upon Buck's, of shaking him back and forth, the while calling him ill names that to Buck were love names. Buck knew no greater joy than that rough embrace and the sound of murmured oaths, and at each jerk back and forth it seemed that his heart would be shaken out of his body so great was its ecstasy" (60). The rough swearing, along with Buck's playful biting of Thornton's hand, seems to be an attempt to lend a "manly" quality to this love-play that is constructed in terms that are later echoed in the character of Wolf Larsen. Buck is described, for example, as being "in perfect condition," the picture of "grit and virility";

"The great breast and heavy fore legs were no more than in proportion with the rest of the body, where the muscles showed in tight rolls underneath the skin. Men felt these muscles and proclaimed them hard as iron" (68–69). Like Wolf Larsen, he is "a magnificent animal" (69), and he participates in intimate rituals with Thornton that on one occasion, at least, make onlookers uncomfortable: "As though animated by a common impulse, the onlookers drew back to a respectful distance, nor were they again indiscreet enough to interrupt" (70).

The relationship between White Fang and Weedon Scott in *White Fang* is portrayed in similar terms. We are told, for example, that White Fang, who is half wolf, experiences love that "manifested itself to him as a void in his being—a hungry, aching, yearning void that clamored to be filled. It was a pain and an unrest; and it received easement only by the touch of the new god's presence."[46] What he experiences is "strange feelings and unwonted impulses" (244), particularly when we find Weedon Scott "squatting down on his heels, face to face with White Fang and petting him—rubbing at the roots of the ears, making long, caressing strokes down the neck to the shoulders, tapping the spine gently with the balls of his fingers" (247). White Fang's response is to initiate a new love ritual: "What of his joy, the great love in him, ever surging and struggling to express itself, succeeded in finding a new mode of expression. He suddenly thrust his head forward and nudged his way in between the master's arm and body. And here, confined, hidden from view all except his ears, no longer growling, he continued to nudge and snuggle" (247). His love is not promiscuous, though, as we are later told that "nobody else ever romped with White Fang. . . . That he allowed the master these liberties was no reason that he should be a common dog, loving here and loving there, everybody's property for a romp and good time. He loved with single heart and refused to cheapen himself or his love" (273).

Critics such as Auerbach and Derrick have noted that London seems to take pains to suppress what could be seen as the homosexual implications of both stories. In *The Call of the Wild*, John Thornton is brutally killed by "Yeehat" Indians, and Buck finds his body hidden in a deep pool of water near the camp. Derrick reads the scene as "a terrible expression and suppression of Buck's love for Thornton."[47] Buck, we are told, makes a pilgrimage to this site each subsequent year even after he has finally heeded "the call" and become the leader of a roaming wolf pack. The mark of Buck's heterosexual "success" at propagation can be seen in "a change in the breed of timber wolves" that is noted in the text, once markings like Buck's appear in the next generation of wolves.[48] White Fang, on the other hand, saves his love-master from a similar fate at the hands of an escaped convict, but his heterosexuality (so the argument goes) is affirmed in the final pages of the novel by the domesticated sheepdog named "Collie." When he follows her into the nearby woods, presumably to have sex, we are given none of the passionate love themes that marked his relationship with Weedon Scott. Instead, we are told, in a rather resigned tone, that they simply run "side by side," just as "his mother, Kiche, and old One Eye had run long years before in the silent Northland forest."[49] The result of this apparently heteronormative affirmation, then, is "a half-dozen pudgy puppies" and the pleasure of his human masters at the performance.[50]

It would be tempting to read London's nonhuman characters simply as cross-dressed human beings, a form of "cross-species drag" in terms of representation.[51] Doing so might point toward some of the liberating possibilities suggested by Garber's work on transvestism, but such a move seems problematic insofar as it would assume no difference between Buck, for example, and the Beast in Henry James. What we have in London's dog/wolf stories, it seems to me, is a different step toward human constructions of "the animal," here with the narratives we might project onto creatures running on four legs rather than two. I do not mean to argue that Buck and White Fang are "real" animals and therefore somehow legible to human beings outside of the epistemology of the jungle. Rather, I want to consider what happens when questions of sexuality are raised in conjunction with questions of "real" animals in London's written texts.

In *The Call of the Wild*, to take one example, we find an erotics of the animal body that is expressed through the thrill of the hunt in descriptions that are at least conceivable as the actions of nonhuman animals. An exultation in the bodies of animals might be seen as more "normal," perhaps, when it describes animals engaged in what is presented as biological destiny, what they were "born to do." Descriptions of Buck's body tingle with excitement, for example, when he is on the hunt, chasing prey, killing instead of being killed, and so on. His "blood lust, the joy to kill" is "infinitely more intimate" than a human hunter's because he can exult in "running the wild thing down, the living meat, to kill with his own teeth and wash his muzzle to the eyes in warm blood."[52] London uses the word "ecstasy" three times in the subsequent passage before plunging into a joyous description of Buck's body pulsing with life: "He was mastered by the sheer surging of life, the tidal wave of being, the perfect joy of each separate muscle, joint, and sinew in that it was everything that was not death, that it was aglow and rampant, expressing itself in movement, flying exultantly under the stars and over the face of dead matter that did not move."[53] Toward the end of the novel Buck is once again portrayed as a glorious body in the wild when he becomes:

> A carnivorous animal, living on a straight meat diet…in full flower, at the high tide of his life, overspilling with vigor and virility. When Thornton passed a caressing hand along his back, a snapping and crackling followed the hand, each hair discharging its pent magnetism at the contact. Every part, brain and body, nerve tissue and fibre, was keyed to the most exquisite pitch; and between all the parts there was a perfect equilibrium or adjustment.…His muscles were surcharged with vitality, and snapped into play sharply, like steel springs. Life streamed through him in splendid flood, glad and rampant, until it seemed that it would burst him asunder in sheer ecstasy and pour forth generously over the world.[54]

Auerbach's assertion that this story reveals "the fact" of London imagining "himself as a dog, an autobiographical projection,"[55] before shifting his narrative sympathies to John Thornton, seems to miss the interspecies physical ecstasy of these scenes almost entirely. Auerbach's brief comment that the "communion between the two grows more problematic once London gives their mutual love a physical basis"[56] is as far as he is willing to go along these lines.[57] The "communion" between a human male and a nonhuman male that London's stories thus evoke is much more interesting to me than humans in animal drag or animals represented "realistically." This kind of interspecies eroticism raises a question I want to consider in the remainder of this chapter, which is, what are the limitations of assuming that animal representation can only construct intra*human* sexualities?

Psychoanalytic readings of Jack London's work would seem to point toward the kinds of readings offered by Derrick and Auerbach. They would follow, in this sense, the work of Freud in his readings of animal dreams and animals more generally in his case studies. His interpretation of the "Wolf Man," for example, assumes that the nature of the Beast must be primarily rooted in such human sexual structures as the Oedipal complex and the fear of castration. Influential critiques of this famous case study by theorists such as Gilles Deleuze and Félix Guattari point toward both different interpretive possibilities today and different conceptions of interspecies sexuality perhaps available at the turn of the century: conceptions that would seem to match the broader discursive possibilities related to human sexuality prior to the condensation of meanings within the homosexual/heterosexual binary.

Deleuze and Guattari's scorn directed toward Freud's "reductive glee" is an important reminder against foregone conclusions in readings of anyone's material, and my own project certainly runs the risk of explaining everything away according to conclusions formed in this way. But their emphasis on "multiplicities," on "becomings-animal," is a crucial tonic to this risk insofar as it allows us to challenge what happens when we interpret "*the* animal," or *l'animot*, to borrow Derrida's term, in less reductive ways.[58] The idea of "becoming-animal" in Deleuze and Guattari provides a significant step toward rethinking representations of animality (and psychoanalysis in general). But it is important to note that the idea is as complex as it is potentially liberating; this is no mere imitative process: "Becomings-animal are basically of another power, since their reality resides not in an animal one imitates or to which one corresponds but in themselves, in that which suddenly sweeps us up and makes us become—a *proximity, an indiscernibility* that extracts a shared element from the animal far more effectively than any domestication, utilization, or imitation could: 'the Beast.'"[59] The problem with psychoanalysts in line with Freud is that they cannot understand these "becomings-animal." Deleuze and Guattari argue that "They killed becoming-animal.... They see the animal as a representative of drives, or a representation of the parents. They do not see the reality of a becoming-animal, that it is affect in itself, the drive in person, and represents nothing. There exist no other drives than the assemblages themselves."[60]

What is missing in Deleuze and Guattari, though, is a more explicit exploration of how these becomings might relate to "plateaus" within interspecies sexualities.[61] I want to suggest that a whole range of erotic pleasures and behaviors between humans and animals are possible, beyond Freud and beyond Deleuze and Guattari, despite the reductiveness of the only available signifier: "bestiality." Pathologizing erotic interactions between humans and animals is certainly more entrenched in turn-of-the-twenty-first-century discourse than is pathologizing homosexuality. My questions about interspecies eroticism, though, provide a means for circling back around to the stories of Jack London and the relationships he depicts between men and their canine or lupine companions: First, why must interspecies erotics be seen only as a substitution for intrahuman desires? Second, why must these erotics be limited to a specific sexual act and/or climax: vaginal or anal intercourse (or, on rare occasions, genital-oral contact that results in the climactic release of sexual fluids)?

Marjorie Garber's *Dog Love* represents a step toward answering these questions, even if she appears to be hesitant in her conclusions. Garber suggests that passages describing the love between John Thornton and Buck, for example, if taken out of context, could be mistaken for a "come-hither excerpt from the back cover of a torrid work of gay fiction."[62] Garber's analysis of the relationship, once the characters are revealed, is that "The love between them is described in the most erotic, if innocent, of terms."[63] But in what sense, I want to ask, must this eroticism be "innocent"? Is it because no genital contact occurs (we assume?) and no seminal fluids are ejaculated? I would point to similar moments in *White Fang* that deserve more nuanced readings, such as White Fang's learning "to romp with the master, to be tumbled down and rolled over, and be the victim of innumerable rough tricks.... This would always culminate with the master's arms going around White Fang's neck and shoulders while the latter crooned and growled his love-song."[64] Garber argues in general that "To allegorize this as a tale about strictly human affairs is to lose much of its affective power,"[65] but there is also more to be considered here.

Garber's larger argument is that "dog love is not an evasion or a substitution. It calls upon the same range and depth of feelings that humans have for humans" (14–15). Garber is perhaps even more useful when she later qualifies such statements by declaring, "The point is perhaps not to argue about whether dog love is a substitute for human love, but rather to detach the notion of 'substitute' from its presumed inferiority to a 'real thing.' Don't all loves function, in a sense, within a chain of substitutions?" (135). There is a confusion about terminology in Garber, though, or perhaps a recognition that we do not have an adequate terminology for discussing interspecies sexualities. Garber suggests, for example, that "human love for dogs is bisexual... dogs occupy an emotional place that is not determined by sex, or gender" (129), and she backs away from exploring the term "homosexual" to describe "male-male cross-species contact" in Alfred Kinsey's *Sexual Behavior in the Human Male*, published in 1948, and *Sexual Behavior in the Human Female*, which followed in 1953 (148–50). But what term should we use to describe the relationship between, say, Buck and John Thornton? The terms "homosexual" and "bisexual" would seem to privilege object choice for genital intercourse, with anatomy trumping species difference. Could "queer" be invoked here without simultaneously evoking the deeply problematic logic that links homosexuality with bestiality in order to condemn both as "unnatural"? Could "bestial" be any better? Considering the history of the Beast I have been tracing in this book, I am inclined to say yes, in the sense that it could be linked with "wolf" sexualities that do not depend upon object choice. But in the sense that "bestiality" also implies genital intercourse and nothing else (petting, stroking, snuggling, kissing, scratching, touching in nongenital areas, etc.), it still seems too limiting.

Even in a study like Midas Dekkers's *Dearest Pet: On Bestiality*, the emphasis is on genital intercourse, albeit a long history of interspecies "sex" in practice and in fantasy.[66] As much as Dekkers's book is useful for calling attention to this taboo subject, it undermines its potential by resorting to biological reasons for condemning it: "Just as an elephant is designed to love elephants, so a human being is naturally attracted only to human beings."[67] For Dekkers, the love of animals, including bestiality, is perhaps "a sign of decadence, a short-circuit in the network of affection, a cry for help from a society which has lost its way."[68] His conclusion is that "Love of animals is very nice, just as all love is nice, but it must not obscure love of human beings, otherwise our human society will disintegrate, creaking in its joints, to the accompaniment of heart-rending meowing and barking."[69] Garber is not so apocalyptic, but her conclusions seem ambivalent when she suggests that "the appeal/repulsion of bestiality is the appeal/revulsion of transgression.... the experience of crossing a forbidden line—taking the pleasures of the body past repression, past morality, even past humanity."[70] Are we prepared, then, to accept such a formulation of, say, human homosexual desire: the appeal/repulsion is all in the transgression?

In order to suggest a different way of thinking about interspecies pleasure, I want to turn to what at first might seem to be an unlikely source: the work of Darwin himself in *The Expression of the Emotions in Man and Animals*. While my focus throughout this book is generally on the Darwinist-Freudian discourse of the jungle, I also want to acknowledge that there are parts of Darwin's own work that suggest alternatives to that discourse. In particular, Darwin's chapter "Joy, High Spirits, Love, Tender Feelings, Devotion" suggests many ways in which human and nonhuman animals seem to exhibit similar emotions, thus providing a starting point for a discussion of interspecies love and pleasure. At times, Darwin not surprisingly frames his study in relation to the evolutionary imperatives of survival and reproduction, such as the suggestion that music has the ability to recall "in a vague and indefinite manner, those strong emotions which were felt during long-past ages, when, as is probable, our early progenitors courted each other by the aid of vocal tones."[71] But powerful emotions can also have a "peculiar effect" that cannot be explained by biological necessity, causing "the muscles to tremble," such as "the thrill or slight shiver which runs down the backbone and limbs of many persons when they are powerfully affected by music..." (168). According to Darwin, nonhuman animals share with humans many of these strong emotions, as well as the "purposeless movements" of a phenomenon such as laughter that "seems to be the expression of mere joy or happiness" (151). Anthropoid apes can thus be tickled (153), the bodies of baboons can shake like humans "when they are much pleased" (154), and the physical expression of laughter can also be "characteristic and expressive of a pleased state of mind in various kinds of monkeys" (160). But Darwin's description of "love" both between and among species is even more interesting for my purposes in this chapter.

According to Darwin, nonhuman animals can derive pleasure—without necessarily aiming toward reproduction—from contact with both humans and other animals: "With the lower animals we see the same principle of pleasure derived from contact in association with love. Dogs and cats manifestly take pleasure in rubbing against their masters and mistresses, and in being rubbed or patted by them. Many kinds of monkeys...delight in fondling and being fondled by each other, and by persons to whom they are attached" (165). Even if this pleasure is derived from "inherited habit, in association with the nursing and tending of our children, and with the mutual caresses of lovers," pleasurable contact between species can come from a desire simply to "clasp in our arms those whom we tenderly love" (165). Darwin emphasizes the pleasure of touch or contact, since love "can hardly be said to have any proper or peculiar means of expression" (165). Among various human populations, for example, Darwin argues that kissing is not always a typical form of "pleasure from close contact with a beloved person... it is replaced in various parts of the world, by the rubbing of noses, as with the New Zealanders and Laplanders, by the rubbing or patting of the arms, breasts, or stomachs, or by one man striking his own face with the hands or feet of another" (166). To illustrate how various kinds of contact can lead to deep forms of pleasure between nonhuman animals, Darwin focuses our attention on a particularly interesting example:

> the behavior of two chimpanzees, rather older animals than those generally imported into this country, when they were first brought together. They sat opposite, touching each other with their much protruded lips; and the one put his hand on the shoulder of the other. They *mutually folded each other in their arms*. Afterwards they stood up, each with one arm on the shoulder of the other, lifted up their heads, opened their mouths, and *yelled with delight*. (165, my emphasis)

Without even telling us whether both of these chimpanzees are male, or whether there is any kind of genital contact, Darwin offers striking language here that I believe can lead us toward a reconceptualization of pleasure experienced by nonhuman animals.

A *mutual folding* that can lead to *yelling with delight*: this kind of formulation has very interesting potential, from my perspective, for helping us to rethink the possibilities of interspecies pleasure or eroticism that might include, but need not be limited to, the forms of sexuality typically associated with "bestiality." While Darwin's understanding of "folding" is very different from Deleuze's more recent theorization of it, my own thinking here is inspired in eccentric ways by both Darwin and Deleuze, with a dash of Haraway thrown in.[72] Mutual folding could be suggestive in many aspects: first, a coming together, a desire on the part of two beings to *en*fold or encircle each other by touching, with a recognition that neither can completely enfold or encompass the other; second, a mutual desire to fold oneself *into* the other, to be folded into a new entity that is more than simply the combination of two essentialized beings; third, a giving up of oneself, a folding, as in a card game, suggesting a willingness to surrender to the course of the game without needing to win; fourth, an openness to being folded or changed in potentially dramatic ways through contact with another; and fifth, a readiness or a desire for the "music" of this mutual folding to provoke pleasure, even to the point of yelling out in delight.[73]

This kind of mutual folding could be used to describe both inter- and intraspecies forms of contact, without needing to determine whether that contact is "innocent" or not. To think of the relationships between Buck and John Thornton or White Fang and Weedon Scott as mutual foldings ultimately allows us to see how these texts can model alternative possibilities that resist the discourse of the jungle. In this way, Jack London's texts offer more than they are often given credit for, even if they only open the door to new questions about issues such as a dog's ability to consent. In *When Species Meet*, Donna Haraway addresses related questions in the context of training with her dog to participate in agility competitions, while offering important caveats: "Obviously, one would hope, it is essential for a human being to understand that one's partner is an adult (or puppy) member of another species, with his or her own exacting species interests and individual quirks, and not a furry child, a character in *Call of the Wild*, or an extension of one's intentions or fantasies."[74] While Haraway thus participates in the characterization of London's novella as essentially "men in furs," she also points the way toward acknowledging both species difference and the possibility of interspecies communication. According to Haraway:

The philosophic and literary conceit that all we have is representations and no access to what animals think and feel is wrong. Human beings do, or can, know more than we used to know, and the right to gauge that knowledge is rooted in historical, flawed, generative cross-species practices.... Disarmed of the fantasy of climbing into heads, one's own or others', to get the full story from the inside, we can make some multispecies semiotic progress. (226)

In addition to challenging the assumption that we cannot ever know what a dog might really want or feel, and therefore should not even try, Haraway also alludes here to psychoanalytic and poststructuralist work in literary and cultural theory that has challenged the assumption that a human being can ever truly know even his or her own "self," or other human others, let alone a non-human other.[75] Recognizing this point, though, leads Haraway to suggest that "people can stop looking for some single defining difference between them and everybody else and understand that they are in rich and largely uncharted, material-semiotic, flesh-to-flesh, and face-to-face connection with a host of significant others. That requires retraining in the contact zone" (235).

Haraway's theorization of "contact zones" resonates with my formulation of mutual folding, although her context of training for agility competitions—and the "joy" it can produce—does not seem to include as much of the erotic element I am focusing on here. Eva Hayward's recent work on contact zones with cup corals in a marine lab at the University of California, Santa Cruz, seems to take a further step into the sensual and sexual. In her article "FINGERYEYES: Impressions of Cup Corals," Hayward explores what she calls "*fingeryeyes* to explain the tentacular visuality of cross-species encounters and to name the synaesthetic quality of materialized sensation.... From this point of view/touch of fingeryeyes, species are impressions, thresholds of emergence."[76] Corals, then, can "make an impression: aesthetically, haptically, ontologically, and...sensually, sexually" (581) when species meet, such as during an encounter that Hayward describes: "Their tentacles reached out as my digits and tools reached toward them. The thickness of the skin on my hands protected me from their sting, but even still I felt a slight tingling at points of contact. For a moment, we, the corals and I, *enfolded elements of each other within ourselves*" (590–91, my emphasis). Yet the potential for mutual folding here is limited by Hayward's first explanation of the retraction of the "fringes": "There is no question that they are responding to predator/prey impulses; the power is decidedly asymmetrical" (591). While I believe the recognition of the power differential is crucial, I think the invocation of a biological framework limits the potential for imagining different possibilities in this contact zone, different forms of experiencing the world that might not require an evolutionary framework to be the first or best explanation of what is going on.

Haraway explores various genealogies and histories of other kinds of contact zones, including the literal space on an agility apparatus where a canine competitor's feet must touch, as well as the theorization of contact zones from fields such as postcolonial studies, science fiction studies, ecology, and biology.[77] A contact zone can also be a site for interspecies interaction, for what Haraway calls "becoming with" a companion species. This mutually constitutive interaction can be purposeless, from a biological perspective, leading to various possibilities stemming from Haraway's own formulation of "the open," which is rather different from the Heideggerian theorization of that term (221). For Haraway, "training with an animal, whether the critter is named wild or domestic, can be part of disengaging from the semiotics and technologies of compulsory reproductive biopolitics" (222). Though she is acutely aware of issues and histories of power relations relevant to this kind of "becoming with," Haraway remains open to "the idea that the experience of sensual joy in the nonliteral open of play might underlie the possibility of morality and responsibility for and to one another in all of our undertakings at whatever webbed scales of time and space" (242).

This move toward the political—if not ethical—implications of interspecies "joy" is one that links Haraway's project with my own in this book. Haraway's "premise is that touch ramifies and shapes accountability. Accountability, caring for, being affected, and entering into responsibility are not ethical abstractions; these mundane, prosaic things are the result of having truck with each other. . . . Touch, regard, looking back, becoming with—all these make us responsible in unpredictable ways for which worlds take shape" (36). Even without an emphasis on the erotic possibilities of mutual foldings, Haraway's focus on "touch" in relation to accountability and responsibility for nonhuman others can offer a new starting point for discussions of how humans should treat various nonhuman animals in specific historical and cultural contexts. My own interest in interspecies sexualities can similarly open the door to new inquiries, without assuming that nonhuman animals, on the one hand, are incapable of feeling love and pleasure, or that human beings, on the other hand, must be engaged in bestiality if there is any erotic element in their interactions with other species. This is only a starting point, then, for beginning to think in subtler ways about the relationship between theorizing nonhuman subjectivity and proposing or legislating practical guidelines for determining which kinds of mutual foldings might be appropriate in various contexts.

An animality studies approach to these questions, from my perspective, need not be focused primarily upon formulating ethical principles that could be applied to all interspecies interactions. Instead, we can explore constructions of animality at specific historical and cultural moments, not only to see how those constructions relate to histories of both human and nonhuman sexuality, for example, but also to see whether various texts provide useful starting points for imagining alternatives to problematic discourses, such as the Darwinist-Freudian jungle. To suggest that mutual foldings in the work of Jack London are transgressive would be to suggest that norms were fully in place at the time of its publication. From my perspective, the more interesting possibility is that texts such as *White Fang* and *The Call of the Wild*, as well as *The Sea-Wolf*, do not quite know what to do with the erotic fireworks I have explored in this chapter. Readers today still do not quite know what to do with these passages, but my hope is that we can now see that the epistemology of the jungle, in flux at the turn of the century, provides a crucial context for understanding the multiplicity of ways that representations of animality and sexuality have been weaved together, or positioned against each other, in the construction of the discourse of the jungle. Prior to the naturalization of intraspecies heterosexuality as "animal instinct," the nature of the beast in writers such as Kipling, James, and London suggests complicated, interesting, and potentially productive alternatives to assumptions about biologically determined sexuality in both human and nonhuman animals.

PART TWO

Survival of the Fittest Market

3

The Octopus and the Corporation

MONSTROUS ANIMALITY IN NORRIS, SPENCER, AND CARNEGIE

AT THE SAME moment that texts by Henry James and Jack London explore alternative relationships between sexuality and animality, corporations in the marketplace are increasingly constructed within a Darwinist-Freudian framework of "survival of the fittest." But there are also representations of corporations at this moment that resist the discourse of the jungle. Figures 3 and 4 illustrate how economic trusts could be represented as an octopus, for example, in rather surprising ways. In figure 3, "Doctor" Roosevelt vaccinates the various tentacles: the Beef Trust, the Railroad Trust, the Steel Trust, and so on.[1] We might at first think about the appropriateness of the analogy: tentacles representing the broad reach of corporations in the age of robber barons, willing to squeeze if not destroy their prey in the pursuit of profit. We might want to quickly situate the representation of the octopus in a narrative of Darwinian survival, where animals must kill or be killed in the survival-of-the-fittest jungle of the business world. In figure 4, the Standard Oil company (or trust) is grabbing and eating people, while encircling Congress and warily eyeing the White House.[2] But a giant corporation represented as an octopus does not quite fit our image of the economic jungle today. What does an octopus eat, for example? Not usually people, and not usually sheep, such as those that are massacred at the beginning of Frank Norris's 1901 novel *The Octopus: A Story of California.* Mostly they eat seafood: crabs, lobsters, and fish. It is hard to imagine an epic battle between a *crab* and an octopus. The relationship between animality and constructions of the corporation, then, is more complicated than often assumed at the turn of the twentieth century in the United States. Various texts from that moment, including essays by Andrew

Figure 3 "Vaccinating the Trusts" (1910). "Give the doctor time; his patient has a lot of arms that need attention." From the *Journal* (Minneapolis).

Figure 4 "Next!" Standard Oil eyes the White House.

Carnegie and Herbert Spencer (who was an earlier influence on Carnegie), illustrate how the marketplace has yet to be fully animalized within the discourse of the jungle. Instead, on the cusp of this new formulation, there is a construction of animality that resonates with Protestant Christian thinking about *monstrous* market forces, on the one hand, or the corporation newly codified as a person, on the other hand, without necessarily constructing either the human or the animal within the Darwinist-Freudian jungle.

The Nature of the Octopus

The first chapter of Frank Norris's *The Octopus* ends with a scene of monstrous terror. Innocent sheep have wandered onto the railroad tracks and are mercilessly slaughtered with the sudden appearance of a train: "the symbol of a vast power, huge, terrible...leaving blood and destruction in its path; the leviathan, with tentacles of steel clutching into the soil, the soulless Force, the iron-hearted Power, the monster, the Colossus, the Octopus."[3] Invoking a range of metaphors, from monster to machine to *the* octopus, the passage culminates in the hyperbolic rhetoric of a force or power that is beyond the understanding of either the innocent sheep or the brooding poet Presley, who witnesses the scene of the crime. Presley's sympathies are first aroused by what he hears: "a confusion of lamentable sounds that rose into the night"; "prolonged cries of agony, sobbing wails of infinite pain, heart-rending, pitiful" (49). But he soon sees the results of the slaughter: "little bodies had been flung; backs were snapped against the fence posts; brains knocked out. Caught in the barbs of the wire, wedged in, the bodies hung suspended" (50). Presley's "quick burst of irresistible compassion for this brute agony" drives him away from the scene, "almost running, even putting his hands over his ears till he was out of hearing distance of that all but human distress" (50). The sympathy that this "all but human distress" might arouse for the sheep themselves is mitigated, perhaps, by the recognition that we are in the realm of metaphor, where the railroad becomes "the symbol of a vast power" otherwise known as the Railroad Trust, and the sheep are stand-ins for "the People," squeezed to death by the tentacles of the Octopus. We do not expect sheep to fight back. But a certain set of assumptions must be embedded in these constructions of the sheep and the octopus in order to have them represent the conflict between "the People" and the elite class of railroad magnates, or monopoly capitalists in general, at the turn of the century. The series of analogies given to illuminate the force of the railroad—monster, machine, octopus—do not each evoke the same set of associations. The driving force behind a machine would be indifferent but knowable, for example, rather than malicious or unknowable, as in the case of a monster.[4] Twenty-first-century readers might assume that an octopus would squeeze its prey out of something like an *a*moral drive to survive rather than malice. But the novel itself spends several hundred pages, I would argue, trying to figure out precisely what the nature of the beast is here.

Whether the octopus-railroad in Norris's novel is slaughtering sheep or squeezing competitors and workers to death, questions are raised about how to interpret this kind of violence, and whether the corporation should stand accountable for these actions. In the final pages, the fictional Pacific & Southwestern Railroad stands trial, figuratively, for a litany of offenses that ring with religious overtones (and serve as a convenient reminder of several of the novel's plotlines):

> The ranches had been seized in the tentacles of the octopus; the iniq-uitous burden of extortionate freight rates had been imposed like a yoke of iron. The monster had killed Harran, had killed Osterman, had killed Broderson, had killed Hooven. It had beggared Magnus and had driven him to a state of semi-insanity after he had wrecked his honour in the vain attempt to do evil that good might come.... It had slain Annixter at the very moment when painfully and manfully he had at last achieved his own salvation and stood forth resolved to do right, to act unselfishly and to live for others. It had widowed Hilma in the very dawn of her happiness. It had killed the very babe within the mother's womb, strangling life ere yet it had been born, stamping out the spark ordained by God to burn through all eternity. (650–51)

Presley, who opens the novel as witness to the slaughter of sheep by the rail-road, has been a witness to all these sins, and he appears to be left with a sense of how futile it is to resist the railroad: "What then was left? Was there no hope, no outlook for the future, no rift in the black curtain, no glimmer through the night? Was good to be thus overthrown? Was evil thus to be strong and to prevail? Was nothing left?" (651). Underlying these questions is a more basic frustration about the nature of the force at work here: whether it can be iden-tified, or judged, or punished. Presley's judgment and the conclusion of the narrative suggest that the railroad is simply an unstoppable force—one that can supposedly contribute to "the greater good"—and that there is no rea-son to punish the octopus. His conclusions are more complicated than they might appear, though, and thus deserving of greater scrutiny.

If the judgment of the railroad-octopus points toward the class politics of the novel, then it would seem appropriate to consider whether the
novel is interested in "true" reform for working-class people or, rather, for
middle-class farmers like Magnus Derrick. This kind of question is certainly
relevant, and it has been pursued most persuasively by critics such as June
Howard. Howard's approach points toward a kind of progressive hypothesis
which argues that trusts and corporations are not in fact unstoppable but
rather driven by class interests that can be regulated and reformed. The threat
of *The Octopus*, from this perspective, is that it suggests corporations must be
either monstrous or indifferent but not subject to explicable motivations or
controllable behaviors, as they would be in the logic of "the jungle," which
could then be the starting point for progressive advocacy in favor of an animalized revolution. Corporations constructed as unstoppable might thus be
troubling from a political perspective, but I am more interested in exploring
what it means that Norris's novel is not fully embedded in social Darwinist
conceptions of human nature, derived supposedly from "real" animals and
applicable supposedly to the behavior of corporations granted the status of
"persons" (who would then be responsible for acting "humanely"). There is
good reason to avoid the assumption that the discourse of animality in this
text is stable in post-Freudian terms, or that the most relevant question to
explore is how progressive the politics of *The Octopus* might be.[5]

The historical development of granting corporations the status of "persons" has been traced by influential critics such as Alan Trachtenberg in *The
Incorporation of America: Culture and Society in the Gilded Age* (1982) and
Walter Benn Michaels in *The Gold Standard and the Logic of Naturalism:
American Literature at the Turn of the Century* (1987), although neither of these
studies considers how the definition of a "person" shifts once "animal instincts"
become hegemonic in constructions of human beings. Trachtenberg describes
how the concept of incorporation shifted from a public charter with the "presumption of public service" to a legal recognition of a profit-seeking entity:
"The corporation embodied a legally sanctioned fiction, that an association of
people constituted a single entity which might hold property, sue and be sued,
enter contracts, and continue in existence beyond the lifetime or membership
of any of its participants."[6] Michaels's chapter titled "Corporate Fiction" traces
the construction of corporations as persons through contemporaneous texts
and then cites *Button v. Hoffman* (1884) as a key Supreme Court ruling in
which the fiction of a corporation was upheld for even a single stockholder.[7]
In this case, the stockholder was found to be not individually responsible for
corporate property, which would otherwise have appeared to be his own.[8] But

there are other significant cases to consider as well, such as *Santa Clara County v. Southern Pacific Railroad* (1886), in which "the Court held, without argument, that corporations were 'persons' within the meaning of the due process clause of the fourteenth amendment, thus opening the door for direct challenges to regulations by corporations."[9] To the extent of my knowledge, *Santa Clara* is the first time a corporation was codified as a "person."

But what kind of "person," exactly, could be seen as the model for the behavior of a corporation? The figureheads of many of these newly minted corporations—Morgan, Carnegie, Rockefeller, et al.—were one possibility. As Howard Zinn reminds us, most of these multimillionaires did not come from poverty: "A study of the origins of 303 textile, railroad, and steel executives of the 1870s showed that 90 percent came from middle- or upper-class families."[10] Their behavior as "robber barons" is far more representative than the "rags to riches" mythology, following instead a common pattern, "in industry after industry," of "shrewd, efficient businessmen building empires, choking out competition, maintaining high prices, keeping wages low, using government subsidies" (257). In 1886 alone, the same year as *Santa Clara*, there were more than 1,400 labor strikes involving five hundred thousand workers (273), mostly because the behavior of corporations at the time was anything but generous toward workers. The armed battle between striking workers and Pinkerton guards at Andrew Carnegie's steel plant in Homestead, Pennsylvania, for example, on July 5, 1892, resulted in the deaths of seven workers (276). Reporting on resumed operations at Homestead for a June 1894 *McClure's Magazine* piece, Hamlin Garland employed an interesting combination of animality and monstrosity to describe both workers and machinery: "The lifting crane fascinated me. A man perched upon it like a monkey on the limb of a tree; and the creature raised, swung, lowered, shot out, opened its monstrous beak, seized the slab of iron, retreated, lifted, swung and dropped it upon the carriers. It was like a living thing, some strange creature unabashed by heat or heavy weights. To get in its way meant death."[11] Looking back as he departs the area, Garland is blasted by "A roar as of a hundred lions, a thunder as of cannons, flames that made the electric light look like a twinkling blue star, jarring clang of falling iron, burst of spluttering flakes of fire, scream of terrible saws, shifting of mighty trucks with hiss of steam!"[12] His final thought, as he leaves the scene behind, is that "the town and its industries lay like a cancer on the breast of a human body."[13]

Describing the behavior of a corporation like Carnegie's thus seems to evoke a range of possibilities, from animals to monsters to a cancerous disease on the body politic. But perhaps we can be more specific. According to

Walter Benn Michaels, a distinction must be made between corporations in general and monopolies: "The whole point of monopolies, like the Railroad (what makes them 'monstrous'), is that they transcend the mechanical laws of the market" and are therefore unregulated by those laws.[14] But this logic does not quite make sense. Or, rather, it reveals how the logic at work in Norris's *The Octopus* is on the cusp between the construction of "natural" laws of the market—responding mechanically to supply and demand—on the one hand, and "natural" laws of "the jungle," on the other: an economic epistemology that would justify price-fixing and "unfair" practices as completely "natural" rather than "monstrous."[15] Derived in large part from Adam Smith, the mysterious "laws of the market," prior to their animalization, are distinct from those "monstrous" practices seen as unethical from a Judeo-Christian perspective. Monstrosity could signify a whole range of signifieds, though, and I do not want to equate "monstrous" too reductively with "evil" in a religious sense. The *body* of the exploitative or oppressive corporation, though, is monstrous in the sense that it is unknowable rather than explicable through a Darwinist-Freudian construction of animality.

In *The Octopus*, the body of the corporation-as-person is embodied most clearly in the figure of Shelgrim, the supreme head of the railroad. As Michaels points out, when Presley confronts Shelgrim in his office toward the end of the novel, "like the octopus he heads,...his body placed in the chair to rest, is all head and hands, a cephalopod."[16] But an octopus is a new and largely unknown animal at the end of the nineteenth century. The first recorded usage of the word "octopus" in the *Oxford English Dictionary* is 1758, defined as "A genus of cephalopod molluscs, characterized by eight 'arms' surrounding the mouth and provided with suckers."[17] It is not until 1882 that the figurative possibilities of this animal are first deployed, once it can be "applied to an organized power having extended ramifications and far-reaching influence, esp. harmful or destructive." Webster's dictionary does not even define "octopus" in 1878, and by 1911 it is merely "a genus of Cephalopods having 8 arms."[18] It remains to be seen what kind of octopus Shelgrim can represent as head of this railroad.

When Presley finds himself outside the San Francisco headquarters of the Pacific & Southwestern Railroad late in the novel, the narrative characterizes the office as "the stronghold of the enemy—the centre of all that vast ramifying system of arteries that drained the life-blood of the State; the nucleus of the web in which so many lives, so many fortunes, so many destinies had been enmeshed."[19] He confronts the place from which "had emanated that policy of extortion, oppression and injustice that little by little had shouldered the ranchers from their rights, till, their backs to the wall, exasperated and despairing they had turned and fought and died" (569). The nature of this force, in other words, is far worse than a morally indifferent animal fighting to survive in the wild. Instead, its power is represented through the metonymy of Shelgrim, "the man whose power was so vast, whose will was so resistless, whose potency for evil so limitless" (570). Once admitted to his office, Presley realizes that Shelgrim is more than seventy years old, though, and he is impressed with his level of energy, even if it is "an ogre's vitality": "Just so is the man-eating tiger strong. The man should have energy who has sucked the life-blood from an entire People" (571). And the description of Shelgrim, as other critics have noted, invokes the creature signified by "octopus":

> He was large, almost to massiveness. An iron-grey beard and a mustache that completely hid the mouth covered the lower part of his face.... But the enormous breadth of the shoulders was what, at first, most vividly forced itself upon Presley's notice. Never had he seen a broader man; the neck, however, seemed in a manner to have settled into the shoulders, and furthermore they were humped and rounded, as if to bear great responsibilities, and great abuse. (571–72)

Later in the interview Presley notices that, "curiously enough, Shelgrim did not move his body. His arms moved, and his head, but the great bulk of the man remained immobile in its place, and as the interview proceeded and this peculiarity emphasised [sic] itself, Presley began to conceive the odd idea that Shelgrim had, as it were, placed his body in the chair to rest, while his head and brain and hands went on working independently" (574). His body, in other words, is largely irrelevant, and we are left with the question of whether this body can or should be punished for the sins of the railroad.

Presley's narrative purpose, in part, is to act as judge of Shelgrim's actions. But he is quickly swayed by the mental state, or *mens rea* in legal terms, of one who might otherwise be deemed a criminal. In what surely could be seen as a performance, or at the very least a rather weak attempt to portray Shelgrim as beneficent to his workers, Presley is initially ignored as he sits in the great office and listens to Shelgrim bequeath leniency toward a bookkeeper of his whose drunkenness continually renders him useless as a worker. While the assistant manager wants to fire the bookkeeper, Shelgrim notes that the man has a wife and three children, and then resolves to almost double his salary. Once Shelgrim turns his attention to Presley, the first thought of the magnate is to denigrate Presley's poem "The Toilers," in comparison with the painting from which Presley had been originally inspired. Presley seems to consider these statements to be mitigating circumstances that might speak to the culpability of this man for the crimes committed by the railroad. Presley is soon convinced that this is a man of taste, a man "not only great, but large; many-sided, of vast sympathies, who understood with equal intelligence, the human nature in an habitual drunkard, the ethics of a masterpiece of painting, and the financiering and operation of ten thousand miles of railroad" (575). If the railroad this man runs has committed crimes such as the literal and figurative slaughter of "sheep" in the first chapter, the logic seems to run, then such acts must be seen as something like involuntary manslaughter, certainly without "malice aforethought," as the law would require. The railroad-*monster* of the first chapter does not massacre the sheep in order to "feed" itself or to survive; rather, it kills wantonly, indifferently, without even a specific plan for wiping out an indirect form of competition in the form of sheep-raising as an industry. And even if the acts of the corporation are the result of malevolent and monstrous motivations, what *body* could be punished? Both the railroad and Shelgrim, in effect, have no recognizable body, just like, supposedly, the unknown creature known as "the octopus."

After exonerating Shelgrim as an individual, Presley turns to judge the railroad according to mitigating circumstances from an earlier historical moment. The mysterious forces of supply and demand, according to Shelgrim, actually create the trusts of the late nineteenth century on their own: "try to believe this—to begin with—*that Railroads build themselves.* Where there is a demand sooner or later there will be a supply" (576). The force behind the wheat is quickly linked to the same process: "The Wheat grows itself.... You are dealing with forces, young man, when you speak of Wheat and the Railroads, not with men" (576). But these forces, I want to emphasize, are not themselves animalized in a Darwinist-Freudian sense; they run because of unstoppable machinery, rather than biological appetites. And the deaths of people and animals along the way are merely incidental, rather than "naturally" consumed:

> The Wheat is one force, the Railroad, another, and there is the law that governs them—supply and demand. Men have only little to do in the whole business. Complications may arise, conditions that bear hard on the individual—crush him maybe—*but the Wheat will be carried to feed the people* as inevitably as it will grow. If you want to fasten the blame of the affair at Los Muertos on any one person, you will make a mistake. Blame conditions, not men. (576)

While Presley might still be inclined to blame Shelgrim, he is soon convinced by such arguments: "Can any one stop the Wheat? Well, then no more can I stop the Road"; "It is a force born out of certain conditions, and I—no man—can stop it or control it" (576).

Presley's conclusion is that the railroad cannot be evil; it is simply indifferent. It may be "natural" in the sense that it presses on without individual human agency, but the corporation, like "the octopus" it supposedly mimics, is more monstrous than animalized in a Darwinist-Freudian formulation. Presley's question, and the question of much of the book, in fact, becomes, "Was no one, then, to blame for the horror at the irrigating ditch? Forces, conditions, laws of supply and demand—were these then the enemies after all?" (576–77). The answer, at least at this point in the novel, is:

> Not enemies; there was no malevolence in Nature. Colossal indifference only, a vast trend toward appointed goals. Nature was, then, a gigantic engine, a vast cyclopean power, huge, terrible, a leviathan with a heart of steel, knowing no compunction, no forgiveness, no tolerance; crushing out the human atom standing in its way, with nirvanic calm, the agony of destruction sending never a jar, never the faintest tremour through all that prodigious mechanism of wheels and cogs. (577)

In the final pages of the novel, after listening to Vanamee's celebration of Christian goodness, Presley concludes that all things can also contribute to the greater good: "The larger view always and through all shams, all wickedness, discovers Truth that will, in the end, prevail, and all things, surely, inevitably, resistlessly work together for good" (652). Such privileged musing obviously overlooks those working-class bodies that are ground up along the way. But it also resists Darwinist-Freudian constructions of "animal instincts" as the only framework for explaining the behavior, or perhaps sins, of a corporation.

Taming a Bull Market

I return to *The Octopus* in the next chapter to indicate more clearly how working-class bodies are the first to be animalized, but first I want to explore other currents at this historical moment that contribute to the eventual animalization of the market as a whole. Social Darwinism as articulated by Herbert Spencer and Andrew Carnegie plays a key role here, even though the rhetoric of these two men in particular is influenced more by Christian discourse than is commonly assumed. Their construction of social Darwinism specifically in economic terms enables a logic that might seem similar to Presley's: monopoly capitalism can ultimately contribute to the greater good. The difference is that competition (or exploitation, depending upon your perspective) eventually comes to be justified as a manifestation of survival-of-the-fittest instincts. Frank Norris's "market Forces" might resist being characterized as "animal" in nature, but the evolution of terms such as "bull" and "bear" market illustrate how animality can signify market behavior as a whole, rather than the behavior of individual investors, at the end of the nineteenth century. The latter definition, according to the *OED*, goes back to at least 1719 in relation to the English stock exchange, when a "bear" was "A speculator for a fall," while a "bull" was "One who endeavours by speculative purchases, or otherwise, to raise the price of stocks."[20] Both terms originally referred to the purchase of the stock itself (and a "bull" was slang for a crown piece as early as 1812). But it is not until 1891 that a "bull market" is recognizable as "a market characterized by the rising price of stock," and 1903 that a "bear market" can be characterized "by the falling price of stock."[21] According to Eric Partridge's *Slang To-Day and Yesterday*, the coinage of "bull" as a signifier for a policeman also becomes recognizable around 1890.[22] The policeman and the market, then, can both be "bulls" by the end of the nineteenth century.

If the market is becoming animalized, then, should it be tamed? Should "humane" restraints be codified by law? If a bear market is to be avoided at all costs, should the bull be held back by concern for workers or those who might not benefit directly from economic "progress"? The figure of Herbert Spencer is instructive and representative here, particularly once we recognize that toward the end of the nineteenth century his theories on "survival of the fittest" had an incalculable influence on economic thinking in the United States. Toward the beginning of his career, though, Spencer justified his philosophy of rugged individualism by appealing to Christian scripture rather than the doctrine of evolution through natural selection, and this shift points toward one possibility for deploying "animality" in the interests, supposedly, of more than just self-interest. In one of his first published pieces in 1836, for example, in response to a defense of the Poor Laws in England at the time, Spencer outlines the familiar conservative belief that laws of this kind actually discourage rugged individuals from working hard: "The whole tenor of your argument implies...that a person is not to be allowed to raise himself by his own exertions. What! is not a man to be benefited by his superior industry?— is he always to be kept down in the ranks of pauperism?—is there no reward to be held out to perseverance, and no punishment to idleness?"[23] The answer, though, might be somewhat surprising from Spencer, who argues that his opponent's "assertions [are] directly opposed to the truth of Scripture," such as, "In the sweat of thy face shalt thou eat bread"; "Six days shalt thou labour"; and "If any will not work neither let him eat" (181). More explicitly, "The whole system of man's responsibility, and of his future reward or punishment, depending upon his being 'diligent in business, fervent in spirit, serving the Lord,' seems completely set aside by your reasoning" (181).

If the individual worker in 1836 is to be rewarded or punished in the after-life, as well as in life, for his divinely sanctioned labor, by the 1880s the goal is shifting toward successful manipulation of one's "survival instincts" and the resulting ability to propagate. In "The Sins of Legislators" (1884), for example, Spencer points toward the need for "rigorous maintenance of those normal relations among citizens under which each gets in return for his labour, skilled or unskilled, bodily or mental, as much as is proved to be its value by the demand for it: such return, therefore, as will enable him to thrive and rear off-spring in proportion to the superiorities which make him valuable to himself and others" (128–29). As early as 1851, in *Social Statics*, Spencer was construct-ing society as an organism, a concept subsequently developed in later works such as *The Principles of Sociology* (1874–1875). In "The Sins of Legislators," he quotes his earlier work, pointing toward the greater good that can come, supposedly, from a society allowed to function according to the law of "sur-vival of the fittest," even if some individuals must necessarily be left behind: "The poverty of the incapable, the distresses that came upon the imprudent, the starvation of the idle, and those shoulderings aside of the weak by the strong, which leave so many 'in shallows and in miseries,' are the decrees of a large, far-seeing benevolence" (130). For the greater good, then, the "process *must* be undergone, and the sufferings *must* be endured"; interfering with this process can, in the long run, "work pure evil" (131). Note the continued usage of "evil" and "sin," even within the framework of evolution here. And, it is important to note, as John Offer has, that Spencer's evolving philosophy was far from consistent: "Endemic conceptual slipperiness meant that Spencer's theory became irrefutable in principle: he produced not the intended bang of a theory of everything but the whimper of what was at best a cumbrous and unreliable *redescription* of everything."[24]

The translation of Spencer into American economic thinking can be seen through figures such as Andrew Carnegie and John D. Rockefeller. According to Rockefeller, "The growth of a large business is merely a survival of the fit-test, the working out of a law of nature and a law of God."[25] Carnegie's collec-tion of essays titled *The Gospel of Wealth and Other Timely Essays*, which was first published in 1900, deploys similar rhetoric of both evolution and moral duty, regardless of Carnegie's own commitments—or resistance—to institutionalized Christianity. The title essay first appeared in the *North American Review* in the June and December 1889 issues, singing the praises of "the law of competition": "it is to this law that we owe our wonderful material development, which brings improved conditions in its train."[26] The focus throughout the collection is the "rising tide lifts all boats" argument, that the "progress" of "the race" (meaning whiteness) must inevitably benefit everyone, even if there are individual hardships: "whether the law be benign or not, we must say of it...it is here; we cannot evade it; no substitutes for it have been found; and while the law may be sometimes hard for the individual, it is best for the race, because it insures the survival of the fittest in every department" (16).[27] Inequality is therefore also inevitable: "We accept and welcome, therefore, as conditions to which we must accommodate ourselves, great inequality of environment; the concentration of business, industrial and commercial, in the hands of a few; and the law of competition between these, as being not only beneficial, but essential to the future progress of the race" (16–17).

Carnegie's philanthropic endeavors are used to justify whatever means might be necessary for his individual financial gain. He spends considerable time in this essay counseling other millionaire capitalists how best to give away their money once they have piled it up. Opposed to simply passing along wealth through inheritances (because the inheritors would then have no incentive to work), Carnegie hopes to adopt a form of Christian duty that has evolved according to the times. Rather than imitating the life of Christ, he aspires toward a life "animated by Christ's spirit, by recognizing the changed conditions of this age, and adopting modes of expressing this spirit suitable to the changed conditions under which we live, still laboring for the good of our fellows, which was the essence of his life and teaching, but laboring in a different manner" (25). The "duty of the man of wealth," then, is not to give handouts to the undeserving but "to help those who will help themselves" (27). How should this be done? By endowing libraries, parks, art museums, universities, hospitals, laboratories, concert halls, and churches. Followed properly, the "gospel of wealth but echoes Christ's words. It calls upon the millionaire to sell all that he hath and give it in the highest and best form to the poor by administering his estate himself for the good of his fellows, before he is called upon to lie down and rest upon the bosom of Mother Earth" (49).

Such apparently noble sentiments, though, have little to do with how Carnegie runs his businesses. In an 1891 essay titled "The Advantages of Poverty" (first published in *Nineteenth Century*), Carnegie can blithely declare, "my 'progress' has inevitably carried with it not the 'growing poverty,' but the growing riches of my fellow-countrymen, as the progress of every employer of labor must necessarily carry with it the enrichment of the country and of the laborer" (52–53). This warm feeling of benevolence comes a year before the Homestead strike previously mentioned. In response to the Haymarket Affair of May 1886, Carnegie, writing in the August issue of *Forum*, characterizes the event as "not, in itself, a very serious matter": "A rash had broken out upon the body politic, but it was only skin-deep, and disappeared as rapidly as it had come" (108). And in "Popular Illusions about Trusts," originally published in 1900 in *Century*, seven years after the Panic of 1893, Carnegie still has unshakable faith in the benevolent and inevitable consolidation of capital as the answer to all social ills:

> this overpowering, irresistible tendency toward aggregation of capital and increase of size in every branch of product cannot be arrested or even greatly impeded, and … instead of attempting to restrict either, we should hail every increase as something gained, not for the few rich, but for the millions of poor, seeing that the law is salutary, working for good and not for evil. Every enlargement is an improvement, step by step, upon what has preceded. It makes for higher civilization, for the enrichment of human life, not for one, but for all classes of men. (83)

Following Spencer, whom Carnegie describes as his teacher (52), the argument justifies the expansion of capital as an "outgrowth of human nature" (91), manifested in the form of "the organism known as human society" (78).

Five years after this essay, in *Lochner v. New York* (1905), the Supreme Court would follow suit in upholding Spencer's philosophy by translating it into a defense of corporations against labor reforms or regulations. In a famous dissent, Oliver Wendell Holmes identified the underlying ideology that could be objected to: "The Fourteenth Amendment does not enact Mr. Herbert Spencer's Social Statics.... A constitution is not intended to embody a particular economic theory, whether of paternalism and the organic relation of the citizen to the State or of *laissez-faire*."[28] In *Lochner*, the court found that a New York statute limiting bakers to sixty hours of work per week and ten hours per day infringed upon the right of contract between an individual worker and a corporation figured as a "person" with a right to make contracts under the Fourteenth Amendment. The *Lochner* case subsequently became precedent for roughly thirty years of rulings that struck down economic regulation on similar grounds.[29]

Restrictions upon corporations figured as persons are thus seen as unnatural. According to the new laws of the jungle, eventually, exploitation might be just another word for survival of the fittest. The Christian morality that underlies not only the evolution of Spencer and Carnegie but also Frank Norris's novel soon fades. Violence becomes the manifestation of animal instincts, but the ability to control those instincts becomes a marker of class identity. *The Octopus* delineates these shifting constructions of animal instincts along class lines, while carving out space for an evolving middle class positioned between the threat of an animalized working-class revolution and the oppression of the predatory economic elite. Representations of instinctual violence, in other words, are deployed in the service of defining class boundaries. The next chapter explores these class distinctions in relation to animality in both *The Octopus* and Upton Sinclair's *The Jungle* (1906).

4

The Working-Class Beast

FRANK NORRIS AND UPTON SINCLAIR

TO THINK OF the entire capitalist marketplace as itself a jungle seems automatic to us at the turn of the twenty-first century. We think of corporations fighting to survive in the market like beasts in the jungle, like wolfish predators ready to exploit new economic niches, as well as their own workers. The nature of the corporate beast, in other words, is supposed to be an instinct for survival at the expense of other competitors, as well as workers who are seen as disposable. As the previous chapter of this book has revealed, though, constructions of the corporation at the turn of the century were not always or exclusively framed within the discourse of the jungle. But representations of workers and the working class were more likely to be animalized in a Darwinist-Freudian sense. Figure 5 illustrates, for example, how workers striking or in revolt could be represented collectively as an animal; in this case a wolf, shot down by President Roosevelt, represents the end of the 1902 anthracite coal strike in Pennsylvania.[1] Striking workers could also be constructed individually as naturally violent, with animal instincts barely contained by their humanity, or simply as animals without any humanity at all.

This chapter explores the relationship between animality and the working class in representations of both "real" animals and animalized working-class figures, particularly in novels such as Frank Norris's *The Octopus* (1901) and Upton Sinclair's *The Jungle* (1906). While these texts thus help to produce the discourse of the jungle, they also include residual Christian discourses that reveal how the nature of the beast could be constructed rather differently in more privileged characters. In addition, the move to construct workers as more animalized than members of other economic classes can be

Figure 5 "Roosevelt's Biggest Game." From the *Herald* (New York).

seen in the logic of many progressive muckrakers and reformers, here exemplified by Sinclair in particular. Progressive-era labor reform, in other words, becomes a way for middle-class reformers to distance themselves from the "animals" for whom they want to advocate. But the larger claim of this book is that constructions of "the animal" are not necessarily stable within the Darwinist-Freudian jungle at the turn of the century. The logic of progressive reform, in other words, can actually help to *produce* the discourse of the jungle, rather than simply responding to it. At times, then, representations of both "real" animals and animalized workers at the turn of the century—from a circus elephant at Coney Island to the novels of Norris and Sinclair—seem rather removed from a twenty-first-century understanding of what it means to be an "animal."

The Elephant in the Market

On January 5, 1903, a circus elephant named Topsy was publicly electrocuted at Coney Island in New York City. A *New York Times* front-page article framed it—a little tongue-in-cheek—as a judicial sentence being executed: "Topsy, the big, man-killing elephant at Luna Park, Coney Island, paid the death penalty at the park yesterday by the agency of a heavy electric current and 460 grains [*sic*] of cyanide of potassium."[2] The mode of execution was originally intended to be hanging, and a scaffold had been built in the park, but the Society for the Prevention of Cruelty to Animals intervened in opposition to such a method.[3] Instead, Thomas Edison was called upon to rig up a suitable contraption, with copper plates attached to wooden sandals that were tied to Topsy's feet. Cyanide-stuffed carrots, as it turned out, had no effect on her, so the electric current was forced to do the job:

> There was a bit of smoke for an instant. Topsy raised her trunk as if to protest, then shook, bent to her knees, fell, and rolled over on her right side motionless. All this took a matter of ten seconds. There had been no sound and hardly a conscious movement of the body, outside the raising of the trunk when the current was first felt. In two minutes from the time of turning on the current Dr. Brotheridge pronounced Topsy dead.[4]

The claim of a "painless" death was emphasized in various newspaper accounts. The *Commercial Advertiser*, for example, proclaimed: "Bad Elephant Killed: Topsy Meets Quick and Painless Death at Coney Island."[5] More than 1,500 people witnessed the 6,600 volts and 460 grams of cyanide given to her "in order to make Topsy's execution quick and sure."[6] The desire to avoid cruelty, to provide an animal with a "humane" death, is a significant aspect of this event. But the public spectacle of such a death, along with Edison's involvement, points to other key aspects as well, including the threat of class violence.

The size of the crowd was small compared with the millions of visitors who annually made summer trips to Coney Island at the turn of the century. But 1,500 was still a sizable number for the off-season park, and we might wonder what kind of people would have been present. The demographics of Coney Island crowds around the time of Topsy's death have been productively analyzed in John F. Kasson's classic study *Amusing the Million: Coney Island at the Turn of the Century* (1978).[7] According to Kasson, the carnival atmosphere of Coney Island suggested "a moral holiday" where "customary roles are reversed, hierarchies overturned, and penalties suspended."[8] In the case of Topsy, where the penalty was itself the attraction, Kasson argues that the electrocution appealed to a "latent cruelty in their audience," an impulse similar to the one that made King, the "diving horse who leapt from a high platform into a tub of water," so appealing (71). The execution might suggest that an elephant could be required to take responsibility for criminal acts: that an animal could possess the agency of a human being. It could thus be read as an example of resisting distinctions between human and nonhuman agency, but in the end, as Kasson notes, Coney Island was ultimately rather adept at reinstating existing norms: "Dispensing standardized amusement, it demanded standardized responses. Beneath the air of liberation, its pressures were profoundly conformist, its means fundamentally manipulative" (105). The threat of an unruly crowd remained palpable, though, to sociologists such as Edward A. Ross, whose fears are summarized by Kasson: "The spectacle of masses of people anonymously congregating to participate in intensely emotional amusements seemed like social dynamite. With frightening ease a peaceful group of pleasure seekers...might erupt into a demonic mob" (97).

The representation of Topsy's life and death in the *New York Times* evokes this threat of mob violence, and the link between animality and violence—specifically class violence—is the aspect I want to emphasize here. Topsy's physical body, I believe, can be seen as representative of the working class, and her death takes place at a historical moment when shifting constructions of animality are changing the way people think about human bodies in the marketplace. Leading up to her death, the *Times* notes the illusion of control over the corporeal force of the elephant: "On either side were four husky attendants making believe that they could really hold her by the neck ropes if she should try to break away."[9] Her crimes, we are told, include the murder of three keepers since 1900, including J. Fielding Blunt on May 28, 1902, "presumably because he had fed her a lighted cigarette."[10] But she is also represented as a threat because of her occasional refusal to do her less glamorous job: "pushing around big beams which were being used in construction at Luna Park, and hauling loads too heavy for ordinary beasts of burden."[11] An earlier story in the *Times* titled "Elephant Terrorizes Coney Island Police," on December 6, 1902, describes how her trainer Whitey took her out on a drunken rampage, threatening to "turn the elephant loose upon the crowd," while a police officer "threatened to shoot him if he set the animal on the people."[12] After arriving at the police station, Topsy tried to enter, but she "became wedged in the door...and set up a terrific trumpeting. The crowd scattered in terror, while the policemen in the station house were not less alarmed, and some of them sought refuge up stairs and in the cells" (5). The sergeant was forced to beg Whitey "to drive the animal back," but "for fifteen minutes he kept the policemen busy obeying his orders to drive the crowd away and fetch dainties for Topsy. They could do nothing with the man and were afraid to lock him up on account of the elephant" (5). It is not until Frederic Thompson, "one of the proprietors of Luna Park," arrives that Whitey can be "induced" to bring the animal back to the park. The charge against Whitey is revealed to be disorderly conduct, and the article ends by noting that the Society for the Prevention of Cruelty to Animals had recently "prosecuted [Whitey] Ault for wounding the elephant near the eye with a pitchfork" (5). Whitey thus stands judged, while the possibility of punishing Topsy's physical threat is delayed. And a tension is suggested between humane treatment—of either animals or human workers—and the possibility that they might revolt.

The execution of Topsy, I believe, belongs to a different discursive regime that is only partially legible to us today; it is difficult to imagine a similar public spectacle taking place in the early twenty-first century. Key constructions of both animality and humanity are in flux in Topsy's time, in part through a new willingness to extend the rhetoric of "humane" reform not only to working animals but also to working people. But the link between animality and violence is not limited to working-class mobs. The "natural" exploitation and competition among corporations in the marketplace is eventually animalized, and Topsy's execution thus introduces the shifting constructions of violence in the market that are the subject of this chapter. In this case, Edison's electric company explicitly equates the life of an elephant with the life of a potential human consumer of electricity as a commodity. As Ed Boland, Jr., notes, Edison was actually fighting for dominance in the electricity market: "In his bitter battle with George Westinghouse for control of America's fledgling electric infrastructure, Edison argued that Westinghouse's alternating current was deadly dangerous, while his direct current was safe. In Topsy, Edison saw an opportunity to show everyone just how deadly alternating current could be," even though "alternating current eventually won out over direct current."[13]

Topsy is a rather unfortunate consumer, then, of a deliberately violent corporation playacting here with the fiction of a judicial mandate. From the perspective of the twenty-first century we might be inclined to describe the Edison-Westinghouse battle as two corporations fighting to survive, as two wolfish predators competing in the jungle of the market. What we think of as instinct in animals today is easily projected onto not just corporations but also human beings working in the marketplace. But this construction of the business world as a "jungle" is actually relatively recent. Freud's later work registers this shift toward naturalizing violent or aggressive drives in addition to sexual instincts. His assertion in *Civilization and Its Discontents* (1930) that "man is a wolf to man" refers to individual human beings rather than the behavior of corporations in the market. But as early as the end of the nineteenth century in the United States, a similar logic was being used to describe both individual and corporate behavior. A neighbor, as Freud notes, might represent a temptation for "wolfishness" to be let out in the form of a desire "to exploit his [neighbor's] capacity for work without compensation" or "to seize his possessions."[14] This link between animality and economic ruthlessness suggests how capitalism comes to exploit the logic of "the jungle": the behavior of human beings and corporations in the marketplace comes to be equated with animals fighting to survive, "naturally" defined by the need to kill or be killed, to exploit or be exploited. Novels such as *The Octopus* might appear to solidify this discourse, but Norris's work is in fact much less settled on the question of the animal.

The Nature of Violence

The Octopus explores four rather distinct representations of instincts through four different kinds of violence. The first is the rape and subsequent death of Vanamee's beloved Angéle by an unknown person referred to as "the Other"; the second is Annixter's sexual aggressiveness toward Hilma Tree, his eventual wife; the third is the "instinctual" slaughter of thousands of rabbits by Spanish-Mexican workers; and the fourth is the armed battle between middle-class ranch owners and agents of the railroad-octopus. While not often analyzed in juxtaposition with each other, these sites of violence together illustrate the ways that animality comes to define not only the nature of violence but also the nature of class identity at the turn of the century. In each, the privileged can resist animal instincts (or "the beast within") or refuse to be defined by them, often with the help of Christian ideology, while working-class, racial, and animal "Others" are essentialized as creatures who can act only according to violent, survival-of-the-fittest instincts.

In the case of Vanamee's "Other," *The Octopus* represents a crisis of faith in the explanatory power of a Christian worldview and displays a resistance to the growing hegemony of Darwinist-Freudian animality. In the first chapter we are given the description of the crime: "One moonless night, Angéle, arriving under the black shadow of the pear trees a little earlier than usual, found the apparently familiar figure waiting for her. All unsuspecting she gave herself to the embrace of a strange pair of arms, and Vanamee arriving but a score of moments later, stumbled over her prostrate body, inert and unconscious, in the shadow of the overspiring trees."[15] While Angéle is left "delirious, all but raving," Vanamee "ranged the countryside like a wolf," and the "whole county rose, raging, horror-struck" (38). But this Other cannot be found:

The Other had withdrawn into an impenetrable mystery. There he remained. He never was found; he never was so much as heard of. A legend arose about him, this prowler of the night, this strange, fearful figure, with an unseen face, swooping in there from out the darkness, come and gone in an instant, but leaving behind him a track of terror and death and rage and undying grief. Within the year, in giving birth to the child, Angéle had died. (38)

Vanamee's insistent role in the novel is to determine the nature of this violent Other, and he agonizes over "the Answer" in several extended passages.

Father Sarria, the priest of the Mission of San Juan de Guadalajara, makes the explicit comparison between Angéle and the wheat grown by ranchers in the area: "God giveth it a body as it hath pleased him, and to every seed his own body.... It is sown a natural body; it is raised a spiritual body.... Your grain of wheat is your symbol of immortality. You bury it in the earth. It dies, and rises again a thousand times more beautiful. Vanamee, your dear girl was only a grain of humanity that we have buried here, and the end is not yet" (144). The older use of the term "humanity" here distinguishes between the human and the divine, rather than the human and the animal, as it will after Darwin and Freud. But Vanamee is not satisfied with this explanation, and the failure of God to prevent this violence calls into question for Vanamee the existence of God: "Your God! There is no God. There is only the Devil. The Heaven you pray to is only a joke, a wretched trick, a delusion. It is only Hell that is real" (146). Sarria condemns these words as "blasphemy," but the language of the narrator points toward the growing use of psychological terms at the end of the nineteenth century. Vanamee's condition is diagnosed, for example, as a "naturally nervous temperament" that is "diseased, beset with hallucinations," "racked with the most violent illusions, beset in the throes of a veritable hysteria," later characterized as "dementia" (147–48). What he wants, we are told, is "an Answer.... Not a vague visitation of Grace, not a formless sense of Peace; but an Answer, something real, even if the reality were fancied, a voice out of the night, responding to his, a hand in the dark clasping his groping fingers, a breath, human, warm, fragrant, familiar, like a soft, sweet caress on his shrunken cheeks" (151). For much of the novel, though, "the Answer was not in the church" (151), nor was it in the Grave, the Earth which had been "so eager, so responsive to the lightest summons, so vibrant with Life" (154). For Vanamee, the Answer that explains violence and rape in the universe is also clearly not an "animal instinct" in the Other.

The other mystery related to Vanamee is his "occult" power of psychically calling out to both Father Sarria and Presley. Sarria heeds his "call" involuntarily, but he is disturbed and frightened by this "strange power": "It troubles me... to think that my own will can count for so little. Just now I could not resist" (138–39). Vanamee soon turns this power toward conjuring "the Answer," which first seems to be a part of the dead Angéle responding to an extension of Vanamee, outside his own body: "somewhere off there over the little valley, far off, the darkness was troubled; that *me* that went out upon my thought—out from the Mission garden, out over the valley, calling for her, searching for her, found, I don't know what, but found a resting place— a companion" (215). Eventually the Answer, also referred to as "the Vision," "the Illusion," and "the Manifestation" (382–83), is embodied in the form of Angéle's daughter, now sixteen years old, but there is a blurred distinction between mother and daughter: "Called forth from out the darkness, from the grip of the earth, the embrace of the grave, from out the memory of corruption, she rose into light and life, divinely pure" (391). Sarria recognizes her as Angéle's daughter and tells him as much, but for Vanamee it makes no difference: "Angéle or Angéle's daughter, it was all one with him. It was She. Death was overcome. The grave vanquished. Life, ever-renewed, alone existed" (392). Vanamee is then returned to the faith, linking Angéle once again with the wheat:

> Angéle was not the symbol, but the *proof* of immortality. The seed dying, rotting and corrupting the earth; rising again in life unconquer- able, and in immaculate purity,—Angéle dying as she gave birth to her little daughter, life springing from her death,—the pure, unconquer- able, coming forth from the defiled. Why had he not had the knowl- edge of God? Thou fool, that which thou sowest is not quickened except it die.... The wheat called forth from out the darkness, from out the grip of the earth, of the grave, from out corruption, rose trium- phant into light and life. So Angéle, so life, so also the resurrection of the dead. It is sown in corruption. It is raised in incorruption. It is sown in dishonor. It is raised in glory. It is sown in weakness. It is raised in power. Death was swallowed up in Victory. (393)

The apparent triumph of a contrived Christian ideology here evokes the theo- ries of Joseph Le Conte, with whom Norris studied zoology and geology as an undergraduate at Berkeley. Le Conte's books, such as *Religion and Science* (1874) and *Evolution, Its Nature, Its Evidences, and Its Relations to Religious Thought* (1888), work to reconcile Christianity with Darwinian evolution by claiming that the Divine Will operated *through* evolution.[16] But I am more interested in how desperate Vanamee's attempt to reconcile his faith with his "reality" seems to be.

According to Mark Seltzer in *Bodies and Machines* (1992), Vanamee's con-juring of Angéle's daughter can be read as a "miracle of re-creation, a simple replacement of daughter for mother."[17] The achievement, then, is "a circum-vention of both the 'defilement' of Angéle's sexuality and the 'birth' of her daughter," as well as a way to explain the "alterity of sexual production in the novel": reproduction is replaced with reincarnation, and "Vanamee's reincar-native power offers finally an emphatically personified and personifying tech-nique of nonbiological and autonomous reproduction, or what amounts to a mechanical reproduction of persons."[18] This is linked with Seltzer's broader claim about "the naturalist machine," but it does not address the nature of the Other. What seems so desperate to me, in other words, is not the anxiety of gendered (re)production but, rather, the desire to explain away violence within a Christian framework. In Vanamee's mind, it is as if the Other never raped his beloved, and she has simply returned to him. Toward the end of the novel he explains to Presley, simply, that "Angéle has returned to me, and I am happy."[19] From Vanamee's perspective, "It was Reality—it was Angéle in the flesh, vital, sane, material.... Not a manifestation, not a dream, but her very self" (638), and he has no qualms when she, "turning her face to his, kissed him on the mouth" and murmured, "I love you, I love you" (639).

Distinctly lacking in the novel's construction of the Other is a post-Freudian reflection that the Other might actually exist *within* either Father Sarria or Vanamee himself in the form of an explosive fusion of sexual desire and violent "wolfishness." Despite the fact that we are told the Other was an "apparently familiar figure," no further evidence would seem to indicate this link. But the novel does indicate certain dark secrets in the character of Father Sarria. While having a drink with the rancher Annixter one day, for example, Sarria is rather anxious and uneasy about a basket he is carrying, which he claims contains poultry. Annixter's dog tips the basket over and reveals "a cock, his head enclosed in a little chamois bag such as are used for gold watches" (205). Annixter calls out the secret: "Game cocks! Fighting cocks! Oh, you old rat! You'll be a dry nurse to a burro, and keep a hospital for infirm puppies, but you will fight game cocks.... There's the Spanish cropping out, after all" (205). Sarria can only hurry off, "speechless with chagrin" (205). But the idea that a secret vice could represent "the Spanish cropping out" suggests a new and dif-ferent way of explaining violent instincts that I will explore later.

Unlike the Other, whose instincts have not been animalized, a figure such as Annixter represents a second kind of instinct constructed in this novel in which white middle-class drives may be animalized but ultimately restrained within the ideology of Christianity. Middle-class sexual instincts, in other words, are on the cusp between a Christian and a Darwinist-Freudian frame-work, drawing upon a much older construction of "the beast" as the representative of sinful lusts and desires. Annixter's instincts are reined in, for example, by a sense of Christian duty in ways that distance him from his racial and class inferiors, according to the logic of the text, but "instinct" is still associated in part with the new discourse of animality. Chasing after Hilma Tree, the daughter of one of his workers in the dairy, Annixter first sees what is described as her "animal nature," and we are reminded that she is from the laboring class: "There was a certain generous amplitude to the full, round curves of her hips and shoulders that suggested the precocious maturity of a healthy, vigorous animal life passed under the hot southern sun of a half-tropical country" (82–83). On the verge of sexually assaulting her later in the novel, Annixter once again is attracted to "a vibrant note of gayety, of exuberant animal life, sane, honest, strong," but he is also attracted to the "whiteness of her skin [which] under the caress of this hale, vigorous morning light was dazzling, pure, of a fineness beyond words. . . . her large, white arms, wet with milk, redolent and fragrant with milk, glowing and resplendent in the early morning light" (166). Through Hilma we begin to see the moral construction of whiteness as "the good," while it is "only wicked people that love the dark. And the wicked things are always done and planned in the dark" (168). Annixter's sexual desire is not appeased, though, and "a certain excitement [was] beginning to gain upon him"; "he owed it to himself as a man to go as far as he could" (169). Rebuffed on this occasion, Annixter later tells himself, "By God, I'll have that girl yet. . . . Ain't I her employer, her boss? I'll show her—and Delaney, too. It would be easy enough—and then Delaney can have her—if he wants her—after me" (233). But here his "instincts" are revealed as functioning within a Christian framework, with "an evil light flashing from under his scowl": "The male instincts of possession, unreasoned, treacherous, oblique, came twisting to the surface. All the lower nature of the man, ignorant of women, racked at one and the same time with enmity and desire, roused itself like a hideous and abominable beast" (233).

But this evil beast can eventually be tamed within Annixter through the wholesome embrace of Hilma as the wife and mother of his children, rather than simply (and sinfully) the object of his desire. His epiphany, as confessed to her, is, "I know what love means now, and instead of being ashamed of it, I'm proud of it. . . . I'd been absolutely and completely selfish up to the moment I realised I really loved you. . . . It's made it easier to do the straight, clean thing. . . . I love you, and if you will forgive me, and if you will come down to such a beast as I am, I want to be to you the best a man can be to a woman, Hilma" (403–04). Once they are married, Annixter's benevolence is exhibited through such examples as taking in Dyke's wife and daughter after Dyke's downfall. Explaining his conversion to Presley, his often-homosocial friend, Annixter exclaims his newfound religion:

> she's made a man of me. I was a machine before, and if another man, or woman, or child got in my way, I rode 'em down, and I never *dreamed* of anybody but myself. But as soon as I woke up to the fact that I really loved her, why, it was glory hallelujah all in a minute, and, in a way, I kind of loved everybody then, and wanted to be everybody's friend. And I began to see that a fellow can't live *for* himself any more than he can live *by* himself. He's got to think of others.... I'm going to get in and *help* people, and I'm going to keep to that idea the rest of my natural life. That ain't much of a religion, but it's the best I've got...(467–68)

Presley calls this "true nobility" (468), and later Annixter grows rhapsodic, with a "vast and humble thankfulness that his God had chosen him of all men for this great joy, had brought him to his knees for the first time in all his troubled, restless life of combat and aggression. He prayed, he knew not what,—vague words, wordless thoughts, resolving fiercely to do right, to make some return for God's gift thus placed within his hands" (497–98). Regardless of whether his newfound religion is institutionally sanctioned, Annixter's "beast" can be wrestled into submission within Christian ideology.

It might appear that Annixter's violent sexual instincts are displaced onto the descriptions of intensely gendered plowing in his fields, and this claim is worth considering. The language of desire is closely linked with the machine once the plows make their assault:

> It was the long stroking caress, vigorous, male, powerful, for which the Earth seemed panting. The heroic embrace of a multitude of iron hands, gripping deep into the brown, warm flesh of the land that quivered responsive and passionate under this rude advance, so robust as to be almost an assault, so violent as to be veritably brutal. There, under the sun and under the speckless sheen of the sky, the wooing of the Titan began, the vast primal passion, the two world-forces, the elemental Male and Female, locked in a colossal embrace, at grapples in the throes of an infinite desire, at once terrible and divine, knowing no law, untamed, savage, natural, sublime. (130–31)

According to Christophe Den Tandt in *The Urban Sublime in American Literary Naturalism* (1998), this scene can be read as "heterosexual copulation of sublime proportions."[20] Fantasy and desire, here in the form of rape, is combined with dread or terror of the wheat itself, a force linked with the railroad through the rhetoric of the sublime.[21] For Seltzer, once the machine displaces "the Male" as a reproductive force, a tremendous amount of gender anxiety is produced, and the result is "the resolutely abstract account of 'force' that governs the naturalist text."[22] The goal of what Seltzer calls "the naturalist machine," then, is to reclaim male power through technology by describing this "force" through the principles of thermodynamics. Once power has been "put back into the hands of the immortal and autonomous male technology of generation," the creation of life, in the form here of the wheat, can be seen as "the work of an inexhaustible masturbator, spilling his seed on the ground, the product of a mechanistic and miraculous onanism."[23] What we see, then, is "the desire to project an alternative to biological reproduction, to displace the threat posed by the 'women people' (the reduction of men to 'mere animalcules' in the process of procreation) and to devise a counter-mode of reproduction (the naturalist machine)."[24]

However useful this identification of "force" as operating according to the laws of thermodynamics may be, I would also emphasize two further issues: first, that for Norris, the "eternal symphony of reproduction" exists within a Christian framework, which he describes as "primordial energy flung out from the hand of the Lord God himself, immortal, calm, infinitely strong."[25] Second, the agency of the plow, and therefore the "naturalist machine," is split between the restrained, military approach of the middle-class farmer, in this case Annixter, and the animalized, grinding bodies of his workers. While Annixter overlooks the thirty-five plows, each with five shears, resembling "a great column of field artillery" (127–28), his workers and his horses become almost interchangeable. On the ground we see "the working of the smooth brown flanks in the harness," and we hear "the sonorous, steady breaths wrenched from the deep, laboring chests, strap-bound, shining with sweat, and all along the line the voices of the men talking to the horses" (129). Soon the picture blurs between men and horses:

Everywhere there were visions of glossy brown backs, straining, heaving, swollen with muscle; harness streaked with specks of froth, broad, cup-shaped hoofs, heavy with brown loam, men's faces red with tan, blue overalls spotted with axle-grease; muscled hands, the knuckles whitened in their grip on the reins, and through it all the ammoniacal

smell of the horses, the bitter reek of perspiration of beasts and men,
the aroma of warm leather, the scent of dead stubble—and stronger
and more penetrating than everything else, the heavy, enervating odour
of the upturned, living earth. (129–30)

Once the day of plowing is done, the men assault their nightly meal with similarly animalized vigor: "The table was taken as if by assault.... One heard the
incessant sounds of mastication, and saw the uninterrupted movement of great
jaws.... It was no longer a supper. It was a veritable barbecue, a crude and primitive feasting, barbaric, homeric" (132). Vanamee can take part in this feasting,
we are told, but Presley would have "abhorred it—this feeding of the People,
this gorging of the human animal, eager for its meat" (132). It is here, then,
that we glimpse the discourse of animality in its Darwinist-Freudian sense, a
conception of what is within the human being that can be distinguished from
Annixter's middle-class battle with the Devil. The result is a new way of constructing the distance between the working class and the middle class.

    Within this distinction, though, is also a further animalization that repre-
sents the third kind of instinct and identity group essentialized in the novel.
The racist construction of "animal instincts" first suggested in the figure of
Father Sarria earlier is deployed more clearly in the slaughter of jackrabbits
perpetrated by "Spanish-Mexicans," whose instincts are animalized even more
so than their animal victims. Among those participating in the rabbit drive,
we are told, are "Spanish-Mexicans from the town itself,—swarthy young men
on capering horses, dark-eyed girls and matrons, in red and black and yellow,
more Portuguese in brand-new overalls, smoking long thin cigars" (492). The
representation of Annixter as a military commander over his harvest marks
him as above the fray, with "marshals" and "wings, under the command of lieu-
tenants" (493). With more than five thousand people present on Osterman's
ranch, the lines of people herd all rabbits in front of the wings of mobile fenc-
ing that will eventually come together to funnel the animals into the corral.
Mrs. Derrick, the white wife of a rancher, encounters one of the rabbits individually when it jumps onto her lap: "for a long time afterward, she retained
upon her knees the sensation of the four little paws quivering with excitement,
and the feel of the trembling furry body, with its wildly beating heart, pressed
against her own" (500). But the rest of the group can only see "a maze of
small, moving bodies, leaping, ducking, doubling, running back and forth—a
wilderness of agitated ears, white tails and twinkling legs" (500); "the disinte-
grated mass of rabbits commenced, as it were, to solidify and coagulate" (501).
Curiously, though, the rabbits become "less wild" at various moments, and

"all wildness, all fear of man, seemed to have entirely disappeared" once they are squeezed into the corral, and they become "packed two, three, and four feet deep. They were in constant movement; those beneath struggling to the top, those on top sinking and disappearing below their fellows" (500–02).

The link between human beings subordinated by race and class and the animals they are pursuing is again constructed by smell: "from the hot and sweating mass there rose a strange odour, penetrating, ammoniacal, savouring of wild life" (502). While Annixter, his new wife, Hilma, and the "guests" withdraw, the Portuguese men and boys proceed to unleash what is supposedly in their blood: "Blindly, furiously, they struck and struck. The Anglo-Saxon spectators round about drew back in disgust, but the hot, degenerated blood of Portuguese, Mexican, and mixed Spaniard boiled up in excitement at this wholesale slaughter" (502). The white folk, then, proceed to "Homeric" feasting and games that are celebrated as feeding the appetite of "the People, elemental, gross, a great appeasing of appetite, an enormous quenching of thirst. Quarters of beef, roasts, ribs, shoulders, haunches were consumed, loaves of bread by the thousands disappeared, whole barrels of wine went down the dry and dusty throats of the multitude" (504). While men light cigars, "the women seized the occasion to nurse their babies" (503), and further race pride ensues:

> It was Homeric, this feasting, this vast consuming of meat and bread and wine, followed now by games of strength. An epic simplicity and directness, an honest Anglo-Saxon mirth and innocence, commended it. Crude it was; coarse it was, but no taint of viciousness was here. These people were good people, kindly, benignant even, always readier to give than to receive, always more willing to help than to be helped. They were good stock. Of such was the backbone of the nation—sturdy Americans everyone of them. Where else in the world round were such strong, honest men, such strong, beautiful women? (505)

The viciousness of the Mexican-Spanish-Portuguese workers is taken for granted; they are not granted the same consideration of motives, mental states, and extenuating circumstances that white "stock" would be given. Instead, they are prejudged by their group identity, which is constructed as biologically determined through the supposed proximity between racial Others and unwanted animals.

Jackrabbit drives were a historical reality in California at the end of the nineteenth century, and detailed accounts of slaughtering rabbits, along with a middle-class desire to condemn the same details that seem so titillating, indicate that Norris's novel was not alone in its fascination with such displays. According to a report made by Dr. T. S. Palmer in 1896 titled *The Jack Rabbits of the United States*, at least 362,000 rabbits were killed in the state of California alone between 1888 and 1895.[26] As assistant chief of the U.S. Department of Agriculture's Division of Ornithology and Mammalogy, Palmer wrote his report in response to the growing threat of rabbits to corporate farms, such as "the firm of Haggin & Carr" and "the great Miller & Lux ranch" (52, 53). The conclusion that rabbits "ordinarily are held in check by natural enemies and by disease" (79) points toward the obvious fact that coyotes and wolves were subject to mass eradication programs at this point as well.[27] The largest drive on record occurred on March 12, 1892, with eight thousand people involved and somewhere between twenty and thirty thousand rabbits killed (54). The earliest accounts of such drives are supposedly from 1839 when Indians in Walla Walla, Washington, killed several hundred rabbits, but the practice did not reach the San Joaquin Valley until 1882 (47). A *Chicago Tribune* account of a drive near Fresno on October 1, 1893, indicates the desire both for horrific details and for "inhumane" condemnation:

> The fence on each side is closing in fast, and although still some distance from the corral the screaming of the poor creatures can be heard as they find their retreat cut off. The climax of the drive is now at hand.... Now the screeching of the rabbits can be heard above everything, and the ground is covered with dead rabbits by the dozen. At the corral entrance the scene is indescribably pitiful and distressing.... To slash and beat the poor screaming animals to death is the work of but a short time, but it brings tears to many an eye and makes the heart sore to witness the finish. It is a relief to everybody when all is still, when the trying day is at an end. The result of the drive at Fresno was 20,000 dead rabbits.[28]

Palmer's own conclusion about an apparent decline in the number of drives in the 1890s is that "It may be questioned whether such frequent scenes of butchery can have anything but an injurious effect on a community, and it is fortunate that the necessity for them does not now exist" (59). Yet a lack of necessity does not necessarily reveal a lack of desire, or a lack of discursive possibility, as Norris's novel reveals.

In *The Octopus*, the link between animal instincts and butchering animals is bracketed off as a lower-class, race-based domain. But there are other ways of linking animal instincts with class identity, including the fourth and final kind of instinct I want to explore. The conflict between the railroad-octopus and the middle-class ranch owners appropriates the discourse of animality in revealing ways, as in the celebration of "Homeric" white laborers mentioned earlier, before ultimately rejecting this kind of common instinct. If pushed too far, "the People" as an animalized force could presumably unleash their animal nature to fight back against the oppression of the octopus. Norris's narrative appropriates this kind of logic for ranchers such as Annixter and Magnus Derrick, although their workers are only nominally included in these descriptions, as both June Howard and Walter Benn Michaels have shown. Once Derrick's League is informed that the railroad has inflated the selling prices of land that the tenant ranchers must now purchase, for example, Norris tells us:

> For a second there was nothing articulate in that cry of savage exasperation, nothing even intelligent. It was the human animal hounded to its corner, exploited, harried to its last stand, at bay, ferocious, terrible, turning at last with bared teeth and upraised claws to meet the death grapple. It was the hideous squealing of the tormented brute, its back to the wall, defending its lair, its mate and its whelps, ready to bite, to rend, to trample, to batter out the life of The Enemy in a primeval, bestial welter of blood and fury.[29]

At the end of the impromptu meeting, which has excluded all workers with the exception of Vanamee, we are told: "It was the uprising of The People; the thunder of the outbreak of revolt; the mob demanding to be led, aroused at last, imperious, resistless, overwhelming. It was the blind fury of insurrection, the brute, many-tongued, red-eyed, bellowing for guidance, baring its teeth, unsheathing its claws, imposing its will with the abrupt, resistless pressure of the relaxed piston, inexorable, knowing no pity" (279). The movement in the description from monster to machine mirrors many of the descriptions of the railroad-octopus and indicates that the battle to come is not merely animalized. Outside the Opera House, before his speech to "the People," Presley encounters this brute once again after being attacked by the "iron" of the railroad: "it was a beginning, the growl of the awakened brute, feeling the iron in its flank, heaving up its head with bared teeth, the throat vibrating to the long, indrawn snarl of wrath" (544).

Working-class individuals do exist in the novel, and they are frequently animalized. But the middle-class appropriation of animal violence is ultimately rejected as too dangerous. A working-class (white) figure like Dyke embodies this kind of brute resistance, for example, as he uses force to fight back against the railroad. As a result, he is hounded by Behrman, the railroad's agent, and frequently animalized as he is hunted down like "a wild animal" (424, 433). In the end he succumbs to Behrman's men, who finally "closed in again, implacable, unconquerable, ferocious, like hounds upon a wolf" (486). But the "evil influence" of Caraher, the "red" saloon-keeper who always advocates "six inches of plugged gaspipe," is ultimately blamed for Dyke's fall: "an honest man, strong, fearless, upright, struck down by a colossal power, perverted by an evil influence" (357–59). Annixter's response is, "God for us all…and the devil take the hindmost" (360), and the narrative judgment toward the end of the novel is to condemn a violent response of "the People," the threat of "the reds," as a crime: "For all the tragedy of his wife's death, Caraher was none the less an evil influence among the ranchers, an influence that worked only to the inciting of crime.…the anarchist saloon-keeper had goaded Dyke and Presley both to murder; a bad man, a plague spot in the world of the ranchers, poisoning the farmers' bodies with alcohol and their minds with discontent" (620). While Presley is saved from ruin by his class privilege, the violence he commits in the name of the people is distinguishable, apparently, from his ability to recognize it as evil. In this way he avoids being punished like the animalized Dyke, the violent representative of the people who ultimately are to be feared by middle-class reformers as well as capitalists. But the middle class is left between two agents of violence: the people and the octopus. If the octopus abides by the laws of the market, as we have seen earlier, rather than the laws of the jungle, then it would be futile to fight back with animalized force. The result would only be the destruction of middle-class bodies and properties under the inexorable wheels of the railroad. While Norris's novel presents evolving constructions of individual instinct, though, its resistance to the logic of the jungle becomes increasingly rare at this historical moment, a moment seemingly defined by the 1906 publication of Upton Sinclair's *The Jungle*. I turn now to that novel to further explore the relationship between animality and class at the turn of the century.

The Hog-Squeal of the Jungle

Among the most striking passages in *The Jungle* is an early description of a continuous flow of pigs ignominiously tortured in a Chicago slaughterhouse. Hog after hog is jerked off his feet, chained to "a great iron wheel" by one leg, and then ignored while he squeals in agony:

> The shriek was followed by another, louder and yet more agonizing—
> for once started upon that journey, the hog never came back; at the top

of the wheel he was shunted off upon a trolley, and went sailing down the room. And meantime another was swung up and then another, and another, until there was a double line of them, each dangling by a foot and kicking in frenzy and squealing. The uproar was appalling, perilous to the ear-drums; one feared there was too much sound for the room to hold—that the walls must give way or the ceiling crack. There were high squeals and low squeals, grunts, and wails of agony; there would come a momentary lull, and then a fresh outburst, louder than ever, surging up to a deafening climax.[30]

The narrative seems to instruct the reader how to respond by suggesting that "somehow the most matter-of-fact person could not help thinking of the hogs; they were so innocent, they came so very trustingly; and they were so very human in their protests—and so perfectly within their rights!"[31] We might be reminded of Presley's apparent sympathy for sheep slaughtered by the railroad in *The Octopus*. But somewhat surprisingly, perhaps, Sinclair refers to this passage in his *Autobiography* rather differently. "I have frequently observed," he laments, "that an advocate of new ideas is not permitted to have a sense of humor.... For fifty-six years I have been ridiculed for a passage in *The Jungle* that deals with the moral claims of dying hogs—which passage was intended as hilarious farce."[32] The treatment of both animals and workers was no laughing matter at the turn of the century, as this chapter and the previous one have shown, even in the lofty rhetoric of capitalist apologists like Carnegie. For reformers like Sinclair, though, the "humane" treatment of workers was most clearly necessary once behavior in the marketplace appeared to be governed by the laws of the jungle. Rather than merely reflecting this discursive construct, though, *The Jungle* helped to produce it. But there are also alternative epistemologies in this novel that resist the biological determinism that inevitably becomes hegemonic within the birth of "the jungle" broadly conceived.

Sinclair's advocacy is clearly for working-class immigrants like his character Jurgis Rudkus in the novel, rather than for the animals that serve as a metaphor for exploited workers. Regardless of Sinclair's intent, though, the hog-squeal passage maintains an ability to evoke tremendous sympathy for the pigs themselves. Carol Adams suggests in *The Sexual Politics of Meat: A Feminist-Vegetarian Critical Theory* (1990) that "the referent—those few initial pages describing butchering in a book of more than three hundred pages—overpowered the metaphor."[33] For Adams, "Butchering failed as a metaphor for the fate of the worker in *The Jungle* because the novel carried too much information on how the animal was violently killed. To make the absent referent present—that is, describing how an animal dies, kicking, screaming, and is fragmented—disables consumption and disables the power of metaphor."[34] In addition to a simplistic insistence on "*the* referent," Adams's analysis overlooks the fact that the dominant metaphor of the novel is "the jungle," rather than "butchering," and that the difference between these terms is highly significant. But her intuition that Sinclair's narrative seems to disrupt itself here is useful to consider, particularly because this scene actually resists the larger "laws of the jungle" that the rest of the novel so effectively constructs.

As an example of what June Howard calls "slumming in determinism,"[35] the novel's narrative quickly distances itself from the events and characters of this world. "Our friends," we are told, "were not poetical, and the sight suggested to them no metaphors of human destiny; they thought only of the wonderful efficiency of it all."[36] Contrary to the simpleminded response of Jurgis, who declares at this point that he's glad he's not a hog, the reader is told that "One could not stand and watch very long without becoming philosophical, without beginning to deal in symbols and similes, and to hear the hog-squeal of the universe."[37] As Howard notes, "the naturalist plays the role of the readers' guide and interpreter in an alien land. But he is not a native of that land either."[38] Certainly one way to read the novel, then, is as yet another ultimately conservative muckraking text that polices, rather than empowers, its presumptive working-class subject. But I want to suggest that the hog-squeal passage represents a more interesting moment within the discourse of the jungle that is being produced in part by Sinclair's novel.

Rather than epitomizing a "survival of the fittest" confrontation between predator and prey, the hog-squeal passage presents us with questions similarly raised by the slaughter of sheep in Norris's novel: What is the nature of this violence? Is it a punishable crime? A sin? What "extenuating circumstances" might mitigate the culpability of the Beef Trust for such torture? Like the railroad, the Beef Trust's actions demand a narrative explanation: "It was like some horrible crime committed in a dungeon, all unseen and unheeded, buried out of sight and of memory."[39] The turn toward a Christian framework might seem rather appropriate, despite Sinclair's claims of irony. The passage equates human and animal suffering, and even human and animal souls: "Was it permitted to believe that there was nowhere upon the earth, or above the earth, a heaven for hogs, where they were requited for all this suffering?" (37). The individuality of each hog is proclaimed, while, unknowingly, "a black shadow hung over him and a horrid Fate waited in his pathway. Now suddenly it had swooped upon him, and had seized him by the leg. Relentless, remorseless, it was; all his protests, his screams, were nothing to it—it did its cruel will with him, as if his wishes, his feelings, had simply no existence at all; it cut his throat and watched him gasp out his life" (37). Like the octopus, the Beef Trust could be judged as a monstrous corporation that leaves death and destruction in its wake, not because of an amoral, social Darwinist drive to survive but rather out of a malice that is almost incomprehensible. I would argue that this kind of explanation, this ability to label horrific acts as malicious rather than natural, suggests a framework for condemning unnecessary violence without simultaneously constructing "animal instincts" as a way to justify or even expand corporate violence.

Jurgis is relieved that he is "not a hog" at the beginning of the novel, even though he later concludes that "a hog was just what he had been—one of the packers' hogs" (299). But the logic of "the jungle" is constructed largely *after* the hog-squeal passage, which instead resists rationalizing this violence as "natural" in a Darwinist-Freudian sense. Even if Jurgis is presented as uninitiated into the exploitation of the Beef Trust, his awe of the Taylorized efficiency of industrial production is significant for the way it resists a construction of the corporation as simply an animal fighting to survive.[40] From a raised gallery above the cattle pens, for example, Jurgis and his relatives "stood, staring, breathless with wonder" (33). The men on the killing floor go about their work with indifference, with everything "all so very businesslike" (36), before the narrative moves into the hog-squeal passage. Jurgis is fascinated by the distinctly "unnatural" disassembly line:

> The carcass hog was scooped out of the vat by machinery, and then it fell to the second floor, passing on the way through a wonderful machine with numerous scrapers, which adjusted themselves to the size and shape of the animal, and sent it out at the other end with nearly all of its bristles removed. It was then strung up by machinery, and sent upon another trolley ride; this time passing between two lines of men, who sat upon a raised platform, each doing a certain single thing to the carcass as it came to him. (37)

Jurgis can only stare, "open-mouthed, lost in wonder. He had dressed hogs himself in the forest of Lithuania; but he had never expected to live to see one hog dressed by several hundred men. It was like a wonderful poem to him, and he took it all in guilelessly..." (38). As he moves on to the slaughtering of cattle, he sees this machine-in-the-garden as "a picture of human power wonderful to watch" (39), and "something to be seen and never forgotten" (40). By the end of the chapter he is in religious awe, anxious only to join the hierarchy and obey: "to Jurgis it seemed almost profanity to speak about the place as did Jokubas, sceptically; it was a thing as tremendous as the universe—the laws and ways of its working no more than the universe was to be questioned or understood. All that a mere man could do...was to take a thing like this as he found it, and do as he was told; to be given a place in it and a share in its wonderful activities was a blessing to be grateful for, as one was grateful for the sunshine and the rain" (42).

Such faith in the benevolence and inevitability of the corporation echoes the construction of the railroad in *The Octopus* once more, but *The Jungle's* skepticism of such logic is clearly visible in the serialized version that appeared in the socialist newspaper *Appeal to Reason*. In an excerpt deleted from the hog-squeal passage cited earlier, for example, we encounter tremendous sarcasm directed toward the worldview apparent in a figure like Presley (or Carnegie):

> For all the while there was a meaning—if only the poor pig could have known it. Perhaps if he had, he would not have squealed at all, but died happy! If only he had known that he was to figure in the bank-account of some great captain of industry, and perhaps help to found a university, or endow a handful of libraries.... It is one of the crimes of commercialism that...delicate women and little children, who toil and groan in factories and mines and sweatshops and die of starvation and loathsome diseases, are not taught and consoled by the reflection that they are adding to the wealth of society, and to the power and greatness of some eminent philanthropist.[41]

Certainly *The Jungle* condemns the kind of logic apparent at the end of *The Octopus*, or in the work of Spencer and Carnegie, but the hog-squeal passage is not the site for justifying the "laws of the jungle" as "natural." Jurgis may be a figurative hog, but a literal hog systematically dismembered in a Taylorized factory seems rather distant from a wild animal instinctually fighting back in the jungle. There is no threat, in other words, that these literal hogs will revolt, any more than the innocent sheep slaughtered in *The Octopus*. The violence of the corporation in both cases must be either monstrous or machinelike, and it can be condemned, but it is not yet explicitly animalized. The seamless link between corporate exploitation and "survival of the fittest," in other words, has not yet been indelibly forged.

The road to forging such a link is most clearly mapped out through the body of Jurgis himself. June Howard argues that he is ultimately saved from becoming a "brute" by his socialist conversion at the end of the novel: "Jurgis's misfortunes come close to turning him into a brute as well as an ignorant victim and destroying him as a human being."[42] The "achievement" of the novel, at least for Howard, is that what it "actually depicts is the preservation of Jurgis's humanity and the enlightenment of the reader..."[43] I find it difficult to see, though, how Jurgis's "humanity" is left in tact. Rather, I would argue that the construction of "the jungle" requires him to remain animalized throughout the novel. Even after he achieves his "conversion," he is transformed from a "beast of burden,"[44] through the voice of a socialist speaker, to an animalized figure who "stood there, with his clenched hands upraised, his eyes bloodshot, and the veins standing out purple in his face, roaring in the voice of a wild beast, frantic, incoherent, maniacal" (292).

The problem for Jurgis is that even though he displays self-righteous indignation at the prostitution of Marija and the sexual assault of his own wife, his animalized body is always threatening to explode in a fit of supposedly instinctual passion. His response to the sexual assault of Ona, for example, turns him into a raging beast who charges into his wife's factory: "Things swam blood before him, and he screamed aloud in his fury, lifting his victim and smashing his head upon the floor"; "it was only when half a dozen men had seized him ... that he understood that he was losing his prey. In a flash he had bent down and sunk his teeth into the man's cheek; and when they tore him away he was dripping with blood, and little ribbons of skin were hanging in his mouth" (148). Compared to a writhing tiger, Jurgis even repeats the feat of biting off this man's flesh once he meets him again, later in the novel (264). From the very beginning, though, Jurgis is presented as a beast with sexual appetites, a working-class animal who cannot control his sexual instincts. He gazes hungrily at his new wife, Ona, as early as the opening scene of the wedding feast, causing her to turn white and tremble (22); much later, once Ona has died in childbirth and Jurgis has hit the road on his own, we are told that upon seeing a prostitute in a saloon, "the wild beast rose up within him and screamed, as it has screamed in the jungle from the dawn of time." He and his friends subsequently spend the night in "wild rioting and debauchery" (209).

Clearly other figures are animalized in the novel as well. African American workers, for example, who come to break the strike once Jurgis returns to Packingtown, are bundles of instinct barely contained: "brawny negroes [were] stripped to the waist and pounding each other for money, while a throng of three or four thousand surged about, men and women, young white girls from the country rubbing elbows with big buck negroes with daggers in their boots, while rows of wooly heads peered down…" (260). In the midst of this wild threat of miscegenation, of "hell let loose in the yard," we see "stabbings and shootings," "whiskey and women," "a saturnalia of debauchery—scenes such as never before had been witnessed in America." More important, for a middle-class audience, "the nameless diseases of vice were soon rife; and this where food was being handled which was sent out to every corner of the civilized world." In short, the stockyards become "the camping-place of an army of fifteen or twenty thousand human beasts.… [a] square mile of abominations" (261). On the killing floor of the slaughterhouse, Jurgis is forced to manage scabs who are described as "a throng of stupid black negroes, and foreigners who could not understand a word that was said to them" (256).[45]

Jurgis appears to distance himself from this world of debauchery to some extent with his moral condemnation of Marija's turn to prostitution, after he has (hypocritically) deserted what is left of his extended family. His response to finding Marija in a brothel is one of despair: "he had somehow always excepted his own family, that he had loved; and now this sudden horrible discovery—Marija a whore, and Elzbieta and the children living off her shame!" (278). Such a judgment links Marija with an earlier description of prostitutes who are also animalized as they are "herded together in a miniature inferno, with hideous, beastly faces, bloated and leprous with disease, laughing, shouting, screaming in all stages of drunkenness, barking like dogs, gibbering like apes, raving and tearing themselves in delirium" (220). The prospect of Jurgis himself as a prostitute is hinted at once he lets his "wolf-hunger" get "the better of him," while Freddie, the son of a rich capitalist, is described as "very handsome" and "a beautiful boy, with light golden hair and the head of an Antinous" (230).[46]

Jurgis's most violent, "animal" outbreaks, though, result in confrontations with the police and his subsequent incarceration. After the first time he attacks his wife's abuser, Jurgis is thrown in jail, on Christmas Eve, and he perceives his punishment as horribly unjust. Described as a "wild beast" in the midst of the "inmost lair" of the police (149), Jurgis is tormented by the thought of his wife's stained honor, to the extent that "within the soul of him there rose up a fiend, red-eyed and cruel, and tore out the strings of his heart" (150). Rather than incarceration to save his soul, Jurgis's punishment is depicted as a battle of strength. He is like "a wild beast that breaks its teeth upon the bars of its cage" (154), and the state's power is "only force, it was tyranny, the will and the power, reckless and unrestrained" (155). Despite the bells of Christmas Eve ringing outside, the agents of the state "had ground him beneath their heel, they had devoured his substance.... They had put him behind bars, as if he had been a wild beast, a thing without sense or reason, without rights, without affections, without feelings. Nay, they would not even have treated a beast as they had treated him! Would any man in his senses have trapped a wild thing in its lair, and left its young behind to die?" (155). Incarceration, then, is here represented as torture, as physical punishment, of the kind to be reserved for beings without reason or agency. Citing Oscar Wilde, whose own sexuality was notoriously punished by the state, the narrative invokes the prison as brute force: "I know not whether Laws be right, / Or whether Laws be wrong; / All that we know who lie in gaol / Is that the wall is strong" (155–56).

In prison Jurgis encounters the thief named Duane and the representative risk of "turning to crime" among all the other "animals" in jail. Although the prison thus appears to be the most naked site of the Darwinist-Freudian jungle, it is still described in terms that register a residue of Christian condemnation. In this "Noah's ark of the city's crime—there were murderers, 'hold-up men' and burglars, embezzlers, counterfeiters and forgers, bigamists, 'shoplifters,' 'confidence-men,' petty thieves and pickpockets, gamblers and procurers, brawlers, beggars, tramps and drunkards" (159–60). But the beasts in this jungle have souls, lusts, and the ability to be corrupted. It is "the inner soul of a city in which justice and honor, women's bodies and men's souls, were for sale in the market-place, and human beings writhed and fought and fell upon each other like wolves in a pit; in which lusts were raging fires, and men were fuel, and humanity was festering and stewing and wallowing in its own corruption. Into this wild-beast tangle these men had been born without their consent, they had taken part in it because they could not help it" (160). There are no Presleys or Cedarquists here, no men of privilege. The prisoners are exhibited for the public in "a long, cement-walled court roofed with glass" (157) and forced to work "all day long...breaking stone" (163), and we might also think here of convict labor in the South at this historical moment, a practice discussed in further detail in the next chapter of this book.

Significantly, though, it is not until after Jurgis's confrontation with the jungle of the prison that the corporation can also be fully animalized. Once he has been released and confronted with a whole series of tragedies, Jurgis sees himself as "the victim of ravenous vultures that had torn into his vitals and devoured him; of fiends that had racked and tortured him.... the enemies that had been lurking for them, crouching upon their trail and thirsting for their blood.... the company that had marked them for its prey and was waiting its chance" (171). Here, then, the company has achieved animality, albeit within a self-righteous condemnation of corruption and malice as well. But Jurgis must submit, for if he "so much as raised a hand against them, back he would go into that wild-beast pen from which he had just escaped!" (171). Jurgis repeats the process, though, of attacking first a bartender, then his wife's abuser once again, and winding up in jail on two subsequent occasions.

If Jurgis and the workers he represents are thus aligned too closely with animality, it is less surprising to consider both the success of the novel and the best-known legislative result: the passage of the Pure Food and Drugs Act, along with the Meat Inspection Act of 1906. No mention is made in these acts of animal welfare or "humane" slaughter (or humane treatment of workers, for that matter). More than fifty years will pass before the landmark Humane Slaughter Act of 1958 will make it through Congress. Sinclair's famous comment, taken from an article also published in 1906 in *Cosmopolitan* titled "What Life Means to Me," is, "I aimed at the public's heart, and by accident I hit it in the stomach."[47] But the result seems less of an accident when we consider the desire of middle- and upper-class readers to distance themselves from the depraved animals who handle their food. According to Sinclair, "Down in the bottom of the social pit were millions of human beings, rotting in squalor and vice, and spreading a slow contagion that was infecting the whole of civilization. But these wretches were ignorant; they did not know what was the matter with them. They were also voiceless, and could not have told even had they known."[48] Certainly Sinclair relates in great detail the diseased and decaying meat, along with rats and rat poison, among other things, that find their way into the food supply, past inept or corrupt meat inspectors. But, as June Howard argues, "The revolting truth about meat revealed an avenue by which the unclean horrors of a world outside the campfire found their way into that well-lighted, respectable circle and exposed a potentially contaminating contact between the disorder of the slaughterhouse district and the haven of the middle-class home."[49] I would only add that the border between these two worlds is not so much threatened as itself constructed.

Even socialist arguments in the Progressive Era, though, deploy the logic of survival of the fittest, as Sinclair indicates: "Those who lost in the struggle were generally exterminated; but now and then they had been known to save themselves by combination—which was a new and higher kind of strength. It was so that the gregarious animals had overcome the predaceous; it was so, in human history, that the people had mastered the kings. The workers were simply the citizens of industry, and the Socialist movement was the expression of their will to survive."[50] What is significant here, in my view, is the fact that the solution reinforces the problem: it "naturalizes" a Darwinist-Freudian construction of "animality" even as it attempts to keep it under control through collective action. Eventually, this discourse of the jungle is not limited to the lower strata of society; instead, it becomes a hegemonic discourse capable of explaining the behavior of all social classes and every attempt at social reform. The Beef Trust, for example, is a "gigantic combination of capital, which had crushed all opposition, and overthrown the laws of the land, and was preying upon the people" (299). Rich capitalists in general, according to a socialist speaker late in the novel, have the "whole of society...in their grip....like fierce wolves they rend and destroy, like ravening vultures they devour and tear!" (290). Little Stanislovas is literally eaten by rats, and Jurgis's son Antanas drowns in the streets of Packingtown that are described as "sewers of inky blackness," as "huge canyons formed by towering black buildings" (168). Even the socialist speaker modeled after Eugene Debs is figured as an animal: "When he spoke he paced the stage, lithe and eager, like a panther. He leaned over, reaching out for his audience; he pointed into their souls with an insistent finger" (310).[51]

In the serialized version of *The Jungle*, the story ends with Jurgis being sent off to prison. Having skipped bail after his last fight, Jurgis is spotted once again at the socialist rally counting ballot returns. The postscript, then, is that "at one o'clock of the afternoon of the same day Jurgis was handcuffed to a detective, and on his way to serve a two years' sentence in state's prison for assault with intent to kill."[52] Jolted back to the criminality of Jurgis, the reader of the *Appeal to Reason* version is left with even further indication that Jurgis—as an animalized representative of the working class—certainly does not belong to the world of the privileged, intellectual elites and comfortable, ballot-box socialists who dominate the end of the novel. More important, though, the return of Jurgis to prison represents a way of containing his animality, his physical body that remains a threat to well-intentioned reformers. Such an ending might serve to indict the capitalist and corrupt system that refuses to make room for figures like Jurgis, but it also represents a rather crude way of maintaining "law and order" for those of the status quo. Like the red threat in *The Octopus*, violence is thus rejected as the method of choice for bringing about social change. But the decision to drop this postscript from the novel in book form does not indicate a resistance to the animalization of the working class. The novel ends instead with the proclamation that "We shall bear down the opposition, we shall sweep it before us—and Chicago will be ours! *Chicago will be ours!* CHICAGO WILL BE OURS!"[53] An argument can certainly be made that the audience here is just as privileged as the narrator. As June Howard argues, "There is no pretense in *The Jungle* that the group Sinclair is writing *about* is the same or even has much in common with the group he is writing *for*."[54] Michael Brewster Folsom also notes the great gulf "between Sinclair, the expensively educated professional writer, and the humble working stiffs who peopled his brilliant early chapters."[55] The class boundary that Sinclair's text helps to construct, in other words, is in part one between middle-class socialists and the working-class beasts they propose to help through the ballot box.

But the logic would not be very different if the novel instead pointed toward violent revolution, toward the conclusion of, say, the Communist Manifesto: "Let the ruling classes tremble at a Communistic revolution. The proletarians have nothing to lose but their chains. They have a world to win. WORKING MEN OF ALL COUNTRIES UNITE!"[56] Even a Marxist revolutionary logic can be constructed around a naturalization of animality at the turn of the century. The rhetoric of revolution itself, in other words, can construct the fundamental order of society as one in which animalized classes are locked in a death struggle. As Shelton Stromquist and Marvin Bergman argue in their introduction to *Unionizing the Jungles: Labor and Community in the Twentieth-Century Meatpacking Industry* (1997), "Since Upton Sinclair's powerful novel first appeared in 1906, 'the Jungle' has been a compelling metaphor for life and work in the nation's meatpacking industry,"[57] and the metaphor can be extended to describe all behavior in the marketplace, as this chapter has shown.[58] The problem, at least discursively, is that naturalizing "animal instincts" also embeds the perfect excuse for ignoring the hog-squeal of either hogs or workers, since pain and suffering, if not death, are nothing if not "natural" in "the jungle."

PART THREE

The Evolution of Race

5

Archaeology of a Humane Society

ANIMALITY, SAVAGERY, BLACKNESS

IN HIS CONCLUSION to *The Descent of Man, and Selection in Relation to Sex* (1871), Charles Darwin addresses the idea of descending from "savages." Darwin first acknowledges that his "main conclusion"—"that man is descended from some lowly organized form"—might be "highly distasteful to many."[1] But he argues that all humans, including "savages," as well as nonhuman animals, have descended from a common "lowly origin" that predates the evolution of humanity (644). According to Darwin, the "rank of manhood" was "attained" before humans "diverged into distinct races, or as they may be more fitly called, subspecies" (633). But he also suggests that contemporary "barbarians" are similar to the primitive ancestors common to all human beings. He proclaims that "there can hardly be a doubt that we are descended from barbarians" (644), and then recalls his "reflection," upon "first seeing a party of Feugians on a wild and broken shore," that "such were our ancestors" (644). In a move apparently designed to appease the racist sensibilities of his audience, though, Darwin suggests that it might be easier to imagine being a descendant of an animal than a "savage": "For my own part, I would as soon be descended from that heroic little monkey...or from that old baboon...as from a savage who delights to torture his enemies, offers up bloody sacrifices, practices infanticide without remorse, treats his wives like slaves, knows no decency, and is haunted by the grossest superstitions" (644). Regardless of the "main conclusion" of *The Descent of Man*, this passage suggests a racist conflation of contemporary "savages" with "barbarian" ancestors that would have been common to all human beings.[2]

This kind of move is echoed in the first paragraph of Sigmund Freud's *Totem and Taboo* (1913): "Prehistoric man...in a certain sense...is still our contemporary. There are men still living who, as we believe, stand very near to primitive man, far nearer than we do, and whom we therefore regard as his direct heirs and representatives. Such is our view of those whom we describe as savages or half-savages; and their mental life must have a peculiar interest for us if we are right in seeing in it a well-preserved picture of an early stage of our own development."[3] Between Darwin and Freud, though, after the end of the "peculiar institution" of slavery in the United States, dominant discourses attempted to sidestep this evolutionary narrative, suggesting instead that white men could indeed be linked more closely with "the animal" than "the savage," in terms of both "animal instincts" and common animal ancestors. A related—but less explored—move to distinguish between "civilized" white men and "savage" black men was to focus specifically on the treatment of "real" animals. Rather than delighting in torture, the civilized man could supposedly be identified by the capacity for treating not just humans but also animals "humanely." This new discourse can be seen, for example, in a letter by William James to the *Nation* on June 29, 1876: "Among the many good qualities of our 'Anglo-Saxon' race, its sympathy with the feelings of brute animals deserves an honorable mention."[4] The discourse of humane reform was born at the same moment that constructions of black men were also shifting, and, more specifically, an explosion of lynchings was being justified by the myth of the black male rapist, which linked an assault on white womanhood with a savage delight in torture. Humane reform actually became a new and flexible discourse for claiming superiority over various human "races," reinforcing the logic that only the more "civilized" group had evolved enough to treat other groups "humanely."

My purpose in this chapter is to explore this complex and even mutually constitutive relationship between humane reform and U.S. race relations at the end of the nineteenth century, indicating a third major aspect of the discourse of the jungle.[5] At the same time that black men were hoping to distance themselves from racist constructions of their animality, privileged white men became more interested in getting in touch with their own "animal instincts" and promoting the humane treatment of "real" animals.[6] The myth of the black male rapist is often assumed to be based upon the black man's "animal instinct" for sex, but I will illustrate how the rape of a white woman by a black man was often constructed as more savage than animal in nature. Savagery became a label not only for the behavior of black rapists, though, but also for the behavior of other groups, in cases such as northerners condemning southern lynch mobs, or men like William James condescending to white men of the lower classes, or even African Americans condemning white lynchers. The discourse of humane reform defined itself against savagery of various kinds, resulting in a "humane society" broadly conceived that was capable of associating whiteness more with animality than savagery and elevating the animal in new and problematic ways.[7]

Birth of a Humane Society

The imperative to treat human beings or animals more "humanely" is actually a relatively recent historical development in the United States. While the word "humane" is older, the logic of humane reform shifted significantly and became more pervasive at the end of the nineteenth century. Previously, the overarching logic tended to be one of Christian duty toward (certain) helpless creatures rather than humane behavior as a way to define the human—as opposed to the animal—in evolutionary terms. The U.S. animal welfare movement grew out of anticruelty statutes that were first enacted in England toward the beginning of the nineteenth century. In 1822, for example, "An Act to Prevent the Cruel and Improper Treatment of Cattle" was introduced by Colonel Richard Martin, an Irish Protestant from Galway, who was nicknamed "Humanity Dick." Once the bill passed Parliament, it became known as "Martin's Act" and led to the founding of the Society for the Prevention of Cruelty to Animals in 1824, with police powers to enforce the law.[8] With Queen Victoria and the Duchess of Kent as lady patronesses, the Society became "Royal" in 1840, and it grew as a club for white noblemen and gentlemen concerned mostly with domestic animals rather than such species as the fox, which many of them continued to hunt.[9]

The American Society for the Prevention of Cruelty to Animals (ASPCA) was founded in 1866, with an emphasis on attention to domestic animals within a Christian framework. According to Henry Bergh, the founder and first president of the ASPCA, for example, "it is a solemn recognition of that greatest attribute of the Almighty Ruler of the Universe, mercy, which if suspended in our own case but for a single instant, would overwhelm and destroy us."[10] In the United States, various SPCAs were established on a state-by-state basis, along with a range of state laws enacted to protect against cruelty to domestic animals. The ASPCA was in effect the SPCA of New York rather than an umbrella or national organization. The Massachusetts SPCA soon became one of the most prominent early SPCAs, founded by George T. Angell of Boston in 1868. In Angell's view, writing in 1864, the purpose of giving money to "Sabbath schools or other schools" should be "to impress upon the minds of youth their duty towards those domestic animals which God may make dependent upon them."[11] John G. Shortall, as president of the Illinois SPCA, branched off in 1877 to form the American Humane Association (AHA), with early attention focused on the transport and slaughter of cattle, but various state organizations directed toward the "humane" treatment of both children and animals were not necessarily affiliated with the AHA.[12] According to Sydney Coleman's 1924 history of the organization, the AHA convention of 1886 included a mission statement that sought "to remedy universal cruelties by universal remedies, to foster a national recognition of the duties we owe to those who are helpless,"[13] and the advocacy of the AHA was directed toward "Millions of suffering brutes which cannot speak for themselves."[14] The initiatives were often explicitly Christian, including the creation of what was called "Humane Sunday," in which "thousands of pulpits proclaim the duty of humanity."[15] Other organizations founded in the 1880s included the American Antivivisection Society in 1883, and the first Audubon Society in 1886. I turn to William James's thoughts about vivisection in particular—as they relate to lynching—toward the end of this chapter.

The first usage of "humanitarian" also indicates Christian roots. In 1819, a "humanitarian" was "One who affirms the humanity (but denies the divinity) of Christ."[16] It could also signify, by 1831, "One who professes the 'Religion of Humanity,' holding that mankind's duty is chiefly or wholly comprised in the advancement of the welfare of the human race."[17] But the connotations outside of theological discourse were usually negative, such as, by 1844, "One who advocates or practises humanity or humane action; one who devotes himself to the welfare of mankind at large; a philanthropist. Nearly always *contemptuous*, connoting one who goes to excess in his humane principles."[18] According to Webster's dictionary, in 1878, a humanitarian was "One who holds that Christ was merely a man."[19] By 1911 Webster's definition had shifted to include "a philanthropist; an anti-Trinitarian; one who believes that the duty of man consists of acting rightly to others; a perfectionist."[20] The *OED* does not register the later shift toward more positive connotations of this term, but it does indicate that by 1904 the word "humane" could be "Applied to certain weapons or implements which inflict less pain than others of their kind, *spec.* applied to an implement for the painless slaughtering of cattle."[21]

While many humane organizations in the United States were established in the 1860s, it was not until the turn of the century that what might be loosely called the "humane movement" flourished, as well as shifted away from an explicitly Christian logic. In the first three years after the founding of the ASPCA in 1866, for example, only a half dozen or so state SPCAs were incorporated. But by December 1907, there were 246 societies nationwide, including some organizations advocating for children as well, while the American

Humane Association claimed that 543 associations had been formed.[22] At the turn of the century, intensive pressure was mounted, for example, on behalf of enforcing the twenty-eight-hour law that required transported livestock to be given food, water, and rest every twenty-eight hours, a law that had been only sporadically enforced since it took effect in 1873. In addition, anticruelty statutes finally made it on the books in every state of the union by 1907.[23] Organizations under a variety of auspices that responded to a Columbia University study by Roswell C. McCrea furnished enough data to suggest that by 1909, with 348 societies reporting, memberships totaled 64,879, and combined budgets exceeded $1 million.[24] Much of the roughly $350,000 in contributions was the result of membership dues, while close to $200,000 came from endowments, together suggesting the class (and presumably race) of most members. Subsidies from state and local governments amounted to close to $250,000, and the amount collected from fines was just over $50,000, the result of more than 28,000 convictions (15). According to McCrea, the majority of the SPCAs acted as "private corporations, exercising delegated police powers," with members granted "powers as peace officers" and "special powers of arrest" (16, 21). Most of this work was directed toward abuses of workhorses in urban areas, cruelty and neglect toward domestic pets, and practices of fighting or baiting animals such as cocks and dogs. Exceptions included the "carnivorous appetite, the extension of science, the providing of exercise for an idle class," so that meat eating, vivisection, and sport hunting, at least for many of the SPCAs, were seen as "weighty enough to justify exceptions in the law of the land" (35). But McCrea noted a general shift in public sentiment by 1910: "conditions have undergone marked change since the earlier days of anti-cruelty work. The grosser forms of cruelty are now exceptional. When they do occur, perpetrators speedily encounter a hostile public attitude" (59).

While a sense of Christian duty persists, what is significant to note is the emergence of the discourse of the jungle at the turn of the century. Once evolutionary thinking challenges the boundaries between the human and the animal, humane behavior apparently becomes a new way to define what it means to be human: to restrain one's animal instincts. In a bulletin put out by the State Normal School of San Diego in 1906, the issue of "rights" is qualified by the "law of nature": "The only right anything possesses is the right to be useful. All living beings must subserve some beneficial purpose or finally be eliminated in the process of evolution. In the long run, the weak, the useless, and the harmful must perish. This is the inevitable law of nature."[25] Humans may be at the top of the food chain, as well as God's creation, but there is need for restraint. "To whose benefit is the world of nature finally to contribute? There can be but one answer. Man, standing at the head of the hierarchy of animal species, rightfully claims sovereignty over this great kingdom.... The rule of nature is that the lower generally serve the ends of the higher."[26] But distinctions can be difficult, since "a study of biology shows such infinitesimal gaps between species, and even between the higher anthropoids and man, [so] that no one dares positively to declare where the one ends and the other begins."[27] Darwinist constructions of the human led to what Marlon Ross has identified as "a hierarchy of races relatively fixed in their relation to each other, but each moving forward at its own pace toward greater civilization, although 'primitive races' were sometimes seen as static, forever left behind in this quick race toward perfected culture."[28] This "race of races" could be used within a certain racist logic to justify the exploitation and oppression of African Americans by a white race that was supposedly more "fit." But a deeper concern, for some, was the implication that black and white Americans were only infinitesimally different, either in terms of both descending from common animal ancestors, or that "civilized" men were actually looking at earlier, more primitive versions of themselves when they looked at black men.

The relationship between cruelty and the discourse of the jungle could lead to constructions of a new kind of hierarchy: *some* human beings have supposedly evolved enough to be "humane" not only toward animals but also toward other human beings. The door was thus opened for claiming humane behavior as a marker of difference *among* human beings: a marker that soon became crucial in terms of U.S. race relations. A "civilized" society, supposedly, would not delight in the *in*humane treatment of either human or non-human animals. The logic of humane reform could then be extended to a broader societal level, including questions such as how a "civilized" society should treat its criminals, as well as other populations. But it is clear that the evolution of a humane society in the United States does not necessarily result in better treatment of black men in particular. Instead, it could be used to justify apparent reforms directed toward black prisoners, for example, that frequently ended up treating them worse than before. It is also clear that the "correctional" system of the South—and increasing numbers of black men thus controlled—became a way to police black freedmen and compensate for the loss of slave labor after the Civil War.[29]

Two examples of humane penal reform in the South illustrate how this logic could perpetuate rather than eliminate racist differences in how criminals were treated. First, the opening of state-controlled plantations to function as penitentiaries in Mississippi and Louisiana was justified, according to Mississippi governor James K. Vardaman, "as both a *humane* and sensible response to Negro crime."[30] As David Oshinsky notes in *"Worse Than Slavery": Parchman Farm and the Ordeal of Jim Crow Justice* (1996), Mississippi's twenty-thousand-acre Parchman Farm, which opened as a state penitentiary in 1904, would have been virtually indistinguishable from a slave plantation.[31] In the first year of its existence it produced a profit of $185,000 from the sale of cotton, other crops, and livestock (109). Mississippi was not alone either in its construction of a state plantation— Angola in Louisiana functioned similarly—or in its continued use of corporal punishment among convicts. According to Oshinsky, most states outside the South had abolished corporal punishment by 1900, but Arkansas, Texas, Florida, and Louisiana routinely whipped convicts "without serious public opposition. It was part of the regional culture, and most prisoners were black" (149). Mississippi was one of the last states to abolish public executions, and the line between mob lynchings and legal executions was often exceedingly narrow well into the 1930s (209–17). While public executions eventually disappeared, plantations such as Parchman and Angola continue to function as working farms up to this day. The point I want to stress here is that working on a plantation-penitentiary was touted as a "humane" alternative to incarceration at the turn of the century: better for the health of the convict, supposedly, than rotting away in jail.

The second example of "humane" penal reform that perpetuates racist cruelties follows similar logic, arguing that convict labor on state-controlled chain gangs provided better alternatives for prisoners. In *Twice the Work of Free Labor: The Political Economy of Convict Labor in the New South* (1996), Alex Lichtenstein reveals how building roads was touted by some as "humanitarian and rehabilitatory" because of the nature of the outdoor work—the virtues of "the strenuous life" valorized by "progressives" like Teddy Roosevelt.[32] Under the previous system of leasing convicts to private companies, daily whippings served as punishment for convicts who failed to complete their assigned "task" for the day. The tasks, which were often deliberately impossible to complete, contributed directly to the profits of private individuals involved in such industries as the extraction of coal or turpentine, or the construction of railroads or bricks (126–51). Complaints about abuses of privately leased convicts with no state oversight resulted in protests at the turn of the century, such as one writer in August 1908 who objected to "punishments, abuses, and suffering...inflicted upon the convicts which were unjustified, unmerciful, cruel and *inhuman*."[33] Yet the protests were directed mostly toward the few white inmates, and the shift from the convict lease system to the state-controlled chain gang simply changed who was doing the whipping of the largely black convict populations. In addition, "Even after the transition from the convict lease to the chain gang, investigators and convicts complained about poor food and sanitation, relentless labor, and brutal punishment in the state's isolated road camps" (182). The actual treatment of convicts hardly became more "humane" in the South, in other words, after the shift to state-controlled convict labor on the chain gang at the turn of the century. But the discourse of humane reform could be used in a variety of ways. Southerners might continue to defend chain gangs as more humane than other forms of incarceration, for example, while northerners could condemn chain gangs as inherently inhumane, thus using humane discourse to claim superiority over southerners in relation to the treatment of prisoners generally and black men more specifically.

Excusing the Animal

The birth of a humane society in the United States also raised questions about whether all human beings were similarly driven by "animal instincts" and how those instincts might relate to culpability for various crimes. Concurrent with the rise of the humane movement at the turn of the century was the rise of "heat of passion" defenses in juridical discourses that essentially excused—or at least mitigated—crimes understood as the acting out of one's animal instincts. The racial implications of these new discourses are complex, and there are distinctions to be made between state-sanctioned punishments and extralegal lynchings of black men in particular at the end of the nineteenth century. But it also becomes clear that a black man's animality is not often seen as a mitigating factor for the alleged crime of raping a white woman. From this perspective, we can begin to see how the question of instincts could be used to distinguish between white and black men: a question that could be related to the formulation of "the savage" in Freud, in which "primitive men," who are not quite animals, can supposedly be distinguished from civilized (white) men by the lack of the ability to discipline themselves.

Foucault's *Discipline and Punish: The Birth of the Prison* (1977) is useful for tracing a relevant history of European penal reform that increases attention to the motivations or mental state of the criminal, leading to more self-policing than corporal punishment, in the context of what appears to be more humane methods of incarceration. But it does not pay enough attention to the shifting discourses I have traced thus far in the United States, particularly at the end of the nineteenth century, or to differences between white and black criminals. According to Foucault, for white men in France at least, "At the beginning of the nineteenth century...the great spectacle of physical punishment disappeared; the tortured body was avoided; the theatrical representation of pain was excluded from punishment."[34] Rather than a simple shift toward "less cruelty, less pain, more kindness, more respect, more 'humanity,'" though, there was a more significant shift in objective: "The expiation that once rained down upon the body must be replaced by a punishment that acts in depth on the heart, the thoughts, the will, the inclinations" (16). In this way, the power of the state is expanded to judge not just acts but also motivations: "Certainly the 'crimes' and 'offenses' on which judgment is passed are juridical objects defined by the code, but judgment is also passed on the passions, instincts, anomalies, infirmities, maladjustments, effects of environment or heredity" (17). These "shadows lurking behind the case" are "judged indirectly as 'attenuating circumstances'" (17). What Foucault breezes past, though, is the difference between "passions" or "instincts" at the beginning of the nineteenth century and the signification of these terms once the discourse of animality has shifted toward Darwinist-Freudian formulations at the beginning of the twentieth century.[35]

According to Freud in *Totem and Taboo* (1913), human beings can be distinguished from animals by their ability to repress—or police—their instincts, but "savages" seem to be stuck somewhere between animality and civilization. In Freud's fantasy about the origins of civilization, brothers band together in the primal horde and act upon the Oedipal impulses that define humanity; they kill the primal father, eat him, regret it, and subsequently establish a prohibition against killing the father by equating him with a totem animal who can only be killed and mourned ritually. Similarly, the incestuous desire for the mother is renounced and subsequently prohibited as the taboo against incest.[36] Freud's primal horde builds upon Darwin's thinking about ancestral animals, but Freud claims the Oedipal impulse (as it leads to totemism and the incest taboo) as the defining characteristic of the human. The implication from Freud, though, is that white civilization developed quickly once the totem and taboo prohibitions were internalized, while contemporary "savages" still have not internalized them, which supposedly explains why similar rituals can still be found among "primitive" people everywhere. Without the achievement of civilized repression, these "savages" supposedly need explicit and external prohibitions against incest, for example, since "these same incestuous wishes, which are later destined to become unconscious, are still regarded by savage peoples as immediate perils against which the most severe measures of defence must be enforced."[37]

In relation to a broader Freudian way of thinking, for white men in the United States at the turn of the twentieth century, the implication could be that white civilization passed through this evolutionary stage quickly, while "savages" are still stuck in the totem and taboo stage. In racist formulations, African Americans could be equated with Darwin's construction of that "savage who delights to torture his enemies,"[38] and an argument could be made that black men needed to be policed because they could not police themselves. There is a difference here, though, between a delight in torture and an animal instinct, since animals are assumed to be *amoral* in the acting out of violent instincts. There are several discursive frameworks for explaining the origins of violence or a crime, then, at the turn of the century: an animal instinct for survival; a savage drive to torture; a devilish impulse for wickedness. As E. P. Evans notes in *The Criminal Prosecution and Capital Punishment of Animals* (1906), "the new system of jurisprudence, based upon more enlightened conceptions of human responsibility, is still in an inchoate state and very far from having worked out a satisfactory solution of the intricate problem of the origin and nature of crime and its proper penalty."[39] But there is a new belief at the end of the nineteenth century that a human being's actions are not always his or her own responsibility, that acting "instinctually" or "in the heat of passion" could be seen as a reason to reduce the punishment for a crime.

In twenty-first-century legal practice, most U.S. states distinguish between first-degree murder and voluntary manslaughter by determining whether there was "malice aforethought," as opposed to "circumstances which would 'mitigate' the homicide."[40] The traditional rule would be "that a killing which would otherwise be murder is mitigated to manslaughter if the defendant acted in a 'heat of passion' caused by legally sufficient provocation. The provocation must be conduct of the victim sufficient to cause a reasonable person in the defendant's situation to lose his customary self-control, and it must actually provoke the defendant into killing before he has time to 'cool off.'"[41] This "reasonable person" standard has often been invoked in cases involving a husband killing the adulterous lover of his wife "in the heat of passion," or an individual whose "honor" is insulted in the midst of a barroom brawl.[42] The state of "temporary insanity" that such scenarios supposedly provoke can be confirmed by psychiatrists and other medical authorities, but the general logic is to focus more on the motivations and mental state, the *mens rea*, of the criminal than on the act itself.[43] At the end of the nineteenth century, this new juridical discourse suggested that violence stemming from one's animal instincts was more "natural," understandable, and excusable. But this logic was not necessarily applied when it came to explaining the motivation of black men supposedly intent upon raping white women, suggesting that this kind of violence might stem from a savage delight in torture rather than an animal instinct.

Lynching the Savage

As the logic of humane reform shifted, it is important to note that various oppositions were established, even if they were sometimes fleeting, overlapping, or even contradictory. The opposite of humane, for example, could actually be seen as savage, rather than inhumane, if the capacity for *either* humane or inhumane behavior is seen as a sign of difference from those savage groups that have not yet evolved this capacity. To describe certain groups as savage is not necessarily the same as calling them animals, or beasts, or brutes, although these terms sometimes seem interchangeable when it comes to the myth of the black male rapist. There are often attempts at distinguishing between the nature and origins of various violent crimes and the people who commit them, leading, for example, to the possibility of associating blackness more with a savage delight in torture than an animalized instinct for sexual reproduction.

As various scholars and activists have pointed out, the myth of the black male rapist existed prior to the end of the nineteenth century, but it exploded as a justification for lynching after Reconstruction. As Martha Hodes notes in *White Women, Black Men: Illicit Sex in the 19th-Century South* (1997), both Ida B. Wells and Frederick Douglass observed how infrequent the allegation of black male rape was before and during the Civil War. According to Hodes, "Although white people in North America had professed beliefs about the greater sexual ardor of black men ever since the colonial era, and although black men had been accused and convicted of raping white women within the racist legal system of the slave South, Wells and Douglass were nonetheless correct that those ideas and inequities did not include relentless, deadly violence toward black men before the late nineteenth century."[44] The rape allegation was overblown in two ways: "Not only was there no postwar wave of such sexual assaults, but rape was not in fact the cause white Southerners recorded most frequently when justifying specific lynchings."[45] Nonetheless, "white apologists relentlessly named the rape of white women as the reason for murdering black men, and fully intended the lynching of black men to sustain an atmosphere of terrorism that was in turn intended to maintain the racial hierarchy that emancipation and Reconstruction had begun to destroy."[46]

According to Sandra Gunning in *Race, Rape, and Lynching: The Red Record of American Literature, 1890–1912* (1996), "while the figure of blackness as the epitome of animalism and sexual energy has always been an overriding preoccupation for white Americans, the dangerously pervasive stereotype of the black rapist—the black as beast—fully emerged in the post–Civil War era."[47] There is more to explore here, though, in relation to these references to "animalism" and "the black as beast."

One of the difficulties might be that "beast" seems to imply both a devilish impulse and a "real" animal in the jungle. It might also suggest that there is little difference between animality and savagery in the construction of black masculinity, and critics tend to see these two discourses as interchangeable. Marlon Ross, for example, cites Winthrop Jordan's classic *White over Black* (1968) in order to argue that "the discourse connecting the African to a regressive *animality* was in place long before the rise of Jim Crow. Just as upper-class Anglo-Saxon women were seen as needing protection by their fathers, husbands, brothers, and sons due to the natural frailty of their flesh, so African American men were conceptualized as needing to be guarded and pre-empted from the masculine privileges of social, political, and economic rule due to the natural *savagery* of their desires."[48] But at times the myth of the black male rapist in particular can be seen as de-emphasizing animality in favor of savagery, classifying the alleged criminal as a torturer rather than an animal whose amoral "heat of passion" could be somewhat excusable. Quincy Ewing's "The Heart of the Race Problem" in the March 1909 issue of the *Atlantic Monthly* illustrates how black people can be aligned more with savagery than animality: "But a little way removed from savagery, [Negroes] are incapable of adopting the white man's moral code, of assimilating the white man's moral sentiments, of striving toward the white man's moral ideals.... They are, in brief, an uncivilized, semi-savage people, living in a civilization to which they are unequal..."[49] The racist logic that follows is outlined by Ida B. Wells in 1895: "Negroes had to be killed to avenge their assaults upon woman. There could be framed no possible excuse more harmful to the Negro and more unanswerable if true in its sufficiency for the white man."[50]

The rape of a white woman by a black man is often constructed as a form of torture—far worse, for some, than any of the atrocities lynchers might commit. Charles H. Smith exemplifies this feeling in a piece for *Forum* in October 1893 titled "Have American Negroes Too Much Liberty?": "The lynching of such a monster... is nothing—nothing compared with what he has done.... there is no torture that could suffice."[51] George Winston, writing in the *Annals of the American Academy of Political Science* in July 1901, evokes white women shuddering in "nameless horror" at the thought that "The black brute is lurking in the dark": "a monstrous beast, crazed with lust."[52] In her infamous speech to the Georgia Agricultural Society on August 11, 1897, Rebecca Latimer Felton proclaims, "if it needs lynching to protect woman's dearest possession from the ravenous human beasts, then I say lynch a thousand times a week if necessary."[53] According to Felton, "The poor girl would choose any death in preference to such ignominy and outrage and a quick death is mercy to the rapist compared to the suffering of innocence and modesty…"[54] Alexander Manly's response to Felton in the *Wilmington Daily Record* on August 18, 1898, dares to suggest that intimacy and attraction between white women and black men are actually common. In Manly's analysis, "Every negro lynched is called 'a big, burly, black brute,' when in fact many of those who have thus been dealt with had white men for their fathers, and were not only not 'black' and 'burly' but were sufficiently attractive for white girls of culture and refinement to fall in love with them, as is well known to all."[55] Manly's response is perceived as so outrageous that it leads to the Wilmington race "riot" of 1898.[56] The references to "brute" and "beast" here illustrate how the discourses of animality, savagery, and even Christianity can overlap, even if these examples also seem to suggest that the greatest threat to white womanhood is a black man reminiscent of Darwin's "savage who delights to torture his enemies."

While white lynch mobs can also be denounced as savage, often in order for northerners to claim "humane" superiority over southerners, the lynchers are sometimes defended as acting out animal instincts "in the heat of passion," or as dispassionate dispensers of justice, much like in the realms of humane vivisection or humane penology, in which supposedly necessary violence is conducted as humanely as possible. According to John Carlisle Kilgo, writing in the *South Atlantic Quarterly* in 1902, "Lynchings are the acts of a temporary social insanity"; southern society is "liable to be outraged suddenly to an uncontrollable point, and thus crazed in its social emotions takes speedy revenge upon the violator of its laws and standards."[57] The response of the lynchers can be seen as an instinct that is difficult to control. Georgia governor Hugh Dorsey, for example, writing to the Colored Welfare League of Augusta in May 1918, explains that "personal outrages and violence, especially against helpless women and children, will not be tolerated by any civilized community, but will provoke prompt retaliation of community vengeance which is difficult, if not impossible, to control…"[58] From his perspective, "the surest way to discourage lynching is to convince the lawless element that such provocative outrages will not be tolerated…"[59] Alternatively, echoes of humane discourse can be heard in the words of lynching apologists claiming that the violence can be done in a calm and detached way. An anonymous letter to the *New York Times* in 1897, for example, signed by "Georgia," argues that "the negro...seems particularly given to this odious crime [of rape].... When it is committed the utmost care is taken to identify the criminal and only when his identity is beyond question is the execution ordered. It is done in a quiet, decided way as a general thing, although in cases of great atrocity sometimes the criminal is shot as well as hanged."[60]

In *A Red Record: Tabulated Statistics and Alleged Causes of Lynchings in the United States, 1892—1893—1894*, Ida B. Wells notes the vast number of lynchings that contradict this description.[61] As Gail Bederman confirms in *Manliness and Civilization: A Cultural History of Gender and Race in the United States, 1880–1917* (1995), lynchings themselves often were not solely about an impatience with the process of justice, which might be solved by a quick and perfunctory execution. Instead, "As lynchings grew in frequency, they also grew in brutality, commonly including burnings alive, castrations, dismemberments, and other deliberate and odious tortures."[62] Wells might be frustrated with the fact that, at times, these "scenes of unusual brutality failed to have any visible effect upon the *humane* sentiments of the people of our land,"[63] but my point is that the logic of humane reform becomes a new and flexible discourse for claiming superiority over those groups one wants to condemn as "savage," even if those people are white. Bederman points out that there was little northern pressure to stop southern lynchings at the turn of the century, despite the movement for other "progressive" reforms.[64] She identifies a shift in the tone of the northern media, but not necessarily any sense that lynching could be stopped: "After 1894, most Northern periodicals stopped treating lynching as a colorful Southern folk-way. They dropped their jocular tones and piously condemned lynching as 'barbarous.' It became a truism that lynching hurt America in the eyes of the 'civilized world.' Nonetheless, journalists still implied one could do little to stop it" (70).[65]

According to Bederman, white antilynching advocates such as William James believed that white lynch mobs were linked with black rapists by common "savage" instincts, such that a lynching became an opportunity "to unleash the savage within them" (73). Bederman cites a letter from James to the *Springfield Daily Republican*, on July 23, 1903, titled "A Strong Note of Warning Regarding the Lynching Epidemic" (subsequently reprinted in the *New York Daily Tribune*). Significantly, James writes about the "carnivore within us," but Bederman can only conclude that, "As James saw it, civilization was far weaker than the primal violence of the natural man" (73).[66] From Bederman's perspective, "The natural man was violent and impulsive. He dominated others through physical force. He lacked any self-control or self-restraint. Above all else, he was untouched by civilization. He was the opposite of civilized—he was natural" (73). But Bederman's analysis misses some of the complexities of how "the natural man" could be constructed. Rather than assuming "savagery" is the common denominator for all human beings, whether white or black, a white man could sometimes equate the "natural" with animality, often in an attempt to distinguish white from black violence, or to associate whiteness more with animality than with Darwinist-Freudian savagery.

According to James, the "epidemic" of lynching was spreading all over the country—not just the South—because it unleashed the carnivore within the human being. The instinct for violence is particularly close to the surface, in James's view, for the "young white American of the lower classes."[67] For those more "civilized," the "blood thirstiness" of the "usual man" seems to be "an exceptional passion, only to be read about in newspapers and romances" (171). There are other contributing factors as well, since "Negro lynching.... appeals to the punitive instinct, to race antipathy and to the white man's pride, as well as to the homicidal frenzy. One shudders to think what roots a custom may strike when *a fierce animal appetite like this* and a perverted ideal emotion combine together to defend it" (172, my emphasis). The "average man," then, who is "predisposed to the peculiar sort of contagion" common to mob violence, is led by "one or two real fanatics" who are "actuated by a maniacal sense of punitive justice" (172). But this emphasis on punishment, rather than a delight in torturing black victims, distinguishes what might otherwise be seen as intentional cruelty. The logic, even in James's discussion, seems to be that lynchings can be about animalized violence, or a necessary policing of black men who cannot police themselves, rather than the lynching itself as an act of savage torture, despite the tremendous amount of evidence to the contrary.

(In)Humane Whiteness

James's thinking about lynching can be related to his thinking about vivisection, and thus serve as an example of how humane discourse could produce a construction of the white race as the only one capable of avoiding, or limiting, the inhumane treatment of either animals or black "savages." Like the dispassionate lyncher, the vivisecting scientist can defend himself by the need, supposedly, to fulfill the white man's "painful duty" under certain circumstances. In a letter to the Vivisection Reform Society, reprinted in the *New York Evening Post* on May 22, 1909, James declines the offer of a vice presidency with the organization but agrees to articulate his views on the issue. He acknowledges the merits of the principle against animal cruelty but seems to invoke a residual Christian framework for thinking about humane behavior. He argues that the "rights of the helpless, even though they be brutes, must be protected by those who have superior power" (191). The risk of unnecessary cruelties comes from "the unspeakable possibilities of callousness, wantonness, and meanness of human nature" (191), and therefore "the public demand for regulation rests on a perfectly sound ethical principle, the denial of which by the scientists speaks ill for either their moral sense or their political ability" (192). But he is generally in favor of scientists regulating themselves as a body (or policing themselves), rather than the legislative prohibition of certain acts. James notes the success of the antivivisection movement in bringing about a general shift in public opinion, even if similar success cannot be claimed for the antilynching "agitation" at this same moment:

> That less wrong is done now than formerly is, I hope, true.... The waste of animal life is very likely lessened, the thought for animal pain less shamefaced in the laboratories than it was. These benefits we certainly owe to the anti-vivisection agitation, which, in the absence of producing actual state-regulation, has gradually induced some sense of public accountability in physiologists, and made them regulate their several individual selves. (191)

As early as 1875, in a letter to the *Nation* on February 25, James sympathizes with the "humane motives" of Henry Bergh, founding president of the ASPCA, even though, significantly, he sees vivisection as a "painful duty" (11). James advocates for the restraint of power, avoiding abuse, arguing that "Our power over animals should not be used simply at our own convenience, but voluntarily limited and sparingly put forth" in order to avoid "blood shed for trifling ends" (12). But in his subsequent letter on June 29, he certainly does not want "this virtue" (which is "Among the many good qualities of our 'Anglo-Saxon' race") to "run to a maudlin excess" (18). Indeed, his race pride does not allow him to condemn vivisection performed "in the course of researches begun with no immediately utilitarian aim" (19). Scientists, as the first letter notes, should not be limited by any outside legislation, since "It is better for many quadrupeds to perish unjustly than for a whole scientific body to be degraded" (13). The key implication seems to be that scientists should be able to perform the "painful duty" of vivisection when they are involved in the dispassionate pursuit of scientific knowledge.[68] James advises the SPCA to lobby for public opinion rather than for new legislation, arguing that "Under this hostile pressure, this constant sense of being challenged—which is very different from the sense of being controlled—the vivisector will feel more responsible, more solemn, less wasteful and indifferent" (13). The deaths of the animals will be more humane, in other words, but not prohibited.

In his analysis of lynching deaths at the turn of the century, James does not equate the dispassionate duty of the presumably white vivisector with the actions of the lower-class lynch mob, even if contemporaries of his might make that analogy. But James is still able to question the animality of the white lynch mob. By July 29, 1903, when he publishes "Epidemic of Lynching" in the *Boston Journal*, James argues that, in order to curb the extralegal outrage of lynching that is spreading throughout the country, the single most important thing to do is to have the newspapers stop printing accounts of the violence. In his construction of mob violence, James once again suggests that the primary motive is an impatience with the process of the legal justice system. He even considers mob violence in comparison with "heat of passion" defenses, implying that both embody animal instincts, before ultimately concluding that the animality of the mob cannot be similarly defended: "we by tradition, exempt from punishment the man who shoots the wrecker of his home and happiness in the moment of extreme provocation; but exemption stops before we reach the mob that is actuated solely by an impatient demand for justice—or by the mere thirst for curiosity" (175). James is thus unwilling to excuse lynching on the basis of animal instinct, but the framework for considering white violence in relation to animality remains in place.

Near the end of James Weldon Johnson's *The Autobiography of an Ex-Coloured Man* (1912), the narrator describes a horrific southern lynching in which a black man is burned alive. The narrator's resulting sense of shame is expressed not only for his country, "the only civilized, if not the only state on earth, where a human being would be burned alive," but also for his race: "Shame at being identified with a people that could with impunity be treated worse than animals. For certainly the law would restrain and punish the malicious burning alive of animals."[69] The narrator wonders why we do not "shudder with horror at the mere idea of such practices being realities in this day of enlightened and humanitarianized thought."[70] By the turn of the century in the United States, the "humanitarianized" or "humane" treatment of at least some animals was increasingly mandated by law, while the torture of black men continued to run rampant. Black bodies were often literally vivisected in the context of lynchings, without being justified in the name of science.[71]

As Darwinist-Freudian constructions of animality and savagery threatened to level the racial playing field, the discourse of humane reform became a productive framework for distinguishing between blackness and whiteness, often in complex and even contradictory ways.

Humane advocacy in its foundational moment can be seen as a significant—but often overlooked—discourse in relation to contemporaneous constructions of racial difference. This history remains an important background for thinking about humane advocacy today, particularly for those scholars and activists interested in advocating for both human racial and nonhuman animal issues. It is also crucial history for those of us uncomfortable with the prospect of animality being elevated over blackness, in which concern for animals becomes more important than concern for various racial groups, for example. In our own moment of "humanitarianized" thought, advocating for animals is not simply equivalent to advocating for racial others, if animal advocacy itself continues to construct racial distinctions among human beings.

6

Black Savage, White Animal

TARZAN'S AMERICAN JUNGLE

THE CHARACTER OF Tarzan, first created by Edgar Rice Burroughs in 1912, is easily one of the most popular fictional figures in twentieth-century U.S. culture. According to Gail Bederman, the original serialized version in *All Story* magazine was quickly reprinted in "at least eight major metropolitan newspapers," and the novel published in 1914 sold 750,000 copies by 1934.[1] Tarzan was reincarnated in twenty-four additional books by Burroughs, roughly fifty film adaptations, "four major television series, a radio serial, and comic books" that continue to keep his popularity alive today.[2] Scholars such as Gail Bederman, John F. Kasson, Marianna Torgovnick, Eric Cheyfitz, and Edward Said have all offered various ways of accounting for the enduring popularity of Tarzan, often identifying the encounters with apes and "savages" in the African jungle as displaced representations of domestic and foreign race relations for the United States. These readings tend to conflate Tarzan's "others," though, suggesting that there is little difference between the apes and the savages (with both groups linked to African Americans back home), or that the primary distinction to make is between Tarzan and everyone else. We are often told that Tarzan evolves from ape to savage to the epitome of a racist, sexist, imperialist, American man, who is defined by the restraint of his animal/savage instincts, which are seen as essentially interchangeable. The implication, then, would appear to be that "the savage" (and therefore the African American) is "higher" in evolutionary terms than the animal, and that white Americans should be seen as closer to savages than animals.

My argument, though, building upon the previous chapter's exploration of the relationship between humane discourse and savagery, is that evolutionary logic is actually disrupted by the novel, suggesting instead that animality can first be distinguished from savagery and second elevated *above* savagery in a disavowal of the evolutionary link between (black) savagery and (white) humanity. Distinguishing between various forms of primate violence in the novel allows us to see a more complicated construction of U.S. race relations, and it also allows us to see the novel as more than just a straightforward allegory of white masculinity defined against all other kinds of darker "races." My analysis tracks not only racist and imperialist implications but also the possibilities stemming from reading the apes and other animals *as* animals, even if we can never distinguish between "real" animals and constructions of them. On the one hand, the novel constructs the black male rapist (and therefore African Americans in general) as more savage than animal, linked more with the cruelties of African torture than the survival-of-the-fittest logic of predator and prey. Tarzan, on the other hand, is more animal than savage (except perhaps as Rousseau's noble savage), but his supposedly inherent class and racial superiority distinguishes him from both other animals and animalized, white, working-class sailors. He is a prolific lyncher of both black men and animals in the novel, but his occasional "cruelty" is constructed as "natural," according to the law of the jungle, rather than "savage." The end result is a broader reinforcement of the discourse of the jungle, in which animality is defined by violent and heterosexual instincts. A construction of white masculinity as closer to animality than savagery, then, becomes a new way of claiming race and class difference among human beings, illustrating how the discourse of the jungle is more complex and inconsistent at the turn of the century than we might otherwise assume.

Apes and Savages

Readers of *Tarzan of the Apes* might open the novel expecting to see immediate peril at the hands of "savage" human beings in the African jungle. That is certainly the fear of Lord and Lady Greystoke, Tarzan's aristocratic English parents, once they are abandoned by mutineers on the west African coast. As darkness falls on their first night in the jungle, Lady Alice sees something "silhouetted dimly against the shadows beyond, a great figure standing upright upon the ridge."[3] Grasping her husband's arm, she asks, in a whisper, "What is it, a man?" (20). When Clayton suggests it might have been just a shadow, she replies, "No, John, if it was not a man it was some huge and grotesque mockery of man. Oh, I am afraid" (21). This question—What is it?—organizes much of the novel as readers encounter various inhabitants of the jungle, including Tarzan, and infer their analogues in domestic and imperialist contexts.⁴ It also suggests a corollary question: Which is to be more feared by whites: animals or black men? But the beginning of the novel does not provide any contact with nonwhite human beings, and Tarzan does not encounter any "savages" until he is at least eighteen years old. The shadowy figure that the Claytons glimpse, and that animates the first quarter of the novel, is an ape, not a man, although key scenes of violence reveal that this ape is a somewhat ambiguous figure.

Two attacks by apes against white women in particular evoke the myth of the black male rapist in the United States, but these attacks are actually better identified as the outbreak of "savage" rather than "animal" instincts. The first comes early when Lady Alice and John Clayton are surprised by a "man-brute," a "ferocious monster" that approaches them "through the jungle in a semi-erect position" (24). The beast is described with mixed animal references, characterized as "a great bull," with "shaggy brows," and "great canine fangs," but his motive seems to be much more than just sex or even food, since his "nasty, close-set eyes gleamed hatred" (25). Although Alice shoots the ape while "it" struggles with Clayton, the ape still manages to attack "the delicate woman, who went down beneath him to merciful unconsciousness," and Clayton desperately tries to "drag the ape from his wife's prostrate form" (25–26). The ape rolls over dead, though, having left "no marks upon her," and she does not regain consciousness for another two hours. "That night," we are told, "a little son was born," but "Lady Greystoke never recovered from the shock of the great ape's attack," and she dies a year later in her sleep (26–28).

The second attack even more clearly evokes the threat of black male rape, yet this time the ape's "cruel" attack is endured without the "mercy" of losing consciousness, suggesting an element of torture that remains significant in other scenes of the novel. The second example involves Jane Porter, the young white woman from Baltimore whose later abandonment on the west African coast replays the story of the Claytons, once Tarzan has grown up. Along with her father, Professor Porter, his homosocial friend Samuel T. Philander, her would-be suitor Cecil Clayton ("actually" Tarzan's cousin), and the mammy/minstrel caricature of Esmeralda, Jane is set ashore by mutineers greedy for her father's treasure chest and their ship in order to flee the authorities. Tarzan at this point has succeeded in killing off Kerchak, king of the apes that have adopted and raised him, but he has abdicated his throne in order to think about what it means to be human (all the while teaching himself to read and write in English) and to study the new white visitors to his jungle. In his absence, the belligerent ape known as Terkoz becomes king, but he is driven out of power by other apes fed up with his "cruel and capricious" personality, his "continued truculence," and his "brutish nature" (171). As a result, Terkoz sets off on his own, "foaming with rage and hatred.... nursing his spite and looking for some weak thing on which to vent his pent anger" (172). When he comes upon Jane and Esmeralda, this "horrible, man-like beast" seems to have only murder on his mind, but then he suddenly shifts into "another mood" and thinks that the "hairless white ape would be the first of his new household" (172), suggesting an ongoing and coerced sexual relationship. Esmeralda swoons, of course, but Jane is carried "away toward a fate a thousand times worse than death" (172).

From my perspective, this represents a critical point of reference for understanding the cruelty of the "savage" rapist as distinct from the cruelty of an animal; the "torture" is constructed as being forced to submit to miscegenation, in which the "savage" delights in the infliction of "rage and hatred," rather than a supposedly straightforward—and dispassionate—enactment of a biological instinct to either reproduce or kill off a rival. Neither of those instincts would seem to involve hatred or a delight in torture. But Terkoz's assault evokes "savage" cruelty and the torture of remaining conscious: "It is true that that awful face, pressing close to hers, and the stench of the foul breath beating upon her nostrils, paralyzed her with terror; but her brain was clear, and she comprehended all that transpired." As Terkoz whisks her away, we are told, "still she did not cry out or struggle" (172). Figure 6, which is an image by Neal Adams that was used as a cover for a 1976 edition of *Tarzan*, evokes this figure of savage cruelty.

Reading Terkoz as the embodiment of the African American male rapist myth seems justified, then, and critics tend to take it for granted. But Tarzan's subsequent battle with Terkoz to save Jane from further torture is too often seen as linking, rather than distinguishing, Tarzan and Terkoz in terms of a "savage" instinct. As they prepare for battle, Jane is most impressed with "the great proportions of the ape and the mighty muscles and the fierce fangs," but she sees Tarzan as an animal too when she wonders, "How could any animal vanquish such a mighty antagonist?" (175). The initial charge employs a variety of animal references: "Like two charging bulls they came together, and like two wolves sought each other's throat. Against the long canines of the ape was pitted the thin blade of the man's knife" (175). Despite the thinner phallic symbol, Tarzan prevails in this "primeval" battle, but we are given no details of the physical struggle, other than the fact that "the long knife drank deep a dozen times of Terkoz's heart's blood" (175). Terkoz is not tortured, in other words, but dispatched quickly, and Jane's "primeval" desire

Figure 6 *Tarzan* cover art. Reprinted with the permission of the artist, Neal Adams.

is met by Tarzan, who takes her in his arms, like "no red-blooded man needs lessons in doing," and smothers "her upturned, panting lips with kisses" (175–76). Jane discovers "the meaning of love," but her desire is quickly policed by "an outraged conscience" and she becomes "a mortified woman," despite Tarzan's continued attempts to "take her" once again (176). She turns on him "like a tigress," and he soon decides to do "just what his first ancestor would have done.... He took his woman in his arms and carried her into the jungle" (176).

The implication could thus be read, apparently, as an imminent rape by Tarzan that would align his "savage" instincts with Terkoz. Gail Bederman finds evidence here that "Tarzan remains a savage defined by his unleashed passions" and "only one course of action is possible."[5] Terkoz is "the most primal 'black beast' rapist of all" (228). But Tarzan also, "Like his first ancestor...has become the original savage rapist," and "the impulse to rape becomes as central to *Tarzan*'s construction of perfect primitive masculinity as the impulse to kill" (229). Eventually, his "inherited instinct for chivalry" prevents the rape, though, since "Burroughs couldn't allow Tarzan to actually rape Jane" (229), and by the end of the novel, he is "no longer the primal rapist" (231). My question, though, is whether he is ever actually equated with the "savage" or "primal rapist." In Bederman's view, the issue is crucial in the context of American constructions of white masculinity at this historical moment: "Turn-of-the-century men found something primal and holy in the evolutionary relationship between civilized white men and their ancient savage past, as represented by men of other races; and they used this 'primitive masculinity' to legitimate their continuing power over women" (239). This helps to explain the conflicted or contradictory nature of white men's reactions to the myth of the black male rapist; supposedly, their newly reenergized sense of masculinity as both savage and animal should link them with the instincts of the rapist, but they must then disavow that link by reverting to a Victorian construction of "manliness" that defines white men as more "civilized."

Bederman thus conflates the apes with the savages of this novel, arguing that the "apes signify the primal origins of the civilizing process, the original archetypal savages" (220). She repeatedly refers to Tarzan's "savage jungle childhood with the primitive apes" (221), which results in his "savage masculine superiority to more civilized men" (226), rather than the "primal unmanly savagery of both apes and Africans" (232). According to Bederman, "Tarzan must live the life of an animal, and then of a savage, in order to become a man who is both masculine and civilized" (223). Marianna Torgovnick echoes this thought in *Gone Primitive: Savage Intellects, Modern Lives* (1990), arguing that "Burroughs believed blacks to be a midway stage of evolution from apes to white humans," and that the scene with Terkoz suggests "certain rules: qualities like lust belong to animals and blacks, not to Euro-Americans..."[6] For John F. Kasson in *Houdini, Tarzan, and the Perfect Man: The White Male Body and the Challenge of Modernity in America* (2001), the link between Tarzan (or white masculinity in general) and both animals and savages is "wildness": "for Burroughs and his readers wildness enhanced white Anglo-Saxons but debased black Africans..."[7]

Wildness, supposedly, becomes the "basis of [Tarzan's] virility, power, and authority,"[8] but "The dark, hairy ape Terkoz provides an occasion for Tarzan to display the courage, strength, chivalry, and sexual self-restraint that supposedly distinguished the finest Anglo-Saxons from the darker races *and beasts.*"[9] From my perspective, though, "wildness" only provides a further way of conflating savagery and animality here, while the text itself suggests more productive distinctions.

The logic of humane discourse, as I have explored it in the previous chapter, organizes these distinctions according to supposedly innate tendencies. Human beings are seen as the only primates capable of acting either humanely or inhumanely; nonhuman primates driven by "natural" instincts have no capacity for ethical principles, only the ability to act *a*morally, according to the logic of the jungle. But within human beings, there is the capacity for both moral and immoral behavior, defined not necessarily by a Judeo-Christian ethic but by the need to distinguish between human and nonhuman animals. Among human beings, though, distinctions can be made between what Darwin identifies in *The Descent of Man* as "distinct races, or as they may be more fitly called, subspecies. Some of these, such as the Negro and European, are so distinct that, if specimens had been brought to a naturalist without any further information, they would undoubtedly have been considered by him as good and true species."[10] The African savage of Tarzan's jungle reinforces the claim that, among human primates, there are indeed radical biological differences. While white human beings have the ability to act either humanely or inhumanely, and black human beings would presumably have similar abilities, *Tarzan* suggests that the African man and his African American counterpart are naturally inclined toward savagery, toward the inhumane, and that a delight in torturing victims is somehow innate. *Tarzan* both reinforces and resists this formulation in its constructions of cruelty within black Africans, apes, and Tarzan himself.

Tarzan's experiences with black Africans are thus crucial. His first encounter with nonwhite human beings comes after he has lived his entire childhood and adolescence exclusively among apes. Because he has lived along the African coast, we are told, with no big river nearby, he has been ignorant of "savage natives of the interior," and his initial contact with "black warriors" breaks the "ancient security of his jungle."[11] These men are fleeing the cruelties of Belgian colonial forces under Leopold II, "who had so harassed them for rubber and ivory that they had turned upon their conquerors one day and massacred a white officer and a small detachment of his black troops" (72). After cannibalizing these troops, they are themselves cannibalized by reinforcements, and the decimated tribe flees into the "freedom" of the jungle, bringing with them destruction that evokes the paranoid fears of white southerners in the United States: "what meant freedom and the pursuit of happiness to these savage blacks meant consternation and death to many of the wild denizens of their new home" (72). While the actions of the Belgians can be labeled as inhumane, these African men are quickly identified as inherently savage. The claims of widespread cannibalism are historically widely exaggerated, of course.[12] But cannibalism is not the worst transgression of these men, as we soon find out. Tarzan's response to these "savages" throughout the novel is either to lynch them with his omnipresent handmade noose or to spy on them and terrorize them with "pranks."

I return to Tarzan as a one-man lynch mob later in this chapter, particularly since his murders are constructed very differently from those of the Mbongan villagers. But first, we need to see how cannibalism compares to the torture of first a black victim and then a white man within their newly established village. While Tarzan is initially wondering what he has in common with the Mbongans, he witnesses a scene reminiscent of the lynching in *The Autobiography of an Ex-Colored Man*. Hiding in the trees, he watches as "a struggling animal" is "half led, half carried" into the village, until he realizes that the "quarry was a man" (89). As women and children throw sticks and stones at the victim, "Tarzan of the Apes, young and savage beast of the jungle, wondered at the cruel brutality of his own kind" (89). He quickly distinguishes other animals from these men by the absence of torture: "The ethics of all the others meted a quick and merciful death to their victims" (89).[13] Rather than a quick death, though, the victim of the Mbongans is tied to a stake, pierced by knives and spears thrown at him, while the villagers "danced in wild and savage abandon to the maddening music of the drums" and the "women and children shrieked their delight. The warriors licked their hideous lips in anticipation of the feast to come, and vied with one another in the savagery and loathesomeness of the cruel indignities with which they tortured the still conscious prisoner" (90). Tarzan recalls the ritual of the "Dum-Dum" in which apes of his own tribe ceremonially beat a dead rival ape before cannibalizing his body, but the key distinction is that the apes do not "spring upon their meat while it was still alive" (90). Tarzan's response to the victim's suffering is to play a "wild prank upon these strange, grotesque creatures" after stealing their arrows and making them think that a strange god is haunting their village (91). He clearly notices the "stake where the dying victim now hung, an inert and bloody mass of suffering," but his prank is to magically throw a "grinning human skull" among the villagers near the "half butchered thing they were preparing to feast upon" (92).

The victim of torture, in this case, is clearly linked with the skin color, at least, of the torturers, and thus receives no sympathy from Tarzan. The case is entirely different, though, once the tribe begins to torture a white victim later in the novel. Tarzan has become, we are told, a frequent witness of other victims' suffering: "Many times had Tarzan seen Mbonga's black raiding parties return from the northward with prisoners, and always were the same scenes enacted about that grim stake, beneath the flaring light of many fires" (199). The difference this time is race, since "Tarzan had looked with complacency upon their former orgies, only occasionally interfering for the pleasure of baiting the blacks; but heretofore their victims had been men of their own color" (199). So well does Tarzan know "their customs" that he can "tell almost to a minute how far the dance had gone.... In another instant Mbonga's knife would sever one of the victim's ears—that would mark the beginning of the end..." (200). In this particular case, further plot developments have brought other white people to the jungle. A French naval cruiser has captured the mutineers who had abandoned Jane and her entourage on the coast, and brought them ashore, only to discover that Jane has been abducted by an ape (Terkoz). One of the officers, D'Arnot, is captured by the Mbongans and dragged toward the "most terrifying experience which man can encounter upon earth—the reception of a white prisoner into a village of African cannibals" (197).

Their "cruel savagery" has been intensified, we are told, because of the "still crueler barbarities practiced upon them and theirs by the white officers of that arch hypocrite, Leopold II of Belgium" (197–98). But this scene of torture is clearly the nadir for Tarzan and his readers, as D'Arnot is first beaten and clawed by women, but then "saved for nobler sport than this" as he is "bound securely to the great post from which no live man had ever been released" (198). D'Arnot remains conscious, although "Half fainting from pain and exhaustion," as he reels from the "horrid night-mare" of "The bestial faces, daubed with color— the huge mouths and flabby hanging lips—the yellow teeth, sharp filed—the rolling, demon eyes—the shining naked bodies—the cruel spears. Surely no such creatures really existed upon earth—he must indeed be dreaming" (198). Significantly, though, the dashed description here epitomizes "the savage" rather than "the animal," while D'Arnot's rules of engagement (and class) require him to "not cry out," to "teach these beasts how an officer and a gentleman died" (199). These "beasts" have much more in mind than killing their prey, and Tarzan's response is completely different because of the whiteness of the victim. Although he does not initially know the race of the victim as he speeds toward the village, he guesses that "Tonight it was different—white men, men of Tarzan's own race—might be even now suffering the agonies of torture in that grim, jungle fortress" (199). And sure enough, when he reaches the village he sees the "figure at the stake" about to be reduced to "a writing mass of mutilated flesh" (200). Readers expecting further titillating details of a tortured body are instead presented with Tarzan's heroic rescue of D'Arnot.

What also needs to be rescued, though, is the white man's fear that he might be descended, in evolutionary terms, from these "savages." The description of them echoes Darwin's at the end of *The Descent of Man* as he recalls encountering "a party of Feugians on a wild and broken shore": "These men were absolutely naked and bedaubed with paint, their long hair was tangled, their mouths frothed with excitement, and their expression was wild, startled, and distrustful."[14] Darwin's reflection is that "such were our ancestors" (644). As I have noted in the previous chapter, Darwin suggests that it might be easier to think about a "heroic little monkey" or an "old baboon" as one's ancestor than a "savage who delights to torture his enemies, offers up bloody sacrifices, practises infanticide without remorse, treats his wives like slaves, knows no decency, and is haunted by the grossest superstitions" (644). Despite claims that Darwin's theories do not suggest a progress narrative with (white) humanity as its epitome and goal, Darwin allows himself to feel "some pride" that "man" has "risen, though not through his own exertions, to the very summit of the organic scale"; and there are grounds for "hope for a still higher destiny in the distant future" (644). His final thought, which is framed as a humbling conclusion, still manages to exalt the kind of "humane" quality in Anglo-Saxon men valorized by William James and others, counting among his "noble qualities" the "sympathy which feels for the most debased" and the "benevolence which extends not only to other men but to the humblest living creature" (644). Even though man's "god-like intellect...has penetrated into the movements and constitution of the solar system," he "still bears in his bodily frame the indelible stamp of his lowly origin" (644). But the nature of the evolutionary path from that "lowly origin"—what kind of primate?—is called into question in Tarzan and broader constructions of "the primitive" at the beginning of the twentieth century in the United States.

Tarzanian Animality

Could white men claim animals rather than savages as their immediate ancestors? Freud's answer appears to be no, but his work is influential in solidifying the belief that contemporary "savages" can be seen as essentially the same as the evolutionary ancestors of white "civilization." As I have noted in the previous chapter, at the very beginning of *Totem and Taboo: Some Points of Agreement between the Mental Lives of Savages and Neurotics* (1913), Freud equates "prehistoric man" with, "in a certain sense":

> men still living who, as we believe, stand very near to primitive man, far nearer than we do, and whom we therefore regard as his direct heirs and representatives. Such is our view of those whom we describe as savages or half-savages; and their mental life must have a peculiar interest for us if we are right in seeing in it a well-preserved picture of an early stage of our own development.[15]

Freud is less focused on torture or cruelty than the essentially instinctual nature of "savages" and the resulting inability, supposedly, to repress sexual instincts. According to Freud, "savages" need enforced rituals like totem sacrifices and the externally enforced taboo of incest, because there are no internalized inhibitions that would check their behavior, which is not governed by reason. But civilization is born, supposedly, with a primal Oedipal scene among a savage "horde" and the subsequent guilt that comes from the killing of the primal father.[16] As Marianna Torgovnick points out, Freud's logic and evidence are obviously suspect when he "imagines primitive prehistory in terms of his own psychological theories.... The procedure is entirely circular and self-generating, yielding not 'results' based on observation, but axioms based on metaphors."[17]

Tarzan's construction of "the primitive," according to Torgovnick, is potentially a "source of empowerment," even though it suggests "multiple meanings" with "no specific ethnographic model in mind"; it is a "composite, free-floating creation" that is used for the text's "social commentary and the projection of alternative possibilities" (45). Like Freud, Burroughs presents the "temporal illusion" that current manifestations of "primitive" cultures can be seen as "civilization's" past, reinforcing one of the "most persistent aspects of primitivism in the West" (46). Torgovnick distinguishes between the early Tarzan novels and the later sequels, suggesting that the original *Tarzan* initially resists typical hierarchies of gender, race, and colonial status that are embedded in the Freudian primitive:

> As the series develops, it increasingly affirms existing hierarchies.... But, especially in the opening volumes of the series (and intermittently

thereafter), the Tarzan materials also expose the shaky basis of these hierarchies by showing how far from "natural" they seem to Tarzan as a boy and young man and how subject they are to cultural variation. In fact, the Tarzan story begins with scenes that dramatize confusion and contradiction about black-white relations, about maleness, and about men's treatment of women. (46–47)

When Tarzan first sees a reflection of himself in a pool of water, and feels inferior to the splendid bodies of his fellow apes, Torgovnick reads the scene as a positive affirmation of cultural relativism and its ability to "defamiliarize axiomatic Western norms and raise the possibility of their radical restructuring" (48). Even though Torgovnick acknowledges that "such radical, relativistic moments are counterbalanced and finally overcome by others" (48), the reading of this scene seems far too optimistic, in my view, particularly considering the ironic tone of the narrative: "Tarzan was appalled.... He turned red as he compared [his nose] with the beautiful broad nostrils of his companion. Such a generous nose! Why it spread half across his face! It certainly must be fine to be so handsome, thought poor little Tarzan" (39).

Certainly there is also room for some homosocial admiration of the black male body, implied here by the ape. But I think the surprise of the reader, aside from the knowing wink at this scene, points more logically to Tarzan's encounter with animality—with the ape as an ape, and the white man with apelike instincts—than a disruption of racist human hierarchies. Tarzan's power, in other words, comes not from what Torgovnick calls "potentially utopian uses of the primitive" (55) but from a construction of animal instincts distinct from the "savagery" associated with "the primitive." That distinction comes in large part through a different formulation of cruelty when committed by nonhuman animals. After Tarzan's inverted Narcissus moment, for example, he and his companion are stalked by Sabor, the name for the female lion in the jungle. Aside from the fact that Edgar Rice Burroughs originally had tigers in the *All Story* version, unaware that tigers are not indigenous to Africa,[18] the animals of the novel are more than simple allegories for various human groups. Part of the fantasy is that Tarzan is a real man confronting real animals. But death at the hands of a female lion would register differently from being killed by an ape, for example, and the novel uses the occasion to articulate a different kind of "cruel death": to be trapped "beneath tearing claws and rending fangs."[19] The cruelty stems neither from a delight in torture nor from a desire to make the death more painful than necessary, but from an animal instinct unaware that its ferociousness might not result in a quick and painless death.

Clearly this construction of animality essentializes the Darwinist-Freudian instincts that other chapters of this book have explored, and other examples support the argument that lions, at least, are not simply allegories of darker-skinned human beings. The key example is when Jane and Esmeralda are trapped in the cabin built by the first Lord Greystoke while Sabor tries to penetrate through the window. Rather than the repeated rape scene it initially seems to suggest, the female lion is portrayed as "a man-eater" intent on killing and eating her prey. Although Jane fires off a revolver, she faints alongside Esmeralda while Sabor continues to claw her way through the too-small window: "She saw her prey—the two women—lying senseless upon the floor; there was no longer any resistance to be overcome. Her meat lay before her, and Sabor had only to worm her way through the lattice to claim it" (131). Tarzan is on his way to rescue them, but, as Jane regains consciousness, she resolves to shoot herself and the unconscious Esmeralda "ere the cruel fangs tore into her fair flesh" (134). Her goal is to avoid the "hideous jaws gaping for their prey," the "merciless, yellow fangs," the "rending claws of the great cat" (134). Such a death might read like the scene in *The Birth of a Nation* when suicide is preferable to the shame of having been raped by a black man. But in this case, the text seems to suggest instead a desire for a quick and painless death because being eaten by a lion might entail prolonged physical suffering. Tarzan, of course, arrives just in time to save them, killing Sabor with a "full-Nelson" that literally breaks Sabor's neck (136). Soon thereafter, Tarzan also saves Jane's father and Samuel T. Philander from Numa, the male lion, whose instinct for hunting runs the risk of overpowering him, even if he is already full: "the one great danger was that one of the men might stumble and fall, and then the yellow devil would be upon him in a moment and the joy of the kill would be too great a temptation to withstand" (141).

Tarzan is linked with this kind of instinct when we are told that "To kill was the law of the wild world he knew" (81). But there are distinctions to be made between the kind of killing done by animals and human beings. Tarzan, we are told, is not cruel: "That he joyed in killing, and that he killed with a joyous laugh upon his handsome lips betokened no innate cruelty" (82). Human beings are the only animals that can be savagely cruel, though, and Tarzan appears to be implicated in some way: "He killed for food most often, but, being a man, he sometimes killed for pleasure, a thing which no other animal does; for it has remained for man alone among all creatures to kill senselessly and wantonly for the mere pleasure of inflicting suffering and death" (82). Despite the implication in this instance, including a potential defense of hunting by privileged white Americans, Tarzan is distinguished by the fact that his kills are "without hysteria": "a very businesslike proceeding which admitted of no levity" (82).

Tarzan's actions seem to undermine this abstinence from delighting in the suffering of others, since he is a prankster, as it turns out, when it comes to terrorizing the Mbongan villagers. He is also a frequent voyeur of Mbongan torture scenes and a prolific lyncher of black men for reasons that include simply the theft of their arrows and their clothes to cover himself. As a result, he can serve as a particularly interesting analogue for both white lynchers back home and all their readers fascinated not only with details of torture but also with the bodies of black men.[20] His first encounter with a black man comes after that man has killed Kala, his ape-mammy figure. Grabbing "the coils of his own long rope," Tarzan tracks him down but remains hidden, staring "with wonder upon the strange creature beneath him...this sleek and hideous thing of ebony, pulsing with life" (75–76). Tarzan watches him the length of an entire day as the man kills prey with his arrows, cooks his food with fire, and finally falls asleep, only to find his bow and arrows stolen. Tarzan's premeditated lynching comes only as Kulonga is about to leave the forest for his village: a "quick noose tightened about his neck" (79). The death is represented as a quick one, although Tarzan must "drag back his prey": "Hand over hand Tarzan drew the struggling black until he had him hanging by his neck in midair; then Tarzan climbed to a larger branch drawing the still threshing victim well up into the sheltering verdure of the tree.... Here he fastened the rope securely to a stout branch, and then, descending, plunged his hunting knife into Kulonga's heart" (79).

After the lynching we are given a snapshot of the dead body that establishes the black man as a savage:

> Tarzan examined the black minutely.... The knife with its sheath and belt caught his eye; he appropriated them. A copper anklet also took his fancy, and this he transferred to his own leg.... He examined and admired the tattooing on the forehead and breast. He marvelled at the sharp filed teeth. He investigated and appropriated the feathered headdress, and then he prepared to get down to business, for Tarzan of the Apes was hungry, and here was meat; meat of the kill, which jungle ethics permitted him to eat. (79–80)

But he gets nauseated and decides that men do not eat other men. What is figured as Tarzan's "hereditary instinct" here seems to have "usurped the functions of his untaught mind and saved him from transgressing a world-wide law of whose very existence he was ignorant" (80). Kulonga's "sharp filed teeth" identify him as a cannibal, though, and the "world-wide law" does not quite seem to make sense. According to Torgovnick, "on this detail, as on others, Burroughs felt little need to be consistent. The really important thing to notice, though, is how unresolved matters are for Tarzan. His first meeting with a black results in murder. And he has yet to understand how far he and Kulonga are related."[21] Whether Tarzan himself is confused at this point or not, though, the logic of the text is not inconsistent in the way Torgovnick suggests. Tarzan's "hereditary instinct" clearly invokes racial difference as much as anything, and the text emphasizes torture over cannibalism as the definitive marker of racial difference.

This distinction can be seen in the cannibalism—but not savagery—of the white mutineers captured by D'Arnot's French ship. After the mutineers have killed off all the officers, as well as their new leader—the "rat-faced" Snipes—they find that no one is skilled enough to navigate the ship, and they get lost at sea, without food and water. "Hunger," we are told, "was changing them from human beasts to wild beasts,"[22] and when the Frenchmen finally board their ship, they find two corpses that "appeared to have been partially devoured as though by wolves" (179). At one point before their rescue, "the men lay glaring at each other like beasts of prey, and the following morning two of the corpses lay almost entirely stripped of flesh" (181). The French officers, however, are distinguished from these animalized sailors, immediately ordering "water, medicine, and provisions" to be sent from their own ship through the "perilous" high seas (180). This kind of "humane" treatment of criminals resonates with humane reforms at the turn of the century in the United States, but it also suggests one of the ways that white animality can be exempted from black savagery; these lower-class whites are presented not as torturers but as hungry animals, suggesting that cannibalism itself need not necessarily be the marker of savagery.

This scene intervenes, significantly, between the description of Tarzan's battle with Terkoz over Jane and Tarzan's subsequent scene with Jane in the safety of the apes' amphitheater. It provides further evidence that Tarzan is not equated with Terkoz's savagery, but rather the animalized nature of white masculine power. Tarzan must restrain his animal instincts, in other words, rather than resist a delight in torture that would be more clearly associated with Terkoz and the savage torturers of the novel. Once again, we see that he is a dispassionate killer: "For, though Tarzan of the Apes was a killer of men and of beasts, he killed as the hunter kills, dispassionately, except on those rare occasions when he had killed for hate—though not the brooding, malevolent hate which marks the features of its own with hideous lines" (182). Tarzan's features, instead, are marked by "extraordinary beauty" (182), and Jane decides she has nothing to fear: "No, he could never harm her; of that she was convinced when she translated the fine features and the frank, brave eyes above her into the chivalry which they proclaimed" (183). Tarzan's "problem" is that he has felt "the first fierce passion of his new found love" (183), but he is suddenly not comfortable recognizing that "it was the order of the jungle for the male to take his mate by force" (184). As he thinks about not wanting to be "guided by the laws of the beasts," Jane notices the "graceful majesty of his carriage, the perfect symmetry of his magnificent figure and the poise of his well shaped head upon his broad shoulders" (184). His "natural" class and racial superiority thus convince her that "There could be naught of cruelty or baseness beneath that godlike exterior" (184). She is relieved to find the "hall-mark of his aristocratic birth, the natural outcropping of many generations of fine breeding, an hereditary instinct of graciousness which a lifetime of uncouth and savage training and environment could not eradicate" (189). Rather than raping her, then, his desire is "to please the woman he loved, and to appear well in her eyes," so he unsheathes his hunting knife and hands it to her "hilt first" (190).

Tarzan's inherent superiority thus distinguishes him, supposedly, not only from savages and African American rapists but also from working-class sailors and the "order of the jungle." He is further distinguished from the apes, though, by the way he most often kills other living things. His omnipresent noose is a technology that has marked him as different from his fellow apes since his boyhood, and he is not afraid to snare a wide variety of victims: his ape companions, his ape foster father, Tublat (44), smaller animals like monkeys (67), Sabor the lioness (69), black villagers for their weapons (100), for their clothes, and their "loot" (108), and countless other occasions. We are given scenes like a black man's "body flying upwards in the trees" (110) before being "propped" up at the gate of the village "in such a way that the dead face seemed to be peering around the edge of the gate-post down the path which led to the jungle" (111). Tarzan's response to D'Arnot's torture by the Mbongans is to snare a random man, a "huge black," as if by "an invisible hand" (or the Ku Klux Klan). Dragged by his neck, "Struggling and shrieking, his body, rolling from side to side, moved quickly toward the shadows beneath the trees," until it "rose straight into the air" (200). Lest we think this death too drawn out, apparently, the soaring, "writhing body of the black" is soon sent "sprawling to earth again— to lie very quietly where he had fallen" (201). And our attention is shifted immediately from the dead black body to Tarzan, "a white body, but this one alighted erect" (201).

Whether we consider Tarzan's pleasure in rescuing whiteness from savagery to be "inhumane" or not, my broader point is that this question only makes sense once the discourse of humane reform has become pervasive as a way of distinguishing among various kinds of human cruelty. Interpretations of colonial violence at this moment participate in this new discourse, including references in *Tarzan*, such as the French "punitive expedition" sent back to the Mbongans after D'Arnot has been rescued. After this "determined and angry company" arrives on the outskirts of the village and sees "natives in the field" who have "dropped their implements" and fled, we are told that the "French bullets mowed them down" (207). As the Frenchmen battle their way through the village, it becomes a "wild rout" and a "grim massacre," including those children and women they are "forced to kill in self-defense" (208). In the end, "there lived to oppose them no single warrior of all the savage village of Mbonga" (208). They have "ransacked every hut and corner of the village" in order to find clues about D'Arnot, but they decide that burning the village down would be too much, even though that had been their "original intention" (208). Humanely, presumably, they decide to leave the remaining survivors with "roofs to cover them and a palisade for refuge from the beasts of the jungle" (208). And with friends like these, who would dare call the French "savages"?

Torgovnick reads this scene as evidence of some of the apparently "antiracist positions" of the text, claiming that the details are "rendered so as to give full weight to the terrors inflicted on blacks by better-armed whites."[23] Whether we accept this judgment or not, along with the apparent blame for the Mbongan torture rituals laid at the door of the "still crueler barbarities" of Leopold II's men, my point is that the framework for any kind of judgment is the discourse of the humane. And the question of who is the most humane— Belgium? France? England? America?—reinforces a logic in which the opposite of being "humane" is embodied in the African "savage."

Readers might be inclined to distance themselves from the various forms of cruelty on display in *Tarzan*, or they might use it to justify various racist, sexist, and imperialist perspectives, if not violent acts. But why do these narratives of torture remain so popular at this historical moment? Why is each reiteration so fascinating if, as Tarzan observes, the basic story remains the same? The answer, in part, is that the discourse of the jungle taps into a new sense of wonder, on the one hand, or anxiety, on the other hand, about what it means for a reader to have "natural" instincts within him or her.

Are all human beings inherently the same animal? Am I essentially an ape? A savage? What would it mean to be an ape or a savage in the "natural" state of the jungle? The question of how to define humane behavior offers a new way of defining difference *among* human beings, and this framework becomes crucial for understanding the consumption of all different kinds of torture narratives, particularly as they construct cruelty in relation to the discourse of the jungle. The fact that "the beast within" could be a signifier of whiteness—as well as monstrosity, queerness, or devilish appetite—indicates how complex and inconsistent constructions of animality remained at the turn of the century, as this book has aimed to reveal.

Epilogue

Animal Legacies

WILLIAM JENNINGS BRYAN AND THE SCOPES "MONKEY TRIAL"

IN JULY 1925, John T. Scopes was put on trial for teaching evolution in a public high school in Dayton, Tennessee, after the state had recently codified antievolutionism into law. On the fifth day of the trial, which made headlines and attracted intense interest all across the country, William Jennings Bryan finally spoke in his role as prosecuting attorney, giving a speech that argued against allowing expert testimony from "outsiders" on the subject of evolution. Among Bryan's most vehement objections to evolution itself was the classification of a human being as just another animal, a mammal among 3,500 others, as described in *A Civic Biology*, the textbook used by Scopes to teach evolution. After directing the court's attention to a diagram indicating mammals as one group among many on the "evolutionary tree," Bryan thunders, "How dare those scientists put man in a little ring like that with lions and tigers and everything that is bad!"[1] His outrage becomes a challenge: "Tell me that the parents of this day have not any right to declare that children are not to be taught this doctrine? Shall not be taken down from the high plane upon which God put man? Shall be detached from the throne of God and be compelled to link their ancestors with *the jungle*, tell that to these children?"[2] For Bryan, the Bible is the only source of expert authority: "That Bible is not going to be driven out of this court by experts who come hundreds of miles to testify that they can reconcile evolution, with its ancestor in *the jungle*, with man made by God in his image, and put here for purposes as a part of the divine plan" (125). In response, defense attorney Dudley Field Malone begins by stating flatly, "whether Mr. Bryan knows it or not, he is a mammal, he is an animal and he is a man."[3] While there is much to discuss in relation to the Scopes Trial that is beyond the scope of this book, the general reaction to

Bryan's argument provides a useful epilogue to the birth of jungle discourse I have explored throughout this book.[4] By 1925, I believe, Bryan's *objection* to jungle discourse—and the suggestion that the human is also an animal—was no longer part of the mainstream in the United States.

The ridicule with which Bryan was treated in media coverage of the Scopes trial, particularly for an audience of educated, urban intellectuals in the North, suggested that anyone objecting to formulations of the human as an animal must be an idiot. Perhaps most famously, H. L. Mencken's reporting on the trial reveals utter disdain for both Bryan and fundamentalists in general. In a piece published on July 18, 1925, in the *Baltimore Sun*, for example, Mencken lambastes what he sees as complete ignorance in Bryan: "When I heard him, in open court, denounce the notion that man is a mammal, I was genuinely staggered and so was every other stranger in the courtroom. People looked at one another in blank amazement. But the native fundamentalists, it quickly appeared, saw nothing absurd in his words."[5] Mencken argues that Bryan was once a reasonable man, but now lacks reason altogether: "The Bryan of today, old, disappointed and embittered, is a far different bird. He realizes at last that the glories of this world are not for him, and he takes refuge, peasant-like, in religious hallucinations. They depart from sense altogether. They are not merely silly; they are downright idiotic. And being idiotic, they appeal with irresistible force to the poor half-wits upon whom the old charlatan now preys."[6] Clarence Darrow, the famous defense attorney for Scopes, echoes this judgment in a *New York Times* article titled "Evolution Battle Rages Out of Court," on July 22, 1925, after the trial had concluded with a guilty verdict for Scopes: "I cannot help having some pity for Mr. Bryan being obliged to show his gross ignorance by the simple and competent questions asked him on the witness stand."[7] And a *New York Times* editorial titled "Ended at Last," printed the same day, declared that Bryan had "fared so ill as to inspire pity.... It has long been known to many that he was only a voice calling from a poorly furnished brain-room. But how almost absolutely unfurnished it was the public didn't know till he was forced to make an inventory."[8]

From this perspective, Bryan's reputation as an important and respected populist reformer seems to die with his passionate defense of antievolutionism in the Scopes trial. One way to read the trajectory of his career, then, is that it moves toward a conservatism increasingly out of touch with the rest of the country, or at least with other Progressive-Era reformers. After Bryan's death shortly following the end of the Scopes trial, for example, Eugene Debs condemns this trajectory: "In the early years of Mr. Bryan's career his views, political or otherwise, were centered around progressivism, but since his first campaign he grew more and more conservative until he finally stood before the country, a champion of everything reactionary in our political and social life. To speak with perfect frankness, the cause of human progress sustains no loss in the death of Mr. Bryan."[9] According to Michael Kazin in *A Godly Hero: The Life of William Jennings Bryan* (2006), "By his death, the core of Bryan's appeal had shrunk to what Americans were calling the Bible Belt. Until World War I, his followers had been numerous nearly everywhere, scarce only in the upper reaches of New England."[10] But the Scopes trial essentially reduced him to "a martyr to people whose conservative faith burned brighter than did any zeal for economic and social change."[11]

What is particularly interesting to note, from my perspective, is not necessarily that Bryan became more conservative but that his objections to jungle discourse—and his affirmation of a strong Christian faith—were deemed more problematic in 1925 than at earlier moments in his career. In a lecture he gave many times in 1908 titled "The Prince of Peace," for example, Bryan addresses himself to "liberals" who think Christianity is not compatible with their "intellectual superiority" and "enlightened" conceptions of morality.[12] Contrary to thinking of the human as an animal in a Darwinist-Freudian formulation, Bryan argues that "Man is a religious being" who is ultimately "restrained from evil deeds by the fear of endless remorse" in the afterlife to come.[13] Bryan's inner beast, in other words, is linked with the Devil and sin, rather than the jungle and survival. As Kazin notes, Bryan's reliance upon Christian rhetoric would have been far more common among other reformers at the turn of the century, as opposed to after the Scopes trial: "During the late nineteenth century, when Bryan was a young man, evangelical rhetoric saturated nearly every mass movement in America," including the Knights of Labor, the Woman's Christian Temperance Union, and the Farmer's Alliance.[14] Bryan invoked Christian imagery in his famous "Cross of Gold" speech at the 1896 Democratic Convention, which secured for him the nomination of the Democratic Party for president of the United States. Arguing for the free coinage of silver, in response to defenders of the gold standard, Bryan defends what he sees as a "righteous cause" that is "on the side of the struggling masses."[15] In dramatic conclusion, he bellows, "You shall not press down upon the brow of labor this crown of thorns, you shall not crucify mankind upon a cross of gold."[16] Although he lost the 1896 election to William McKinley, Bryan went on to be the Democratic nominee again in 1900 as well as 1908, losing both elections but earning more than six million votes each time he ran: 47.7 percent, 45.5 percent, and 43.1 percent of the popular vote, respectively.[17] His rejection of jungle discourse, though, was far less of a problem for a progressive audience at the turn of the century, as opposed to later in his career.

Bryan's record as a populist reformer included advocacy for a range of issues, but his activism intersects in interesting ways with jungle discourse. He railed against imperialism in the Spanish-American War, for example, as well as economic inequality in a variety of ways, giving hundreds of speeches each year and publishing dozens of books. As Edward J. Larson notes in *Summer for the Gods* (1997), Bryan eventually resigned his position as secretary of state under Woodrow Wilson in 1915, "in protest over the drift toward war. He spent the next two years criss-crossing the country campaigning against American intervention."[18] While he was unsuccessful in this campaign, "he helped to secure ratification of four constitutional amendments designed to promote a more democratic or righteous society: the direct election of senators, a progressive federal income tax, Prohibition, and female suffrage."[19] According to Kazin, Bryan "preached that the national state should counter the overweening power of banks and industrial corporations by legalizing strikes, subsidizing farmers, taxing the rich, banning private campaign spending, and outlawing the 'liquor trust.'"[20] For Kazin, this record is enough to redeem Bryan, even if his racial prejudices were often glaring: "His one great flaw was to support, with a studied lack of reflection, the abusive system of Jim Crow—a view that was shared, until the late 1930s, by nearly every white Democrat."[21] Rather than excusing Bryan's racism, though, I want to illustrate how it relates to a broader racial subtext of jungle discourse. Bryan's objections to being associated with the jungle, in other words, are generated both by his racism and by his wariness of social Darwinist justifications of economic exploitation and military conquest.

In his 1908 "Prince of Peace" speech, Bryan's resistance to evolution is less absolute than it becomes in the Scopes trial, but it is also clear that he objects to being associated with animals or an animal ancestor at that point: "I have not yet been able to convince myself, that man is a lineal descendant of the lower animals. I do not mean to find fault with you if you want to accept it; all I mean to say is that while you may trace your ancestry back to the monkey if you find pleasure or pride in doing so, you shall not connect me with your family tree without more evidence than has yet been produced."[22] Bryan argues, "It is true that man, in some physical qualities, *resembles the beast*, but man has a mind as well as a body and a soul as well as a mind. The mind is greater than the body and the soul is greater than the mind, and I object to having man's pedigree traced on one-third of him only—and that *the lowest third*."[23] He objects to the "Darwinian theory" as "the merciless law by which the strong crowd out and kill off the weak."[24] But his primary uneasiness seems to be the association between the "lower" third of the human—the body—and "the beast," particularly once we consider his views on race.

The connection, for Bryan, between "the beast" and black men can be seen in his commentary on race, "The Race Problem," in 1903, as well as his later thoughts on the Scopes trial. While Bryan condemns extralegal lynchings of black men in "The Race Problem," he also expresses approval of President Roosevelt's denunciation of "the horrible crime," "the unspeakable *beastiality*," the "crimes against women" that supposedly provoke "mob law."[25] While he might be in favor of allowing "the less advanced" race[26] to make progress, Bryan does not want to give black people false hope: "It is a grievous mistake to turn the negro's thoughts from the substantial advantages of industrial, intellectual and moral progress to the unsubstantial promises of social recognition."[27] Why, he asks, should white people "arouse the colored people to expect social equality or agitate the whites with the fear of it?"[28] In the speech he wanted to give as his closing argument in the Scopes trial—which he was never allowed to deliver, since Darrow's defense team waived its own closing argument—Bryan was prepared to decry Darwin's own arguments linking all human beings back to animals in Africa. In the speech that was subsequently published, Bryan condemns Darwin's logic in *The Descent of Man* when he "tries to locate his first man—that is, the first man to come down out of the trees—in Africa," thus "leaving man in company with gorillas and chimpanzees..."[29] The problem, for Bryan, is that "Darwin attempts to trace the mind of man back to the mind of lower animals.... he endeavors to trace man's moral nature back to the animals. It is all animal—animal—animal, with never a thought of God or of religion."[30] And Bryan, as we know, does not want to be called an animal. He wants to uphold Tennessee's law that would "forbid the teaching of any theory that makes man a descendant of any lower form of life."[31]

The racial hierarchy that Bryan believes in suggests that not only animals but also black people should be seen as a "lower form of life." When Bryan died, many members of the Ku Klux Klan honored him by burning crosses in his memory.[32] But this kind of racism, evident in many of the writers explored in this book, could be justified by both antievolutionists and evolutionists. In George W. Hunter's *A Civic Biology* (1914), for example, which is the textbook supposedly used by Scopes to teach evolution,[33] students are told that there are five "races of man," with white people at the top of the hierarchy: "the Ethiopian or negro type, originating in Africa; the Malay or brown race, from the islands of the Pacific; the American Indian; the Mongolian or yellow race, including the natives of China, Japan, and the Eskimos; and finally, the highest type of all, the Caucasians, represented by the civilized white inhabitants of Europe and America..."[34] A letter to the editor of the *Baltimore Sun* on July 13, 1925, seeks to reassure racist white men with a similar hierarchical logic. "The opponents of the theory of evolution," we are told, "are the ones that make the claim man descends from the monkey—not the men of science" (185). The comparison between (white) man and monkey leads to their becoming "horrified at the revolting idea of any blood relationship between the two…" (185). But they need not worry, we are told, because "There is actually more difference between the white gentleman and those [Fuegian or Australian] savages than between those savages and the higher apes" (185).

W. E. B. Du Bois illustrates how an evolutionist need not be racist, though, suggesting instead that antievolution advocacy is a tool used by white supremacists to keep black people ignorant, as part of a general pattern. In a piece for the *Crisis* titled "Scopes," in September 1925, for example, Du Bois argues, "The folk who leave white Tennessee in blank and ridiculous ignorance of what science has taught the world since 1859 are the same ones who would leave black Tennessee and black America with just as little education as is consistent with fairly efficient labor and reasonable contentment; who rave over the 18th Amendment [for Prohibition] and are dumb over the 15th [giving African American men the right to vote]; who permit lynching and make bastardy legal in order to render their race 'pure'" (183). From the perspective of an editorial titled "If Monkeys Could Speak" in the *Chicago Defender*, on May 23, 1925, evolution actually levels the playing field among all human beings; if Tennessee legislators actually understand Darwinism, we are told, "they will have to admit that there is no fundamental difference between themselves and the race they pretend to despise. Such admission would, of course, play havoc with the existing standards of living in the South" (181).

Evolution could thus be used to either condone or condemn racism, but the general consensus by 1925 was that it no longer made sense to deny that there is an "animal" aspect of being human, most often formulated as both a physical manifestation (in which human and nonhuman animals must eat, for example, in order to survive) and a psychological internalization (in which a human being's "animal instincts" explain some, if not all, aspects of human behavior). There might be debate about whether the "animal" part or the "human" part of a human being is more powerful in determining how humans act. But there is still consensus that the "animal" aspect, regardless of how influential it is within an individual body, can be associated with the discourse of the jungle generally, and with violent and heterosexual instincts in particular. This key aspect of jungle discourse thus distinguishes it from debates over both evolution and social Darwinism; beneath both there often remains the fundamental assumption that "the animal" within "the human" signifies Darwinist-Freudian instincts.

Evolution and social Darwinism have fluctuated over the course of the twentieth century in terms of the extent of their dominance as broad cultural discourses. As Ronald L. Numbers notes in *Darwinism Comes to America* (1999), antievolutionism did not necessarily die with the conclusion of the Scopes trial and Bryan's own death. Mississippi and Arkansas outlawed the teaching of evolution in 1926 and 1928, respectively, and the high point of the antievolution crusade, at least legislatively, could be seen as 1928.[35] Christian fundamentalist advocacy against evolution has certainly persisted, with ebbs and flows, until the turn of the twenty-first century, even if its tactics have shifted in various ways.[36] From the perspective of Richard Hofstadter in *Social Darwinism in American Thought* (1944), social Darwinist thinking largely disappeared as a dominant discourse by the end of World War I.[37] World War II certainly led to social Darwinism being seen as a deeply problematic discourse for its justification of eugenics culminating in Nazism and the Holocaust. But social Darwinism seemed to reappear in the 1980s, as Eric Foner notes in his introduction to Hofstadter's work, with the "resurrection" of "biological explanations for human development and of the social Darwinist mentality, if not the name itself: that government should not intervene to affect the 'natural' workings of the economy, that the distribution of rewards within society reflects individual merit rather than historical circumstances, that the plight of the less fortunate, whether individuals or races, arises from their own failings."[38] Historians such as Robert C. Bannister, in *Social Darwinism: Science and Myth in Anglo-American Social Thought* (1979), argue that the charge of social Darwinism has often been inaccurate and unfair, particularly when it is equated with biological determinism, whether at the turn of the twentieth century or in the sociobiology debates stemming from the publication of Edward O. Wilson's *Sociobiology* in 1975.[39]

Whether one wants to claim social Darwinism or not, though, the discourse of the jungle continues to justify an emphasis on the "animal" side of "human nature" in both best-selling and scholarly texts at the turn of the twenty-first century.[40] A general acceptance of Darwinist-Freudian animality, in other words, seems to remain in the United States, drawing upon the legacy of the Scopes trial that captured the rapt attention of so many Americans. Even a harsh critic of social Darwinism such as Hofstadter can conclude that "the life of man in society, while it is incidentally a biological fact, has characteristics that are not reducible to biology and must be explained in the distinctive terms of a cultural analysis."[41] Despite the defense of characteristics "not reducible to biology," the references to "biological fact" still evoke the "animal" part of the human in ways that only a fundamentalist Christian would presumably object to today. But contemporary critics of biological determinism can continue to associate animality—and the "beast" within the human—with the Darwinist-Freudian jungle, even as they argue vehemently against an oversimplification or reduction of the human to animal instincts.[42]

Recent work in animal studies from a wide range of academic disciplines has complicated our understanding of the human/animal binary in important ways. It has not only undermined various attempts to distinguish humans from other animals (which is usually done by invoking an evolving definition of what is seen as quintessentially human), but also challenged traditional ways of thinking about which nonhuman animal behaviors should be seen as "natural." Bruce Bagemihl documents extensive evidence of "homosexuality" among hundreds of animal species, for example, while Frans de Waal reveals that both humans and animals have evolved cooperative and altruistic behaviors that eventually lead to morality.[43] Jacques Derrida, particularly in *The Animal That Therefore I Am* (2008), indicates how the history of Western philosophy relies upon problematic attempts to distinguish "the human" from "the animal" that can be revealed as deeply flawed in terms of logic, if not also ethics.[44] In *When Species Meet* (2008), Donna Haraway explores how dogs in particular can experience joy, for example, as well as profoundly complex interactions with humans that actually construct or define both of the "critters"—human and nonhuman—involved in the interaction. And Marc Bekoff has published numerous books that reveal the complexities of animal emotions and behavior, based upon studies in cognitive ethology from the perspective of an evolutionary biologist.[45] These kinds of interdisciplinary animal studies work have opened the door even further to thinking about animals as more than just bundles of instincts.

The animality studies approach I have taken in this book reveals other reasons for resisting a hegemonic association of "the animal" with instincts for violence and heterosexuality, particularly within human beings. With wide-ranging impacts on various human groups, the discourse of the jungle has naturalized problematic constructions of human behavior for roughly a century. But the history of animality at the turn of the twentieth century, when "the beast" in U.S. culture was evolving in new and complicated ways, also includes alternative constructions of animality that are important to consider today. My hope is that these alternatives can help us glimpse the possibilities related to thinking about *neither* humans *nor* nonhumans as "beasts," at least in terms of the way that "the animal" has been constructed in the Darwinist-Freudian discourse of the jungle.

Notes

INTRODUCTION

1. John Rolfe and Peter Troob, *Monkey Business: Swinging through the Wall Street Jungle;* Richard Conniff, *The Ape in the Corner Office: Understanding the Workplace Beast in All of Us;* Shelton Stromquist and Marvin Bergman, *Unionizing the Jungles: Labor and Community in the Twentieth-Century Meatpacking Industry.*

2. Freud, *Complete Pyschological Works,* vol. 21, III. Freud adds a note indicating that *homo homini lupus* is taken from Plautus's *Asinaria* (ca. third century B.C.E.). The phrase is also cited in Hobbes's *De Cive* (*On the Citizen*) in 1651.

3. Ibid.

4. Shannon, "Eight Animals in Shakespeare," 472–79.

5. In *Homo Sacer,* Giorgio Agamben seems to lack this kind of historical distinction in his discussion of the "law of nature" for Hobbes. Agamben's focus, though, is on the "state of nature" that can actually be seen as internal to the State: "for Hobbes it is this very identity of the state of nature and violence (*homo hominis lupus*) that justifies the absolute power of the sovereign" (35).

6. Jennifer L. Fleissner, among others, has argued for a recasting of literary naturalism to include some of these texts. See Fleissner, *Women, Compulsion, Modernity.*

7. I use "Darwinist" rather than "Darwinian" here to underscore my interest in discourse loosely based upon Darwin's work rather than Darwin's "actual" ideas. I will distinguish between jungle discourse, social Darwinism, and Darwin's own work later. On the latter, see Levine, *Darwin Loves You.* Levine's project in *Darwin and the Novelists* is closer to my own here, in the sense that Levine explores what he calls "a sort of gestalt of the Darwinian imagination" (13), although his focus is on Victorian novels and science rather than U.S. texts at the turn of the century. Gillian Beer, in *Darwin's Plots,* with a different focus, explores the "ways in which some nineteenth-century novelists who read his work responded to, and resisted, Darwinian insights" (xxvii). For more on Freud's debts to Darwin, see Ritvo, *Darwin's Influence on Freud.*

8. On Freud's 1909 Clark lectures, see Rosenzweig, *Historic Expedition to America;* and Hale, *Freud and the Americans.*

9. Quoted in Bender, *Evolution,* 20

10. Freud, *Complete Psychological Works,* vol. 17, 137.

11. Ibid.

12. Donna Haraway, in *When Species Meet,* adds what she calls "a fourth wound" to Freud's discussion: "the informatic or cyborgian, which infolds organic and technological flesh and so melds that Great Divide as well" (12).

13. In *The Open: Man and Animal,* Agamben describes a split within the human as the distinction between bare life (*zoē*) and political life (*bios*). In Agamben's well-known formulation, the attempt to distinguish between human and animal produces the "anthropological machine" (37), which remains fundamentally problematic within contemporary forms of humanism and neohumanism.

14. Bowler, *Evolution,* 274.

15. Numbers, *Darwinism Comes to America,* 24.

16. Ibid., 2. Numbers is particularly useful for his detailed analysis of a wide range of responses to Darwinism, particularly in terms of various religious theologies and different reactions in different geographic regions in the United States.

17. Russett, *Darwin in America,* 147.

18. Larson, *Summer for the Gods,* 19–20.

19. x, my emphasis.

20. According to Bender in *Evolution and "the Sex Problem,"* "Sex had become a problem first because it had emerged as the essential element of human nature in the context of evolutionary thought" (12).

21. Quoted in Bender, *Evolution,* 20

22. Ibid., 6. Bender also claims, in *The Descent of Love,* that American writers such as William Dean Howells and Henry James were exploring "the sex problem" in the immediate aftermath of Darwin's *Descent of Man* in the 1870s and 1880s.

23. Ibid., 5.

24. London, *Novels and Stories,* 59–60.

25. Ibid., 244.

26. For Seltzer's discussion, see *Bodies and Machines,* 166–72.

27. Hofstadter, *Social Darwinism,* 6.

28. Larson, *Summer,* 27.

29. Hofstadter, *Social Darwinism,* 7. Subsequent text references are to page numbers in this edition.

30. Bannister, *Social Darwinism,* xii. Subsequent text references are to page numbers in this edition.

31. Seitler, *Atavistic Tendencies,* 1. Subsequent text references are to page numbers in this edition.

32. Tracking what she calls "degeneration narratives" and "regeneration narratives," Seitler explores fascinating examples of texts that construct "atavistic tendencies" as character traits handed down as an inheritance, skipping generations and manifesting themselves in animal-like features or behaviors. Seitler reads "the appearance of these signs as a reversion to some earlier moment of species

history.... Dramatizing the human return to the form of an animal" (7). But many of Seitler's most interesting examples—the resurfacing of undesirable traits such as homosexuality, perversity, criminality, and susceptibility to disease—do not fit within Darwinist-Freudian formulations of "the animal" within "the human." She reads *Vandover and the Brute* and *Nightwood* as examples "where sexual perversity as a form of atavism is literally enacted as a character's return to the form of an animal (a wolf, a barking dog)" (27). But what kind of "species" are these? It would be very difficult to reconcile a Darwinist-Freudian "animal" with a proclivity toward sexual perversity; in the discourse of the jungle, animality is associated with "natural" heterosexuality rather than perversions that would threaten the propagation of an animal's offspring. The difficulty with claiming atavism as a dominant discourse at the turn of the century is that it has the potential to evoke both pre- and post-Darwinian understandings of heredity, thus conflating very different constructions of animality.

33. A growing number of scholars in the humanities and social sciences have been addressing "the question of the animal," often building upon the late work of Jacques Derrida. See, for example, Derrida, "Eating Well"; "The Animal That Therefore I Am"; "And Say the Animal Responded?"; *The Animal That Therefore I Am*; and *The Beast and the Sovereign*. See also Calarco and Atterton, *Animal Philosophy*; Calarco, *Zoographies;* Cary Wolfe, *Animal Rites* and *What Is Posthumanism?*, which is part of the "posthumanities" book series edited by Wolfe. Other titles in that series include Haraway, *When Species Meet,* and Shukin, *Animal Capital*. See also DeKoven and Lundblad, *Species Matters*.

34. Recent work in cognitive ethology provides one form of evidence to show that various animal species are much more than bundles of instincts. See, for example, the work of Marc Bekoff in *Minding Animals* and *Emotional Lives of Animals*.

35. For a sharp critique—from the perspective of a methodology identified as "critical animal studies"—of animal studies as not oriented *enough* toward animal advocacy, see Institute for Critical Animal Studies, "About ICAS." For other resources, organizations, and journals related to animal studies, see the "Resources" page of the H-Animal Discussion Network website. See also Animality Studies @ CSU, "Resources," online.

36. Haraway, *When Species Meet*, 29.

37. Ibid., 313n36, 27 (my emphasis). For a broader critique of Deleuze and Guattari's "becoming-animal," see also 27–30. It is important to note here that Haraway's "ordinary" is far from it: "The ordinary is a multipartner mud dance issuing from and in entangled species.... [T]he partners do not preexist their constitutive intra-action at every folded layer of time and space" (32). For a critique of Haraway's reading of Deleuze and Guattari, see Beckman, "(Be)Coming Animal, or the Posthuman Orgasm," in *Between Pleasure and Desire* (forthcoming).

38. Ibid., 19–20. For a broader critique of Derrida's essay, see also 19–27.

39. Derrida, "The Animal," 394.

40. Wolfe, *Animal Rites,* 190. Subsequent text references are to page numbers in this edition.

41. Wolfe, *Posthumanism,* 8. Subsequent text references are to page numbers in this edition.

42. In this regard, Giorgio Agamben's desire in *The Open: Man and Animal* to stop the "anthropological machine"—in its attempt to distinguish between the human and the animal in the production of the biopolitics of what it means to be "human"—could be seen as closer to animality studies than animal studies, even if its *anti*humanism is not *post*humanist enough in Wolfe's sense (and it remains more committed to philosophy than historicized cultural studies, from my perspective). Matthew Calarco, in *Zoographies,* criticizes this aspect of Agamben's work for the "kind of performative anthropocentrism in his texts…" because "Agamben's writings…never explore the impact the machine has on various forms of animal life" (98, 102). Calarco's critique, then, can itself be seen as an example of animal studies rather than animality studies.

43. Haraway, *When Species Meet,* 5.

44. Ibid.

45. Ibid., 6

46. Several parts of this section on animality studies were previously published as part of my "From Animal to Animality Studies," 496–502.

47. Fleissner, *Women, Compulsion,* 22. Fleissner's general goal is a "rereading of the 'naturalist' project" (8), which she enacts brilliantly by shifting away from traditional readings in four ways: moving "from a macho masculinity to the centrality of the modern young woman"; reading nature as a "post-Darwinian location *within* historical time"; identifying the characteristic plot of naturalism as "ongoing, non-linear, repetitive motion"; and seeking to "replace the notion of naturalist determinism with the more nuanced concept of *compulsion*" (9).

48. Michaels, *Gold Standard,*173.

49. Fleissner, *Women, Compulsion,* 45.

50. Ibid.

51. Other scholars of literary naturalism are engaged in subsequent chapters of this book, but examples of other influential work in the field can be found in Donald Pizer, *Companion to American Realism and Naturalism* and *Documents of American Realism and Naturalism.*

52. The cartoon is reprinted in Walter Benn Michaels, *Gold Standard,* 152. For further background on debates related to the gold standard at the end of the nineteenth century—particularly in relation to arguments for the free coinage of silver, as articulated by William Jennings Bryan—see Kazin, *Godly Hero.*

53. Michaels, *Gold Standard,* 151. Subsequent text references are to page numbers in this edition.

54. Part 3 of this book explores humane discourse in greater detail, particularly in relation to concurrent constructions of human racial distinctions.

55. The specific context for figure 2 is President Roosevelt's 1907 autumn bear-hunting trip in Louisiana. The cartoon is reprinted in Ralph H. Lutts, *Nature Fakers*, 136.

56. Lutts, *Wild Animal Story*, 1, 6.

57. According to Donna Haraway, in "Teddy Bear Patriarchy," at least two different versions of the "teddy bear" origin story can be identified. In one, "T.R. returned empty-handed from a hunting trip to [the Deauvereaux or Hotel Colorada in Glenwood Springs, Colorado], and so a hotel maid created a little stuffed bear and gave it to him. Word spread, and the Bear was manufactured in Germany shortly thereafter. Another version has T.R. sparing the life of a bear cub, with the stuffed version commemorating his kindness" (284–85n5).

58. Long, "Preface to *Northern Trails*," 74.

59. Ibid.

60. Ibid., 75.

61. J. Burroughs, "Real and Sham," 129. Subsequent text references are to page numbers in this edition.

62. For an invaluable resource that collects these primary texts, along with critical commentaries, see Ralph H. Lutts, *Wild Animal Story*.

63. Long, "Modern School," 146.

64. Quoted in Clark, "Roosevelt," 167. Roosevelt's interest in "real" animals is mostly to hunt them, but his role in the early conservation movement is relevant here as well, particularly in terms of establishing national parks and other forms of government-protected habitats. Along with the birth of institutions such as the zoo and the natural history museum, the conservation movement offers further evidence of the broader cultural interest in animals at the turn of the century. On these histories, see Haraway, "Teddy Bear Patriarchy," 237–91; Malamud, *Reading Zoos*; Rothfels, *Savages and Beasts*; Worster, *Nature's Economy*; and Cronon, *Uncommon Ground: Rethinking the Human Place in Nature*.

65. Ibid., 171.

66. Long, "I Propose," 176.

67. For more on U.S. imperialist foreign policy at the turn of the century, see Kaplan and Pease, *Cultures of United States Imperialism*; and Kaplan, *Anarchy of Empire*.

68. Quoted in Hofstadter, *Social Darwinism*, 180.

69. Quoted in ibid., 181.

70. Roosevelt, "Nature Fakers," 194. There are important differences, of course, between constructions of Native Americans and other groups constructed as "savage" at the turn of the century, such as Africans and African Americans. While this book focuses on the latter rather than the former, my hope is that future work might explore constructions of animality by and in relation to Native Americans at this same historical moment.

71. London, "The Other Animals," 207; subsequent text references are to page numbers in this edition. For more on London in the context of imperialism, see Ahuja, "Contradictions of Colonial Dependency," 15–28.

72. For more on racial issues in London's work, see Reesman, *Jack London's Racial Lives*.
73. See, for example, the chapter-length studies of Gilman in Bederman, *Manliness and Civilization;* Fleissner, *Women, Compulsion;* and Seitler, *Atavistic Tendencies*.
74. Other fascinating texts and discourses are beyond the scope of this book as well. I have chosen not to focus, for example, on a cluster of texts in which gender and sexuality issues could be linked with the representation of birds or birdlike women but not necessarily the discourse of the jungle: Sarah Orne Jewett's "A White Heron" (1886), Henry James's *The Bostonians* (1886), Mabel Osgood Wright's *Birdcraft* (1895) and *Citizen Bird* (1897), as well as the relationship between the Woman's Movement and women instrumental in the early Audubon Society. On this last relationship, see, for example, Price, "When Women Were Women," in *Flight Maps*, 57–109.
75. Roosevelt, "Nature Fakers," 192.
76. Quoted in Foucault, *Order of Things,* xv.
77. Foucault, ibid.
78. For a useful history of American studies scholarship, including excerpts from early figures such as Henry Nash Smith, see Maddox, *Locating American Studies*.
79. An earlier version of this chapter appeared as my "Epistemology of the Jungle," 747–73.
80. A slightly different version of this chapter was published in DeKoven and Lundblad, *Species Matters*, 75–102.

1 PROGRESSIVE-ERA SEXUALITY AND
THE NATURE OF THE BEAST IN HENRY JAMES

1. Sedgwick, *Epistemology of the Closet*, 83.
2. Foucault, *History of Sexuality: An Introduction,* 43. According to Foucault, "The sodomite had been a temporary aberration; the homosexual was now a species."
3. Sedgwick, *Epistemology*, 9.
4. Ibid., 72.
5. As Donna Haraway in *When Species Meet* notes, "The ability to interbreed reproductively is the rough and ready requirement for members of the same biological species; all those lateral gene exchangers such as bacteria have never made very good species" (17). The *Oxford English Dictionary* gives fourteen definitions of "species," including one germane to zoology and botany: "A group or class of animals or plants (usually constituting a subdivision of a genus) having certain common and permanent characteristics which clearly distinguish it from other groups." But this definition is appended with a significant note: "The exact definition of a species, and the criteria by which species are to be distinguished (esp. in relation to genera or varieties), have been the subject of much discussion." Foucault explores the historical development of biological classification systems in *The Order of Things: An Archaeology of the Human Sciences*.

6. Notable and recent exceptions include Terry, "'Unnatural Acts'" (151–93); Lancaster, *Trouble with Nature*; Giffney and Hird, *Queering the Non/Human;* and Stacy Alaimo, "Eluding Capture" (15–36).

7. For a good summary of the Darwinian "modern synthesis" that eventually shifts the focus of natural selection from the individual organism to the gene, see Larson, *Evolution,* 267–86.

8. H. James, "Beast in the Jungle," 365.

9. Beer, *Darwin's Plots*, 15.

10. Ibid.

11. Darwin, *Origin of Species*, 169.

12. Ibid., 198.

13. See, for example, Levine, *Darwin Loves You.*

14. Darwin, *Descent of Man*, vol. 22, 639.

15. Lancaster, *Trouble with Nature,* 85. Other scholars, of course, have also suggested the significance of Darwin in the history of sexuality. Jeffrey Weeks, in *Sexuality and Its Discontents*, for example, has argued that the contribution of Darwinism was "to fuel speculation on the origins of phenomena, and hence stimulate the search for the prime motor of behaviour. The concept of 'the instinct' usefully filled the gap" (83). But the emphasis in this kind of work is often on *human* instinct and its relationship to subsequent constructions of human sexuality rather than the ongoing relationship between representations of animality and human sexuality.

16. Freud, *Complete Psychological Works*, vol. 7, 153.

17. Halperin, *History of Homosexuality*, 29.

18. Abelove, "Freud, Male Homosexuality," 382.

19. Ibid., 385. As Abelove points out, the history of the American Psychiatric Association in the twentieth century has seen "two sets of moralistic psychoanalysts, each opposing the other, each claiming to stand in the tradition of Freud, and each espousing a position which Freud himself rejected as wrong and repressive" (391). Abelove refers here to analysts such as Irving Bieber and Charles Socarides, who argued that homosexuality is an illness, as well as analysts such as Judd Marmor and Robert Stoller, who denied that it is an illness but maintained that homosexuality is manifested only in a minority of the population, as opposed to Freud's claim that it is a universal possibility. The American Psychiatric Association, as Abelove also points out, did not remove homosexuality from its official list of illnesses until 1973.

20. Freud, *Complete Psychological Works*, vol. 7, 150.

21. For more on the history of these apparently conflicting meanings of "jungle," see Zimmerman, *Jungle and the Aroma.*

22. Said, *Culture and Imperialism,* 8. Said cites the research of Henry Magdoff from *Imperialism,* 29, 35.

23. In *The Jungle and The Aroma of Meats*, Zimmerman suggests that Kipling's construction of the jungle is a "mirage of exoticism and primitivism"(ix).

24. Kipling, *Jungle Books*, 250.

25. Slater, "Amazonia as Edenic Narrrative," 117.

26. Karlin, Introduction to *Jungle Books,* 11–12.

27. Kipling, *Jungle Books,* 191.

28. Ibid.

29. Said, *Culture and Imperialism,* 143.

30. Kipling, *Jungle Books,* 152. Subsequent text references are to this edition.

31. See Bagemihl, *Biological Exuberance*; Roughgarden, *Evolution's Rainbow*; and Zuk, *Sexual Selections.*

32. Partridge, *Slang To-Day and Yesterday,* 467.

33. Chauncey, *Gay New York,* 89. Subsequent text references are to page numbers in this edition.

34. David Halperin, in *How to Do the History of Homosexuality,* also complicates sweeping generalizations about the shift from acts to identity in the history of sexuality, arguing that character types were associated with certain same-sex sexual relationships long before the construction of "the homosexual" as defined by Foucault; as a result, it would be inaccurate to say that there was absolutely no relationship between "acts" and "identity" before the nineteenth century (29–32). For complexities related to various constructions of African American male sexuality at the turn of the century, see Marlon B. Ross, *Manning the Race.*

35. Sedgwick, *Epistemology,* 87.

36. Chauncey, *Gay New York,* 89.

37. Ibid., 85.

38. Freud, *Complete Psychological Works,* vol. 17, 26–27. Subsequent text references are to page numbers in this edition.

39. For a provocative reading of the primal scene as fundamentally engaged with cross-dressing, see Garber, *Vested Interests,* 382–90.

40. Deleuze and Guattari, *Thousand Plateaus,* 28–29. Marjorie Garber, in *Dog Love,* writes about the dogs in Freud's own life, from "Wolf," the first black Alsatian dog that he gives to his daughter Anna in 1925, to "a succession of chows" who "became in his later years his closest companions" (136–37).

41. H. James, "Beast in the Jungle," 401.

42. Sedgwick, *Epistemology,* 201. Subsequent text references are to page numbers in this edition.

43. Recent work in queer studies tends to affirm Sedgwick's reading. Roger Lancaster, in *The Trouble with Nature,* for example, states that "in James's coded text, the beast that lurks within is closeted homosexual desire" (264), with the implication that the beast eventually enforces the closet.

44. H. James, "Beast in the Jungle," 379, 385–87. Subsequent text references are to page numbers in this edition.

45. Sedgwick, *Epistemology,* 207.

46. H. James, "Beast," 401.

47. Sedgwick, *Epistemology,* 208.

48. Freud, *Complete Psychological Works*, vol. 10, 166. Subsequent text references are to page numbers in this edition.

49. In support of her reading, Sedgwick quotes an interesting passage from James's *Notebooks*, written in 1905, that could actually be seen, from my perspective, as resonating with Chauncey's indication that the partners of queer "wolves" were often called "lambs" and "kids." In what Sedgwick calls a "pregnant address to James's male muse," the entry invokes "the full summer days of L[amb] H[ouse]" (H. James, "Notebooks," 318, quoted in *Epistemology*, 208n33).

50. H. James, "Beast," 359–60.

51. Sedgwick, *Epistemology*, 212.

52. H. James, "Beast," 361. Subsequent text references are to page numbers in this edition.

53. Kipling, *Jungle Books*, 257. Subsequent text references are to page numbers in this edition.

2 BETWEEN SPECIES

1. See Mark Seltzer, *Bodies and Machines*, 166–72.

2. Auerbach, *Male Call*, 9.

3. Derrick, "Making a Heterosexual Man," 255n21. Derrick draws upon biographies of London, such as Andrew Sinclair's *Jack: A Biography of Jack London* (1977), to support these claims, and also provides a good condensed summary of debates in the scholarship over suggestions of homosexuality in London's life.

4. Auerbach, *Male Call*, 179–80.

5. Ibid., 179.

6. Partridge, *Slang To-Day and Yesterday*, 467.

7. Ibid., 446.

8. London, *Novels and Stories*, 494. Subsequent text references are to page numbers in this edition.

9. See, for example, Auerbach, *Male Call*, 178–226; Derrick "Making"; and Howard, *Form and History*, 111–14.

10. Partridge, *Slang*, 444.

11. London, *Novels and Stories*, 593. Subsequent text references are to page numbers in this edition. For an example of a reading that resists any suggestions of homosexuality in the novel, see Baskett, "Sea Change in *The Sea Wolf*." Other critics in this vein have linked Wolf's "beauty" to the evolution of elaborate ornamentation in males of a species, such as the peacock, in relation to sexual selection. Bert Bender, for example, reads *The Sea Wolf* as a "narrative of sexual love" in which Maud ultimately chooses Hump over Wolf, who represents not only male beauty but also an animalized brutality that has not yet evolved a human sense of morality. Bender also suggests that homosexuality, bisexuality, androgyny, and hermaphroditism are essentially all linked together and "normal" from a Darwinian perspective. See Bender, *Evolution*, 76–78.

12. For more on colonial dimensions of the "South Seas" here, see Neel Ahuja, "Contradictions." See also Colleen Lye, *America's Asia*.

13. Auerbach, *Male Call*, 212.

14. Ibid., 213.

15. Derrick, "Making," 110.

16. Ibid., 111.

17. Howard, *Form and History*, 174.

18. Ibid., 173.

19. Ibid., 174.

20. Baskett, "Sea Change," 108.

21. Derrick, "Making," 254n9. For a good summary of other limitations of the "androgyny" argument, see also 256n23.

22. Auerbach, *Male Call*, 214–15.

23. Derrick, "Making," 114–15.

24. Ibid., 118.

25. London, *Novels and Stories*, 687.

26. Ibid.

27. Garber, *Vested Interests*, 11.

28. Ibid., 16

29. Ibid., 16, 17 (original emphasis).

30. Mark Seltzer's reading of this scene in *Bodies and Machines* emphasizes it as a mechanical problem Hump must figure out. Seltzer's conclusion is that "The problem in mechanics is the appropriate form of the making of men in machine culture, the form of virgin birth proper to that culture.... This is what sex in machine culture looks like" (171). While Seltzer's larger arguments about naturalism and turn-of-the-century anxieties over the lines between bodies and machines, between the natural and the unnatural, are useful for my own project, they do not pay enough attention, in my view, to the histories of "the jungle" I am suggesting here.

31. London, *Novels and Stories*, 757.

32. Ibid., 757–58.

33. I owe the formulation of this question to Donald Pease, and I am grateful for his comments on an earlier version of this discussion.

34. Partridge, *Slang*, 463.

35. London, *Novels and Stories*, 758 (my emphasis). Subsequent text references are to page numbers in this edition.

36. Chauncey, *Gay New York*, 27.

37. Ibid.

38. Derrick, "Making," 126. Subsequent text references are to page numbers in this edition.

39. See Sedgwick, *Between Men*.

40. Auerbach, *Male Call*, 216.

41. Ibid., 215–22.

42. London, *Novels and Stories*, 580. Subsequent text references are to page numbers in this edition.

43. Chauncey, *Gay New York*, 70.

44. Ibid., 85.

45. London, *Novels and Stories*, 59–60. Subsequent text references to *Call of the Wild* are to page numbers in this edition.

46. London, *Novels and Stories*, 244. Subsequent text references to *White Fang* are to pages numbers in this edition.

47. Derrick, "Making," 122.

48. London, *Novels and Stories*, 85.

49. Ibid., 276.

50. Ibid., 283–84.

51. I borrow and extend the idea of "cross-species drag" here from David Mazel, who uses the phrase in a narrower sense in his study of the social construction and performance of "wilderness" in the work of James Fenimore Cooper and the field of ecocriticism. Mazel focuses on what might be called "literal" drag performances in *The Last of the Mohicans*, in which a beaver colony, for instance, is originally mistaken for an Indian village, or Chingachgook dresses up and passes as a beaver. See Mazel, "Performing 'Wilderness,'" 101–14.

52. London, *Novels and Stories*, 33.

53. Ibid., 34.

54. Ibid., 77–78.

55. Auerbach, *Male Call*, 84.

56. Ibid., 105.

57. Auerbach's basic argument, that London's human and nonhuman stories are as much about constructing his own identity as a writer as anything else, is provocative and interesting. But any investment in discourses of sexuality is quickly subordinated to a methodology that relies upon biographical material to an extent I find less useful for placing London's work in the context of turn-of-the-century constructions of animality.

58. See Derrida, "Animal," 415–16.

59. Deleuze and Guattari, *Thousand Plateaus*, 279 (original emphasis).

60. Ibid., 259. For an explanation, as well as a critique, of the idea of "becoming-animal," see Haraway, *When Species Meet*, 27–30. For an important critique of Haraway's reading of Deleuze and Guattari in this regard, however, along with a cogent explanation of Deleuze and Guattari's broader project, see Frida Beckman, *Between Pleasure and Desire*.

61. For a good introduction to issues of sex in Deleuze and Guattari, see Frida Beckman's introduction to *Deleuze and Sex* titled "What Is Sex? An Introduction to the Sexual Philosophy of Gilles Deleuze."

62. Garber, *Dog Love*, 120.

63. Ibid.

64. London, *Novels and Stories*, 273.

65. Garber, *Dog Love*, 121. Subsequent text references are to page numbers in this edition.

66. Garber cites the research of Dekkers, as well as others, for literary examples of cross-species sex back to the third century in Rome. See *Dog Love*, 143–44.

67. Dekkers, *Dearest Pet*, 31. See also Alphonso Lingis, who takes a cue from Deleuze and Guattari in his experimental vision of a sexuality that includes both human and nonhuman sexual objects ("Animal Body," 165–82); his piece is undermined, from my perspective, by "biological" distinctions between "the animal" and "culture."

68. Ibid., 189.

69. Ibid., 189–90.

70. Garber, *Dog Love*, 158.

71. Darwin, *Expression of the Emotions*, 168. Subsequent text references are to page numbers in this edition.

72. Deleuze writes about foldings in relation to Foucault in "Foldings, or the Inside of Thought (Subjectivation)," which is the last chapter of his *Foucault*. For more on this aspect of Deleuze's work in relation to sexuality, see Beckman, *Deleuze and Sex*.

73. I am thinking of "music," "yelling," and "folding" here more figuratively than literally, such that "yelling" could encompass various kinds of sounds produced by various species, and "folding" could relate to various kinds of touch or contact, regardless of whether a being has arms, paws, flippers, and so on. Other sensory modes could take priority as well. As a result, "folding" would not necessarily require a "hand" that can grasp an other (in Heidegger's sense that only humans have a "hand" that goes beyond merely a biological or utilitarian function). For more exploration of Derrida's critique of Heidegger on this point, see Cary Wolfe, *What is Posthumanism?*, 203–05. I want to thank an anonymous reader for Oxford University Press for reminding me of Darwin in this context, and Dan and Kristy Beachy-Quick for suggesting other metaphors for foldings that are intriguing to think about here as well: brain matter and bread dough.

74. Haraway, *When Species Meet*, 213. Subsequent text references are to page numbers in this edition.

75. Jacques Derrida's *The Animal That Therefore I Am* makes this point perhaps most forcefully in the context of Continental philosophy in order to show how human and nonhuman others need not be distinguished categorically. For an extended and useful discussion of Derrida's late work on "the question of the animal," see Wolfe, *What Is Posthumanism?*; see also Haraway's discussion of Derrida in *When Species Meet*, 19–27.

76. Hayward, "FINGERYEYES," 580. Subsequent text references are to page numbers in this article.

77. Haraway, *When Species Meet*, 215–19. Subsequent text references are to page numbers in this edition.

3 THE OCTOPUS AND THE CORPORATION

1. The cartoon is reprinted in Albert Shaw, *Cartoon History of Roosevelt's Career*, 76.

2. The cartoon is reprinted in Jacqueline Goldsby, *Spectacular Secret*, 31.

3. Norris, *Octopus*, 51. Subsequent text references are to page numbers in this edition.

4. For a collection of essays that explores "the monster" (with a tendency to universalize rather than call for historical and cultural specificity), see Jeffrey Jerome Cohen, *Monster Theory*. On the significance of "machine culture" at this historical moment, see Mark Seltzer, *Bodies and Machines*.

5. Other novels by Norris, such as *McTeague* and *Vandover and the Brute*, also raise significant questions about the shifting nature of animality that could be explored further. But *The Octopus* is my focus here partly because it has been the subject of influential criticism by Walter Benn Michaels that seems most relevant to thinking about the emerging discourse of the jungle.

6. Trachtenberg, *Incorporation of America*, 83.

7. Michaels, *Gold Standard*, 188–206. Michaels cites John P. Davis, *Corporations* (1905); Arthur W. Machen Jr., "Corporate Personality" (1911); George F. Canfield, "The Scope and Limits of the Corporate Entity Theory" (1917); and I. Maurice Wormser, *Disregard of the Corporate Fiction* (1927).

8. Ibid., 197.

9. Stone et al., *Constitutional Law*, 712.

10. Zinn, *People's History*, 254. Subsequent text references are to page numbers in this edition.

11. Garland, *Homestead*.

12. Ibid.

13. Ibid.

14. Michaels, *Gold Standard*, 211.

15. For more on constructions of animality within capitalism, particularly in relation to Marxist theory, see Nicole Shukin, *Animal Capital*.

16. Michaels, *Gold Standard*, 208.

17. *Oxford English Dictionary*.

18. *Webster's New Standard Dictionary*.

19. Norris, *Octopus*, 569. Subsequent text references are to page numbers in this edition.

20. *Oxford English Dictionary*.

21. Ibid.

22. Partridge, *Slang To-Day and Yesterday*, 426. See also Don Luskin, *History of "Bull" and "Bear"*; and Robert B. and J. Bradford De Long Barsky, "Bull and Bear Markets," 265–81.

23. Spencer, *Political Writings*, 179. Subsequent text references are to page numbers in this edition.

24. Offer, Introduction to *Political Writings*, xx–xxi.

25. Quoted in Trachtenberg, *Incorporation of America*, 84–85.

26. Carnegie, *Gospel of Wealth*, 16. Subsequent text references are to page numbers in this edition.

27. As Gail Bederman points out in *Manliness and Civilization*, the related anxiety over "race suicide" can be seen in such figures as Theodore Roosevelt, who was worried about "native-born white Americans' falling birth rate" and the possibility that the white race would "lose power and allow inferior races to surpass it in the Darwinistic quest for global supremacy" (200). See Bederman, *Manliness and Civilization*, 200.

28. Lochner v. New York, 54.

29. See Stone et al., *Constitutional Law*, 710–28.

4 THE WORKING-CLASS BEAST

1. The cartoon is reprinted in Shaw, *A Cartoon History of Roosevelt's Career*, 78.

2. "Coney Elephant Killed," 1.

3. On the birth of the animal welfare movement at the end of the nineteenth century, see chapter 5 of this book.

4. Ibid.

5. "Bad Elephant Killed," 5.

6. Ibid.

7. For a more recent history of Coney Island—one that lacks Kasson's emphasis on class politics—see Immerso, *Coney Island*.

8. Kasson, *Amusing the Million*, 50. Subsequent text references are to page numbers in this edition.

9. "Coney Elephant Killed," 1.

10. Ibid.

11. Ibid. Luna Park opened on May 16, 1903, lit up with 200,000 electric lights. During the first five years there were 31 million admissions collected, and 20 million in 1909 alone (including visits by Freud and Jung). See Immerso, *Coney Island*, 60, 81.

12. "Elephant Terrorizes," 5. Subsequent text references are to page numbers in this article.

13. Boland, "Elephant's Demise." The commentary was in response to a letter about Errol Morris's 1999 documentary *Mr. Death*, which includes footage of the electrocution.

14. Freud, *Complete Psychological Works*, vol. 21, 111.

15. Norris, *Octopus*, 38. Subsequent text references are to page numbers in this edition.

16. Starr, Introduction to *Octopus*, xxvi–xxvii.

17. Seltzer, *Bodies and Machines*, 33.

18. Ibid.

19. Norris, *Octopus*, 636. Subsequent text references are to page numbers in this edition.

20. Den Tandt, *Urban Sublime*, 76.

21. On the history of American encounters with "the machine," the classic source is Leo Marx's *Machine in the Garden*.

22. Seltzer, *Bodies and Machines*, 28.

23. Ibid., 31.

24. Ibid., 32.

25. Norris, *Octopus*, 634. Subsequent text references are to page numbers in this edition.

26. Palmer, *Jack Rabbits*, 54, 58. Subsequent text references are to page numbers in this report.

27. Donald Worster, in *Nature's Economy,* has shown that wolf eradication programs were intense during the Progressive Era, arguing that "for several decades, a major feature of the crusade for resource conservation was a deliberate campaign to destroy wild animals—one of the most efficient, well-organized, and well-financed such efforts in all of man's history" (261). With the creation of the Bureau of the Biological Survey in the Department of Agriculture in 1905, pamphlets were produced describing how to eliminate various animals. See, for example, Vernon Bailey, "Destruction of Wolves."

28. Quoted in Palmer, 51

29. Norris, *Octopus,* 272–73. Subsequent text references are to page numbers in this edition.

30. Sinclair, *Jungle*, 36.

31. Ibid.

32. Sinclair, *Autobiography*, 164.

33. Adams, *Sexual Politics*, 62–63.

34. Ibid., 63.

35. Howard, *Form and History*, 125.

36. Sinclair, *Jungle*, 34.

37. Ibid., 37.

38. Howard, *Form and History,* 159.

39. Sinclair, *Jungle,* 36. Subsequent text references are to page numbers in this edition.

40. On Frederick Winslow Taylor's *The Principles of Scientific Management* (1911) and the impact of his theories, see Howard, *Form and History*, 136–37.

41. De Gruson, *Lost First Edition,* 29. It is interesting to note that in the *Appeal to Reason* edition, "pig" is used throughout, rather than "hog," so that the initial phrase was the "pig-squeal of the jungle." According to the *OED*, "pig" could signify a female animal, as well as a police officer, or an ingot of metal. A "hog," though, would have been a "swine reared for slaughter; spec. a castrated male swine," or "a ten-cent piece," or a "railway locomotive" (by 1888). According to Godfrey Irwin's *American Tramp and Underworld Slang* (1931), both a "hog" and a "pig" could signify a locomotive; see also Eric Partridge, *Slang To-Day and Yesterday*. Sinclair's revision could thus be seen as ensuring that the gender of

the animal is male, and shifting the connotation from a police officer to an economic unit of measure.

42. Howard, *Form and History*, 158.

43. Ibid.

44. Sinclair, *Jungle*, 287. Subsequent text references are to page numbers in this edition.

45. Rick Halpern, among others, has written about the historical precedents of using black workers to break strikes in Chicago's Union Stock Yards. In 1894 they were used to defeat the Knights of Labor, and in 1904 they were used to defeat the Amalgamated Meat Cutters as well as the Butcher Workmen. See Halpern, "Race and Radicalism," 75.

46. See part 1 of this book for discussion of "wolf" sexualities at the turn of the century.

47. Sinclair, "What Life Means," 594.

48. Ibid., 592–93.

49. Howard, *Form and History,* 160. In *Monumental Anxieties*, Scott Derrick argues that *The Jungle* records "an aversion to the body and all of its fluids, smells, and processes": his general argument is that the novel registers a "gynephobic fear of the maternal body" that comes from "Sinclair's own abject dread of the feminine sources of his writing and the conflicted struggle for authority this dread produces"; "As it proceeds, *The Jungle*'s hatred of the capitalist burdens of social injustice, poverty, and suffering is increasingly indistinguishable from a gynephobic aversion to the body and all of its fluids, smells, and processes" (159–70). I find Derrick's argument interesting and useful, but I believe the aversion to the smells and fluids of the body derives more directly from constructions of animality at this moment.

50. Sinclair, *Jungle*, 309–10. Subsequent text references are to page numbers in this edition.

51. Just before introducing the speaker modeled after Debs, Sinclair describes the Pullman Strike of 1894, although not specifically mentioning it by name: "a strike of a hundred and fifty thousand railroad employees, and thugs had been hired by the railroads to commit violence, and the President of the United States had sent in troops to break the strike, by flinging the officers of the union into jail without trial" (310).

52. De Gruson, *Lost First Edition*, 318.

53. Sinclair, *Jungle*, 328.

54. Howard, *Form and History,* 159.

55. Folsom, "Sinclair's Escape from *The Jungle*," 248.

56. Quoted in Tucker, *Marx-Engels Reader,* 500.

57. Stromquist and Bergman, "Introduction," 1.

58. The titles of various labor histories continue to use the metaphor of "the jungle." See, for example, James R. Barrett, *Work and Community* and Thomas J. Jablonsky, *Pride in the Jungle*.

5 ARCHAEOLOGY OF A HUMANE SOCIETY

1. Darwin, *Descent of Man*, 644. Subsequent text references are to page numbers in this edition.
2. Whether or not Darwin himself was a racist is beside the point here, which is to highlight the racist *construction* of contemporary "savages" as somehow simultaneously living in the present but also representing the white man's evolutionary past, even if that kind of temporal disconnect seems to contradict Darwin's other conclusions about the evolution of human races or "subspecies." For more on Darwin's own thinking about race, including in relation to his British audience, see Beer *Darwin's Plots*. See also Desmond and James, *Darwin's Sacred Cause*.
3. Freud, *Complete Psychological Works*, vol. 13, 1.
4. W. James, *Essays, Comments, and Reviews*, 18.
5. I am tremendously grateful to Marlon Ross and Marianne DeKoven for their very helpful insights and suggestions in response to earlier versions of this chapter.
6. For an example of the white male fantasy of getting in touch with his wild animality, see the next chapter of this book on *Tarzan*. See also Bederman's chapter on G. Stanley Hall in *Manliness and Civilization*, 77–120.
7. Following Jacques Derrida in *The Animal That Therefore I Am*, I am conscious of the need for specificity when talking about animals, rather than reducing all species to *the* animal: "Confined within this catch-all concept, within this vast encampment of the animal, in this general signifier, within the strict enclosure of this definite article ('the Animal' and not 'animals'), as in a virgin forest, a zoo, a hunting or fishing ground, a paddock or an abattoir, a space of domestication, are all living things that man does not recognize as his fellows, his neighbors, or his brothers" (34). But there is a dominant discourse of animality that I have in mind here that constructs "the animal"—in both human and nonhuman animals—as naturally violent in the name of survival and heterosexual in the name of reproduction. In the case of humane reform, even when directed toward domesticated animals and persistent stereotypes of the loyal plantation Negro as a domesticated pet, there is still a construction of a white man's "animal instincts" that can be either restrained or indulged.
8. Carson, *Men, Beasts, and Gods*, 50–54.
9. Ibid., 55–58. For more on the history of animal welfare in England, see Harriet Ritvo, *The Animal Estate*.
10. Quoted in Coleman, *Humane Society Leaders*, 37.
11. Quoted in McCrea, *Humane Movement*, 12.
12. Carson, *Men, Beasts, and Gods*, 116–18. For more on the history of linking "humane" advocacy for animals with children, see Susan J. Pearson, *Rights of the Defenseless*.
13. Coleman, *Humane Society Leaders*, 259.
14. Ibid., 252.
15. Ibid., 264.

16. *Oxford English Dictionary.*

17. Ibid.

18. Ibid.

19. Webster et al., *Dictionary of the English Language*, 206.

20. Webster et al., *New Standard Dictionary.*

21. *Oxford English Dictionary.*

22. McCrea, *Humane Movement*, 12–15.

23. Finsen and Finsen, *Animal Rights*, 52.

24. McCrea, *Humane Movement*, 15. Subsequent text references are to page numbers in this edition.

25. Quoted in McCrea, *Humane Movement,* 91–92.

26. Ibid., 92.

27. Ibid.

28. M. Ross, *Manning the Race*, 41. For more on Darwinist constructions of race that could be used for either racist or antiracist arguments, see the epilogue to this book. In Darwin's own work, of course, one of the purposes of evolutionary theory is to explain how species evolve or change over time, which could then be used to argue against fixed differences between human races. In addition, Darwin's claim that all human races evolve from common ancestors could be used to argue for more equality, rather than "natural" hierarchies.

29. See Edward L. Ayers *Vengeance and Justice*; Donald R. Walker, *Penology for Profit*; and Mark Colvin, *Penitentiaries, Reformatories, and Chain Gangs.*

30. Quoted in Oshinsky, *"Worse Than Slavery,"* 110 (my emphasis).

31. Oshinsky, ibid., 109. Subsequent text references are to page numbers in this edition.

32. Lichtenstein, *Twice the Work*, 179. Subsequent text references are to page numbers in this edition.

33. Quoted in ibid., 159 (my emphasis).

34. Foucault, *Discipline and Punish*, 14. Subsequent text references are to page numbers in this edition.

35. Foucault's larger argument, that "man" as a knowing and knowable subject is first constructed at the beginning of the nineteenth century, similarly overlooks the significance of how "man" or "humanity" is changed through the later deployment of "animality." The link between the humane treatment or discipline of criminals and the humane treatment of animals that we see at the turn of the twentieth century in the United States has its roots in the work of Jeremy Bentham at the end of the eighteenth century, although Foucault does not make this connection. Foucault notes that Bentham's Panopticon prison design was likely inspired by Le Vaux's menagerie at Versailles, but Foucault does not mention Bentham's simultaneous advocacy for animals. Often quoted by historians of animal welfare movements, Bentham's famous statement in *Introduction to the Principles of Morals and Legislation* (1780) is: "The question is not, *Can they reason?* nor, Can they *talk?* but, Can they *suffer?*"

(qtd. in Salt, *Animals' Rights*, 145–46). Animal welfare historians follow Foucault, in a sense, by not juxtaposing these two sides of Bentham's "humane" (in the earlier Christian sense) impulse for reform. But the two sides continue to be related after humane discourse shifts.

36. Freud, *Complete Psychological Works*, vol. 13, 141–42.

37. Ibid., 17. For more on Freud's construction of "the primitive," see Marianna Torgovnick, *Gone Primitive*; Anne McClintock, *Imperial Leather*; and Ranjana Khanna, *Dark Continents*.

38. Darwin, *Descent of Man*, 644.

39. Evans, *Criminal Prosecution*, 15–16. Evans provides a fascinating history of "animal trials" in Europe in which animals seem to be granted agency and therefore responsibility for various "crimes."

40. P. E. Johnson, *Criminal Law*, 164.

41. Ibid.

42. Heat of passion defenses have been used, as Eve Sedgwick points out, even in cases where the concept of "homosexual panic" has been distorted to defend violence against gays and lesbians after alleged "come-ons." See Sedgwick, *Epistemology*, 20–21.

43. On legal definitions of "reasonable" or "unreasonable" emotions in such cases, see Kahan and Nussbaum, "Two Conceptions of Emotion in Criminal Law."

44. Hodes, *White Women, Black Men*, 2.

45. Ibid., 176.

46. Ibid.

47. Gunning, *Race, Rape, and Lynching*, 5.

48. M. B. Ross, *Manning the Race*, 10–11 (my emphasis). Ross's brilliant study has different priorities than mine in this chapter, such as his desire to "show how struggles to reform the notion of black manhood—in terms of citizenship, patriarchy, patronage, companionship, romance, militance, and male entitlement—have constantly worried, disrupted, and altered the dominant discourse on race and masculinity" (8).

49. Quoted in Bederman, *Manliness and Civilization*, 49.

50. Wells, "Case Stated," 6. Wells's work is excerpted in *Lynching in America: A History in Documents*, edited by Christopher Waldrep, which is an invaluable collection of documents and essays illustrating the complexities and differences among many different kinds of lynchings. For important studies of lynching, see Ayers, *Vengence and Justice*; Gunning, *Race, Rape, and Lynching*; Goldsby, *Spectacular Secret*; Gussow, *Seems Like Murder Here*; Hale, *Making Whiteness*; and Stokes, *Color of Sex*.

51. Quoted in Hodes, *White Women*, 204.

52. Quoted in ibid., 201.

53. Felton, "Needs of the Farmers' Wives," 144.

54. Ibid.

55. Manly, "Mrs. Fellows's Speech," 147.

56. For more on the Wilmington riot, see Hodes, *White Women,* 193–97.

57. Kilgo, "Inquiry Concerning Lynchings," 10.

58. Dorsey, "Answers," 199.

59. Ibid.

60. "Georgia," 7.

61. Wells, "Case Stated," 4. As Jacqueline Goldsby notes in *A Spectacular Secret,* the term "lynching" can represent not only hangings but also any form of extralegal murder perpetrated by white people against those identified as black. There are many racial atrocities that are not typically included when determining the number of lynchings in this period, suggesting that the violence was much more widespread than often acknowledged: "Despite the word's imprecision, and despite the fact that black people were 'lynched' in any number of ways (hanging, shooting, stabbing, burning, dragging, bludgeoning, drowning, and dismembering), similar atrocities that occurred in the course of race riots aren't called 'lynching,' nor are they factored into established inventories of lynching's death toll. Hundreds of murders and assaults occurred under the regimes of convict lease labor and debt peonage too, the accounts of which often describe what we would consider lynchings. Like the rapes of black women by white men, however, those atrocities aren't considered part of lynching's history" (10–11).

62. Bederman, *Manliness,* 47.

63. Wells, "Case Stated," 4 (my emphasis).

64. Bederman, *Manliness,* 71. Subsequent text references are to page numbers in this edition.

65. Other strategies could be seen as successful, though, such as what Goldsby identifies as "raising public consciousness about the violence, funding publication of a vibrant literature of resistance, and mobilizing select sectors of the national public for mass political action," along with the "state-based anti-lynching laws" successfully achieved through the work of Ida B. Wells after 1893–95 (317n12).

66. James does write about an "aboriginal capacity for murderous excitement," but it is at least a stretch to assume that the reference is to an "uncivilized savage" rather than something like an animal instinct.

67. W. James, *Essays, Comments, and Reviews,* 171. Subsequent text references are to page numbers in this edition.

68. For more on the antivivisection movement, see Mason, *Civilized Creatures,* 164–65.

69. J. W. Johnson, *Autobiography of an Ex-Colored Man,* 188, 191.

70. Ibid., 189.

71. For examples of lynching victims—both alive and dead—cut up for souvenirs, see Tolnay and Beck, *Festival of Violence.* Black bodies were often vivisected in the context of medical experiments as well, leading up to, perhaps most infamously, the Tuskegee Syphilis Study that began in 1932. See Reverby, *Tuskegee's Truths.*

6 BLACK SAVAGE, WHITE ANIMAL

1. Bederman, *Manliness and Civilization*, 219.

2. Kasson, *Houdini, Tarzan, and the Perfect Man*, 7.

3. Burroughs, *Tarzan*, 20. Subsequent text references are to page numbers in this edition.

4. As Rachel Adams points out in *Sideshow U.S.A.*, P. T. Barnum's famous exhibit known as "What Is It?" drew upon questions about the "missing link" between human and nonhuman primates, exhibiting a creature supposedly somewhere between "a lower order of MAN" and "a higher order of MONKEY," with characteristics of both an orangutan and a human being (36–37).

5. Bederman, *Manliness*, 228. Subsequent text references are to page numbers in this edition.

6. Torgovnick, *Gone Primitive*, 53.

7. Kasson, *Houdini, Tarzan*, 212.

8. Ibid.

9. Ibid., 214 (my emphasis).

10. Darwin, *Descent*, 633.

11. Burroughs, *Tarzan*, 71. Subsequent text references are to page numbers in this edition.

12. On the historically hyperbolic construction of all Africans as cannibals, see Torgovnick, *Gone Primitive*, 258n47. See also Berglund, *Cannibal Fictions*, 80–85.

13. The leopard is noted as the exception, calling to mind references to "the leopard's spots" in Jeremiah of the Christian Bible, Kipling's "just so" tale (1902), and Dixon's *Leopard's Spots* (1902).

14. Darwin, *Descent*, 644. Subsequent text references to this page number refer to this edition.

15. Freud, *Complete Psychological Works*, vol. 13, 1.

16. Ibid., 141–42. The banishment of Terkoz by the other apes when he is their ruler is thus reminiscent of Freud's primal scene fantasy in *Totem and Taboo*.

17. Torgovnick, *Gone Primitive*, 203. Subsequent text references are to page numbers in this edition.

18. Bederman, *Manliness*, 220.

19. Burroughs, Tarzan, 41. Subsequent text references are to page numbers in this edition.

20. I have in mind here Eric Lott's analysis of lynching photographs that not only problematize the desire to avoid being implicated in their violence but also register the complex context of forbidden interracial desire: "Look at the liberties taken with black men's bodies in these pictures, the murderous intimacy they reveal. The bodies oiled, roped, undressed; suspenders undone, belts askew, crotches exposed, genitals cut out. The bold sexual transgressions of which these men have been accused become the bold sexual transgressions of the lynchers themselves: hard not to feel

the charge of desire here, or white men's sympathetic identification with black out-laws of their own imaginations. To be sure, these are rites of exorcism that attempt to banish the 'shadow' of the black man. But this may be because black men are so intimately imagined in the first place—the lynching itself seems a way to convert interracial desire to disavowal" ("Strange and Bitter Spectacle").

21. Torgovnick, *Gone Primitive,* 50.
22. Burroughs, *Tarzan,* 180. Subsequent text references are to page numbers in this edition.
23. Torgovnick, *Gone Primitive,* 50.

EPILOGUE

1. Quoted in Moran, *Scopes Trial,* 121. Moran's work is particularly useful as both a transcript of the trial and a collection of media coverage and related materials.
2. Quoted in ibid., 122 (my emphasis).
3. Quoted in ibid., 126 (my emphasis).
4. Edward J. Larson has explored the Scopes trial, along with subsequent histories of evolution debates, in several influential books. See, for example, *Summer for the Gods; Trial and Error; Evolution;* and *Creation-Evolution Debate.*
5. Quoted in Moran, *Scopes Trial,* 170.
6. Ibid.
7. "Evolution Battle," 2.
8. "Ended at Last," 18.
9. Quoted in Leinwand, *William Jennings Bryan,* xvii.
10. Kazin, *Godly Hero,* 300.
11. Ibid., 301.
12. Bryan, "Cross of Gold Speech," 136, 137.
13. Ibid., 136, 146.
14. Kazin, *Godly Hero,* xv–xvii.
15. Bryan, "Cross of Gold," 38, 45.
16. Ibid., 46.
17. Boyer, *Enduring Vision,* vol. 2, 607, 641.
18. Larson, *Summer for the Gods,* 35.
19. Ibid., 38.
20. Kazin, *Godly Hero,* xix.
21. Ibid. For a powerful critique of a trend among scholars such as Kazin that priori-tizes the "common dreams" of ordinary people—centered on class solidarity—over racial differences, see Lott, *The Disappearing Liberal Intellectual.*
22. Bryan, "Prince of Peace," 139.
23. Ibid. (my emphasis).
24. Ibid., 140.
25. Bryan, "Race Problem," 170 (my emphasis).

26. Ibid., 73.

27. Ibid., 72

28. Ibid.

29. Bryan, *Last Message*, 30.

30. Ibid., 30–31.

31. Ibid., 17.

32. Leinwand, *William Jennings Bryan*, xvi.

33. According to Ronald L. Numbers in *Darwinism Comes to America*, it's doubtful that Scopes ever actually taught evolution from this textbook; he was primarily a teacher of algebra, physics, and chemistry when he volunteered to test the new anti-evolution law (86).

34. Quoted in Moran, *Scopes Trial*, 187. The quotations that follow from the *Baltimore Sun,* Du Bois, and the *Chicago Defender* are also taken from Moran; the page numbers cited in the text are from this edition.

35. Numbers, *Darwinism*, 88, 91.

36. For a brief sketch of the history of fundamentalist activism in relation to evolution after the Scopes trial, see Moran, *Scopes Trial*, 50–56.

37. Hofstadter, *Social Darwinism*, 202–03.

38. Foner, Introduction to *Social Darwinism,* xx.

39. Bannister, *Social Darwinism*, xxix–xxxi. On the history of the sociobiology debate, see Larson, *Evolution* (86); Levine, *Darwin Loves You* (93–128); and Andrew Ross, *Chicago Gangster*. On the subsequent "science wars" and the Sokal hoax, see Sokal's website, http://www.physics.nyu.edu/faculty/sokal/; Fromm, "My Science Wars"; Trindle, "The Missing Document"; Lott, "Blinded by Science"; and my "Emersonian Science Studies."

40. See, for example, Steven Pinker's *The Blank Slate: The Modern Denial of Human Nature* (2006) and Edward O. Wilson's *Consilience: The Unity of Knowledge* (1998). Both books are best sellers produced by Harvard scholars. See also the even more popular work, for example, of Helen Fisher, including *The Sex Contract* (1982); *Anatomy of Love* (1992); *The First Sex* (1999); and *Why We Love* (2004). Among so-called Literary Darwinists in the academy, the approach is not necessarily any more subtle. In *Literary Darwinism: Evolution, Human Nature, and Literature* (2004), for example, Joseph Carroll argues that "Darwin succeeds in analyzing human psychology and culture in ways that lead back through unbroken causal sequences to the elementary biological drives toward survival and reproduction. He is thus the first sociobiologist and the first evolutionary psychologist..." (viii). In the near future, according to Carroll, all social scientists (and presumably literary critics) "will have to accommodate themselves to the reality of what is empirically known about the biological basis of human behavior" (x).

41. Hofstadter, *Social Darwinism*, 204.

42. To be fair, influential work in evolutionary biology and cognitive neuroscience resists the charge of biological determinism by focusing on the complexities of

genes—and their ability to be switched on or off in response to environmental vari-ables—rather than animal instincts. As E. O. Wilson notes in his "Foreword from the Scientific Side" in *The Literary Animal: Evolution and the Nature of Narrative* (2005), "the brain is in fact intricately wired from birth. Human behavior is deter-mined by neither genes nor culture but instead by a complex interaction of these two prescribing forces, with biology guiding and environment specifying" (viii). Harold Fromm gives a good summary of this way of explaining consciousness, drawn from the cognitive neurosciences and the work of Wilson, Pinker, Daniel Dennett, and others, in "Muses, Spooks, Neurons, and the Rhetoric of Freedom."

43. See Bagemihl, *Biological Exuberance*; de Waal et al., *Primates and Philosophers*.

44. See also Giorgio Agamben on the human/animal binary in *The Open: Man and Animal*.

45. See, for example, Bekoff, *Minding Animals* and *Emotional Lives of Animals*.

Bibliography

Abelove, Henry. "Freud, Male Homosexuality, and the Americans." In *The Lesbian and Gay Studies Reader*, edited by Henry Abelove, Michele Aina Barale, and David M. Halperin, 381–93. New York: Routledge, 1993.

"About ICAS." *Critical Animal Studies*. Inst. for Critical Animal Studies. Accessed August 13, 2008. http://www.criticalanimalstudies.org/about/.

Adams, Carol J. *The Sexual Politics of Meat: A Feminist-Vegetarian Critical Theory*. 1990. New York: Continuum, 2000.

Adams, Rachel. *Sideshow U.S.A.: Freaks and the American Cultural Imagination*. Chicago: University of Chicago Press, 2001.

Agamben, Giorgio. *Homo Sacer: Sovereign Power and Bare Life*. Translated by Daniel Heller-Roazen. Palo Alto, CA: Stanford University Press, 1998.

———. *The Open: Man and Animal*. Translated by Kevin Attell. Palo Alto, CA: Stanford University Press, 2004.

Ahuja, Neel. "The Contradictions of Colonial Dependency: Jack London, Leprosy, and Hawaiian Annexation." *Journal of Literary and Cultural Disability Studies* 1.2 (2007): 15–28.

Alaimo, Stacy. "Eluding Capture: The Science, Culture, and Pleasure of 'Queer' Animals." In *Queer Ecologies: Sex, Nature, Biopolitics, Desire*, edited by Catriona Mortimer-Sandilands and Bruce Erickson, 15–36. Bloomington: Indiana University Press, 2010.

Allen, James, Hilton Als, Congressman John Lewis, and Leon F. Litwack. *Without Sanctuary: Lynching Photography in America*. Santa Fe: Twin Palms, 2000.

American Psychological Association, American Psychiatric Association, National Association of Social Workers, and Texas Chapter of the National Association of Social Workers. *Brief for Amici Curiae, in Support of Petitioners John Geddes Lawrence and Tyron Garner v. State of Texas*. January 2003. U.S. Supreme Court, No. 02–102. Accessed February 21, 2004. http://supreme.lp.findlaw.com/supreme_court/briefs/02-102/02-102.mer.ami.apa.pdf.

Animality Studies @ CSU. "Resources." Colorado State University, 2009–12. Accessed April 29, 2012. http://animalitystudies.colostate.edu/resources.htm.

Auerbach, Jonathan. *Male Call: Becoming Jack London*. Durham, NC: Duke University Press, 1996.

Ayers, Edward L. *Vengeance and Justice: Crime and Punishment in the 19th Century American South*. New York: Oxford University Press, 1984.

"Bad Elephant Killed: Topsy Meets Quick and Painless Death at Coney Island." *Commercial Advertiser*, January 5, 1903.

Bagemihl, Bruce. *Biological Exuberance: Animal Homosexuality and Natural Diversity*. New York: St. Martin's, 1999.

Bailey, Vernon. "Directions for the Destruction of Wolves and Coyotes." *Bureau of Biological Survey, U.S. Department of Agriculture* 55 (March 13, 1907): 1–6.

Baker, Steve. *The Postmodern Animal*. London: Reaktion, 2000.

Bannister, Robert C. *Social Darwinism: Science and Myth in Anglo-American Social Thought*. Philadelphia: Temple University Press, 1979.

Barrett, James R. *Work and Community in the Jungle: Chicago's Packinghouse Workers, 1894–1922*. Urbana: University of Illinois Press, 1987.

Barsky, Robert B., and J. Bradford De Long. "Bull and Bear Markets in the Twentieth Century." *Journal of Economic History* 50.2 (June 1990): 265–81.

Baskett, Sam S. "Sea Change in *The Sea-Wolf*." In *Rereading Jack London*, edited by Leonard Cassuto and Jeanne Campbell Reesman, 92–109. Palo Alto, CA: Stanford University Press, 1996.

Beckman, Frida. *Between Pleasure and Desire: Deleuze, Sexuality and (Be)coming*. Edinburgh: Edinburgh University Press, forthcoming.

———, ed. *Deleuze and Sex*. Edinburgh: Edinburgh University Press, 2011.

———. "What is Sex? An Introduction to the Sexual Philosophy of Gilles Deleuze." In *Deleuze and Sex*, edited by Frida Beckman, 1–29. Edinburgh: Edinburgh University Press, 2011.

Bederman, Gail. *Manliness and Civilization: A Cultural History of Gender and Race in the United States, 1880–1917*. Chicago: University of Chicago Press, 1995.

Beer, Gillian. *Darwin's Plots: Evolutionary Narrative in Darwin, George Eliot, and Nineteenth-Century Fiction*. 2nd ed. Cambridge: Cambridge University Press, 2000.

Bekoff, Marc. *Minding Animals: Awareness, Emotions, and Heart*. New York: Oxford University Press, 2002.

———. *The Emotional Lives of Animals: A Leading Scientist Explores Animal Joy, Sorrow, and Empathy—and Why They Matter*. Novato, CA: New World Library, 2007.

Bender, Bert. *The Descent of Love: Darwin and the Theory of Sexual Selection in American Fiction, 1871–1926*. Philadelphia: University of Pennsylvania Press, 1996.

———. *Evolution and "the Sex Problem": American Narratives during the Eclipse of Darwinism*. Kent, OH: Kent State University Press, 2004.

Berglund, Jeff. *Cannibal Fictions: American Explorations of Colonialism, Race, Gender, and Sexuality*. Madison: University of Wisconsin Press, 2006.

Bleakley, Alan. *The Animalizing Imagination: Totemism, Textuality and Ecocriticism*. New York: St. Martin's Press, 2000.

Boland, Ed, Jr. "An Elephant's Demise." *New York Times*, July 8, 2001, sec. F.Y.I.: CY2.

Bowler, Peter J. *Evolution: The History of an Idea*. 3rd ed. Berkeley: University of California Press, 2003.

Boyer, Paul S., et al. *The Enduring Vision: A History of the American People*. Vol. 2. 4th ed. Boston: Houghton Mifflin, 2000.

Bradford, Phillips Verner, and Harvey Blume. *Ota Benga: The Pygmy in the Zoo*. New York: St. Martin's, 1992.

Bryan, William Jennings. "The Cross of Gold Speech." In *William Jennings Bryan: Selections*, edited by Ray Ginger, 37–46. Indianapolis: Bobbs-Merrill, 1967.

——. *The Last Message of William Jennings Bryan*. New York: Fleming H. Revell, 1925.

——. "The Prince of Peace." In *William Jennings Bryan: Selections*, edited by Ray Ginger, 135–50. Indianapolis: Bobbs-Merrill, 1967.

——. "The Race Problem." In *William Jennings Bryan: Selections*, edited by Ray Ginger, 69–74. Indianapolis: Bobbs-Merrill, 1967.

Buell, Lawrence. *The Environmental Imagination: Thoreau, Nature Writing, and the Formation of American Culture*. Cambridge: Harvard University Press, 1995.

"A Bungling Experiment." *New York Times*, August 7, 1890, 4.

Burroughs, Edgar Rice. *Tarzan of the Apes*. 1914. New York: Penguin, 1990.

Burroughs, John. "Real and Sham Natural History." *Atlantic Monthly* 91 (March 1903): 298–309. Reprinted in *The Wild Animal Story*, edited by Ralph H. Lutts, 129–43. Philadelphia: Temple University Press, 1998.

Calarco, Matthew. *Zoographies: The Question of the Animal from Heidegger to Derrida*. New York: Columbia University Press, 2008.

Calarco, Matthew, and Peter Atterton, eds. *Animal Philosophy: Essential Readings in Continental Thought*. London: Continuum, 2004.

Carby, Hazel V. *Reconstructing Womanhood: The Emergence of the Afro-American Woman Novelist*. New York: Oxford University Press, 1987.

Carnegie, Andrew. *The Gospel of Wealth and Other Timely Essays*. 1900. Cambridge: Harvard University Press, 1962.

Carroll, Joseph. *Literary Darwinism: Evolution, Human Nature, and Literature*. New York: Routledge, 2004.

Carson, Gerald. *Men, Beasts, and Gods: A History of Cruelty and Kindness to Animals*. New York: Scribner's, 1972.

Chauncey, George. *Gay New York: Gender, Urban Culture, and the Makings of the Gay Male World, 1890–1940*. New York: Basic Books, 1994.

——, Nancy F. Cott, John D'Emilio, Estelle B. Freedman, Thomas C. Holt, John Howard, Lynn Hunt, Mark D. Jordan, Elizabeth Lapovsky Kennedy, and Linda P. Kerber. *Amicus Brief of Professors of History, in Support of Petitioners John Geddes Lawrence and Tyron Garner v. State of Texas*. January 2003. U.S. Supreme Court, No. 02–102. Accessed February 21, 2004. http://supreme.lp.findlaw.com/supreme_court/briefs/02–102/02–102.mer.ami.hist.pdf.

Cheyfitz, Eric. *The Poetics of Imperialism: Translation and Colonization from the Tempest to Tarzan*. Expanded ed. Philadelphia: University of Pennsylvania Press, 1997.

Clark, Edward B. "Roosevelt on the Nature Fakirs." *Everybody's Magazine* 16 (June 1907), 770–74. Reprinted in *The Wild Animal Story*, edited by Ralph H. Lutts, 164–71. Philadelphia: Temple University Press, 1998.

Cohen, Jeffrey Jerome, ed. *Monster Theory: Reading Culture*. Minneapolis: University of Minnesota Press, 1996.

Coleman, Sydney H. *Humane Society Leaders in America, with a Sketch of the Early History of the Humane Movement in England*. Albany, NY: American Humane Association, 1924.

Colvin, Mark. *Penitentiaries, Reformatories, and Chain Gangs: Social Theory and the History of Punishment in Nineteenth-Century America*. New York: St. Martin's, 1997.

"Coney Elephant Killed: Topsy Overcome with Cyanide of Potassium and Electricity." *New York Times*, January 5, 1903, 1.

Conniff, Richard. *The Ape in the Corner Office: Understanding the Workplace Beast in All of Us*. New York: Crown Business, 2005.

Crist, Eileen. *Images of Animals Anthropomorphism and Animal Mind*. Philadelphia: Temple University Press, 1998.

Cronon, William, ed. *Uncommon Ground: Rethinking the Human Place in Nature*. 2nd ed. New York: Norton, 1996.

Curtin, Deane W. *Chinnagounder's Challenge: The Question of Ecological Citizenship*. Bloomington: Indiana University Press, 1999.

Darwin, Charles. *The Descent of Man, and Selection in Relation to Sex*. 1871. Vols. 21 and 22 of *The Works of Charles Darwin*. Edited by Paul H. Barrett and R. B. Freeman. New York: New York University Press, 2010.

———. *The Expression of the Emotions in Man and Animals*. 1872. Vol. 23 of *The Works of Charles Darwin*. Edited by Paul H. Barrett and R. B. Freeman. New York: New York University Press, 2010.

———. *The Origin of Species*. 1859. Edited by Gillian Beer. Oxford: Oxford University Press, 1998.

Daston, Lorraine, and Gregg Mitman, eds. *Thinking with Animals: New Perspectives on Anthropomorphism*. New York: Columbia University Press, 2005.

Davis, Janet M. *The Circus Age: Culture and Society under the American Big Top*. Chapel Hill: University of North Carolina Press, 2002.

De Gruson, Gene, ed. *The Lost First Edition of Upton Sinclair's "The Jungle."* Memphis: Peachtree, 1988.

Dekkers, Midas. *Dearest Pet: On Bestiality*. Translated by Paul Vincent. London: Verso, 1994.

DeKoven, Marianne, and Michael Lundblad, eds. *Species Matters: Humane Advocacy and Cultural Theory*. New York: Columbia University Press, 2012.

Deleuze, Gilles. *Foucault*. Translated by Sean Hand. Minneapolis: University of Minnesota Press, 1988.

———, and Félix Guattari. *A Thousand Plateaus: Capitalism and Schizophrenia*. 1980. Translated by Brian Massumi. Minneapolis: University of Minnesota Press, 1987.

"Denounced in England." *New York Times*, August 7, 1890, 2.

Den Tandt, Christophe. *The Urban Sublime in American Literary Naturalism*. Urbana: University of Illinois Press, 1998.

Derrick, Scott. "Making a Heterosexual Man: Gender, Sexuality, and Narrative in the Fiction of Jack London." In *Rereading Jack London*, edited by Leonard Cassuto and Jeanne Campbell Reesman, 110–29. Palo Alto, CA: Stanford University Press, 1996.

———. *Monumental Anxieties: Homoerotic Desire and Feminine Influence in 19th Century U.S. Literature*. New Brunswick, NJ: Rutgers University Press, 1997.

Derrida, Jacques. "And Say the Animal Responded?" Translated by David Wills. In *Zoontologies: The Question of the Animal*, edited by Cary Wolfe, 121–46. Minneapolis: University of Minnesota Press, 2003.

———. *The Animal That Therefore I Am*. Edited by Marie-Louise Mallet. Translated by David Wills. New York: Fordham University Press, 2008.

———. "The Animal That Therefore I Am (More to Follow)." Translated by David Wills. *Critical Inquiry* 28.2 (2002): 369–418.

———. *The Beast and the Sovereign*. 2 vols. Edited by Michel Lisse, Marie-Louise Mallet, and Ginette Michaud. Translated by Geoffrey Bennington. Chicago: University of Chicago Press, 2009–10.

———. "'Eating Well,' or The Calculation of the Subject: An Interview with Jacques Derrida." In *Who Comes after the Subject?*, edited by Eduardo Cadava, Peter Connor, and Jean-Luc Nancy, 96–119. New York: Routledge, 1991.

Desmond, Adrian, and James Moore. *Darwin's Sacred Cause: How a Hatred of Slavery Shaped Darwin's Views on Human Evolution*. New York: Houghton Mifflin, 2009.

Dorsey, Hugh. "Hugh Dorsey Answers the Colored Welfare League of Augusta." *Augusta Chronicle*, May 25, 1918. Reprinted in *Lynching in America: A History in Documents*, edited by Christopher Waldrep, 198–99. New York: New York University Press, 2006.

"Elephant Terrorizes Coney Island Police." *New York Times*, December 6, 1902, 5.

"Ended at Last." *New York Times*, July 22, 1925, 18.

Evans, E. P. "Bugs and Beasts before the Law." *Atlantic Monthly* 54.322 (August 1884): 235–46.

———. *The Criminal Prosecution and Capital Punishment of Animals*. 1906. London: Faber, 1987.

———. *Evolutionary Ethics and Animal Psychology*. New York: D. Appleton, 1898.

———. "Medieval and Modern Punishment." *Atlantic Monthly* 54.323 (September 1884): 302–08.

"Evolution Battle Rages Out of Court." *New York Times*, July 22, 1925, 2.

"Far Worse Than Hanging: Kemmler's Death Proves an Awful Spectacle." *New York Times*, August 7, 1890, 1–2.

Felton, Rebecca Latimer. "Needs of the Farmers' Wives and Daughters." *Atlanta Journal*, August 12, 1897. Reprinted in *Lynching in America: A History in Documents*, edited by Christopher Waldrep, 143–44. New York: New York University Press, 2006.

Finsen, Lawrence, and Susan Finsen. *The Animal Rights Movement in America: From Compassion to Respect*. New York: Twayne, 1994.

Fisher, Helen. *Anatomy of Love: The Natural History of Monogamy, Adultery, and Divorce*. New York: Norton, 1992.

———. *The First Sex: The Natural Talents of Women and How They Are Changing the World*. New York: Random House, 1999.

———. *The Sex Contract: The Evolution of Human Behavior*. New York: Morrow, 1982.

———. *Why We Love: The Nature and Chemistry of Romantic Love*. New York: Holt, 2004.

Fleissner, Jennifer L. *Women, Compulsion, Modernity: The Moment of American Naturalism*. Chicago: University of Chicago Press, 2004.

Folsom, Michael Brewster. "Upton Sinclair's Escape from The Jungle: The Narrative Strategy and Suppressed Conclusion of America's First Proletarian Novel." *Prospects* 4 (1979): 237–66.

Foner, Eric. Introduction to *Social Darwinism in American Thought*, by Richard Hofstadter, ix–xxviii. Boston: Beacon, 1992.

Foucault, Michel. *Discipline and Punish: The Birth of the Prison* (originally published as *Surveiller et Punir*, 1975). Translated by Alan Sheridan. New York: Pantheon, 1977.

———. *The History of Sexuality, Volume 1: An Introduction* (originally published as *La Volenté de Savoir*, 1976). Translated by Robert Hurley. New York: Pantheon, 1978.

———. *The Order of Things: An Archaeology of the Human Sciences* (originally published as *Les Mots et les Choses*, 1966). New York: Vintage, 1994.

Freud, Sigmund. *The Standard Edition of the Complete Psychological Works of Sigmund Freud*. 24 vols. London: Hogarth Press, 1953–75.

Fromm, Harold. Letter to the Editor. *PMLA* 121.1 (2006): 297.

———. "Muses, Spooks, Neurons, and the Rhetoric of 'Freedom.'" *New Literary History* 36 (2005): 147–59.

———. "My Science Wars." *Hudson Review* 49.4 (1997): 599–609.

Fudge, Erica. *Brutal Reasoning: Animals, Rationality, and Humanity in Early Modern England*. Ithaca, NY: Cornell University Press, 2006.

———. *Perceiving Animals: Humans and Beasts in Early Modern English Culture*. Urbana: University of Illinois Press, 2002.

Gandal, Keith. *The Virtues of the Vicious: Jacob Riis, Stephen Crane and the Spectacle of the Slum*. New York: Oxford University Press, 1997.

Garber, Marjorie. *Dog Love*. New York: Simon and Schuster, 1996.

———. *Vested Interests: Cross-Dressing and Cultural Anxiety*. New York: Routledge, 1992.

Garland, Hamlin. *Homestead and Its Perilous Trades: Impressions of a Visit*. Originally published in *McClure's Magazine* (June 1894). Reprinted in *eHistory*. Ohio State University, 2012. Accessed August 3, 2012. http://ehistory.osu.edu/osu/mmh/HomesteadStrike1892/GarlandHomestead/GarlandHomestead.cfm.

"Georgia." *New York Times*, September 16, 1897. Reprinted in *Lynching in America: A History in Documents*, edited by Christopher Waldrep, 6–9. New York: New York University Press, 2006.

Giffney, Nora, and Myra J. Hird, eds. *Queering the Non/Human*. London: Ashgate, 2008.

Ginger, Ray, ed. *William Jennings Bryan: Selections*. Indianapolis: Bobbs-Merrill, 1967.

Glotfelty, Cheryll. "Introduction: Literary Studies in an Age of Environmental Crisis." In *The Ecocriticism Reader: Landmarks in Literary Ecology*, edited by Cheryll Glotfelty and Harold Fromm, xv–xxxvii. Athens: University of Georgia Press, 1996.

———, and Harold Fromm, eds. *The Ecocriticism Reader: Landmarks in Literary Ecology*. Athens: University of Georgia Press, 1996.

Goldsby, Jacqueline. *A Spectacular Secret: Lynching in American Life and Literature*. Chicago: University of Chicago Press, 2006.

Gottschall, Jonathan, and David Sloan Wilson. "Introduction: Literature—a Last Frontier in Human Evolutionary Studies." In *The Literary Animal: Evolution and the Nature of Narrative*, edited by Jonathan Gottschall and David Sloan Wilson, xvii–xxvi. Evanston, IL: Northwestern University Press, 2005.

———, eds. *The Literary Animal: Evolution and the Nature of Narrative*. Evanston, IL: Northwestern University Press, 2005.

Guha, Ramachandra. *Environmentalism: A Global History*. New York: Longman, 2000.

Gunning, Sandra. *Race, Rape, and Lynching: The Red Record of American Literature, 1890–1912*. New York: Oxford University Press, 1996.

Gussow, Adam. *Seems Like Murder Here: Southern Violence and the Blues Tradition*. Chicago: University of Chicago Press, 2002.

Hale, Grace Elizabeth. *Making Whiteness: The Culture of Segregation in the South, 1890–1940*. New York: Pantheon, 1998.

Hale, Nathan G. *Freud and the Americans: The Beginnings of Psychoanalysis in the United States, 1876–1917*. New York: Oxford University Press, 1971.

Halperin, David M. *How to Do the History of Homosexuality*. Chicago: University of Chicago Press, 2002.

Halpern, Rick. "Race and Radicalism in the Chicago Stockyards: The Rise of the Chicago Packinghouse Workers Organizing Committee." In *Unionizing the Jungles: Labor and Community in the Twentieth-Century Meatpacking Industry*, edited by Shelton Stromquist and Marvin Bergman, 75–95. Iowa City: University of Iowa Press, 1997.

Ham, Jennifer, and Matthew Senior, eds. *Animal Acts: Configuring the Human in Western History*. New York: Routledge, 1997.

H-Animal Discussion Network. "Resources." *H-Net: Humanities and Social Sciences Online*. Michigan State University, 1995–2006. Accessed August 13, 2008. http://www.h-net.org/~animal/resources.html.

Haraway, Donna. *The Companion Species Manifesto: Dogs, People, and Significant Otherness*. Chicago: Prickly Paradigm Press, 2003.

———. *Primate Visions: Gender, Race, and Nature in the World of Modern Science*. New York: Routledge, 1989.

———. *Simians, Cyborgs, and Women: The Reinvention of Nature*. New York: Routledge, 1991.

———. "Teddy Bear Patriarchy: Taxidermy in the Garden of Eden, New York City, 1908–1936." In *Cultures of United States Imperialism*, edited by Amy Kaplan and Donald E. Pease, 237–91. Durham. NC: Duke University Press, 1993.

———. *When Species Meet*. Minneapolis: University of Minnesota Press, 2008.

Hayward, Eva. "FINGERYEYES: Impressions of Cup Corals." *Cultural Anthropology* 25.4 (2010): 577–99.

Hochman, Jhan. *Green Cultural Studies: Nature in Film, Novel, and Theory*. Moscow: University of Idaho Press, 1998.

Hodes, Martha. *White Women, Black Men: Illicit Sex in the 19th-Century South*. New Haven: Yale University Press, 1997.

Hofstadter, Richard. *Social Darwinism in American Thought*. 1944. Boston: Beacon, 1992.

"Hope Again for Kemmler: Snatched from Death at the Last Moment." *New York Times*, April 30, 1890, 1.

Howard, June. *Form and History in American Literary Naturalism*. Chapel Hill: University of North Carolina Press, 1985.

Immerso, Michael. *Coney Island: The People's Playground*. New Brunswick, NJ: Rutgers University Press, 2002.

Institute for Critical Animal Studies. "About ICAS." *Critical Animal Studies*. Accessed August 13, 2008. http://www.criticalanimalstudies.org/about.htm.

Irwin, Godfrey. *American Tramp and Underworld Slang*. New York: Sears Publishing, 1931.

Jablonsky, Thomas J. *Pride in the Jungle: Community and Everyday Life in Back of the Yards Chicago*. Baltimore: Johns Hopkins University Press, 1993.

James, Henry. "The Beast in the Jungle." 1903. In Vol. 11 of *The Complete Tales of Henry James*, edited by Leon Edel, 351–402. Philadelphia: Lippincott, 1964.

———. *The Notebooks of Henry James*. Edited by F. O. Matthiessen and Kenneth B. Murdock. New York: Oxford University Press, 1947.

James, William. *Essays, Comments, and Reviews*. Cambridge: Harvard University Press, 1987.

Jameson, Fredric. *Postmodernism, or, the Cultural Logic of Late Capitalism*. Durham, NC: Duke University Press, 1991.

Johnson, James Weldon. *The Autobiography of an Ex-Coloured Man.* 1912. New York: Vintage, 1989.

Johnson, Phillip E. *Criminal Law: Cases, Materials, and Text.* 6th ed. St. Paul, MN: West Group, 2000.

Jordan, Winthrop D. *White over Black: American Attitudes toward the Negro, 1550–1812.* Chapel Hill: University of North Carolina Press, 1968.

Kahan, Dan M., and Martha C. Nussbaum, "Two Conceptions of Emotion in Criminal Law." *Columbia Law Review* 96.2 (1996): 269–374.

Kaplan, Amy. *The Anarchy of Empire in the Making of U.S. Culture.* Cambridge: Harvard University Press, 2002.

Kaplan, Amy, and Donald E. Pease, eds. *Cultures of United States Imperialism.* Durham, NC: Duke University Press, 1993.

Karlin, Daniel. Introduction to *The Jungle Books*, edited by Daniel Karlin, 7–27. New York: Penguin, 1987.

Kasson, John F. *Amusing the Million: Coney Island at the Turn of the Century.* New York: Hill and Wang, 1978.

———. *Houdini, Tarzan, and the Perfect Man: The White Male Body and the Challenge of Modernity in America.* New York: Hill and Wang, 2001.

Kazin, Michael. *A Godly Hero: The Life of William Jennings Bryan.* New York: Knopf, 2006.

Khanna, Ranjana. *Dark Continents: Psychoanalysis and Colonialism.* Durham, NC: Duke University Press, 2003.

Kilgo, John Carlisle. "An Inquiry Concerning Lynchings." *South Atlantic Quarterly* 1 (January 1902): 4–9. Reprinted in *Lynching in America: A History in Documents*, edited by Christopher Waldrep, 9–11. New York: New York University Press, 2006.

Kinsey, Alfred C. et al. *Sexual Behavior in the Human Female.* 1953. Bloomington, IN: Indiana University Press, 1998.

———. *Sexual Behavior in the Human Male.* 1948. Bloomington, IN: Indiana University Press, 1998.

Kipling, Rudyard. *The Jungle Books.* New York: Penguin, 1987.

Lancaster, Roger N. *The Trouble with Nature: Sex in Science and Popular Culture.* Berkeley: University of California Press, 2003.

Larson, Edward J. *The Creation-Evolution Debate: Historical Perspectives.* Athens: University of Georgia Press, 2007.

———. *Evolution: The Remarkable History of a Scientific Theory.* New York: Modern Library, 2004.

———. *Summer for the Gods: The Scopes Trial and America's Continuing Debate over Science and Religion.* New York: Basic Books, 1997.

———. *Trial and Error: The American Controversy over Creation and Evolution.* 3rd ed. New York: Oxford University Press, 2003.

Lasch, Christopher. *The True and Only Heaven: Progress and Its Critics*. New York: Norton, 1991.

Legman, Gershon. "The Language of Homosexuality: An American Glossary." In *Sex Variants: A Study of Homosexual Patterns*. Vol. 2. Appendix VII, edited by George W. Henry, 1149–79. New York: P. B. Hoeber, 1941.

Leinwand, Gerald. *William Jennings Bryan: An Uncertain Trumpet*. Lanham, MD: Rowman and Littlefield, 2007.

Levine, George. *Darwin and the Novelists: Patterns of Science in Victorian Fiction*. 2nd ed. Chicago: University of Chicago Press, 1991.

———. *Darwin Loves You: Natural Selection and the Re-enchantment of the World*. Princeton: Princeton University Press, 2006.

Lichtenstein, Alex. *Twice the Work of Free Labor: The Political Economy of Convict Labor in the New South*. London: Verso, 1996.

Lingis, Alphonso. "Animal Body, Inhuman Face." In *Zoontologies: The Question of the Animal*, edited by Cary Wolfe, 165–82. Minneapolis: University of Minnesota Press, 2003.

Lippit, Akira Mizuta. *Electric Animal: Toward a Rhetoric of Wildlife*. Minneapolis: University of Minnesota Press, 2000.

Lochner v. New York. 198 U.S. 45. U.S. Supreme Court 1905.

London, Jack. *Jack London: Novels and Stories*. New York: Library of America, 1982.

———. "The Other Animals." *Collier's* 41 (September 1908): 10–11, 25–26. Reprinted in *The Wild Animal Story*, edited by Ralph H. Lutts, 199–210. Philadelphia: Temple University Press, 1998.

Long, William J. "I Propose to Smoke Roosevelt Out." *New York Times Magazine*, June 2, 1907, 2. Reprinted in *The Wild Animal Story*, edited by Ralph H. Lutts, 172–81. Philadelphia: Temple University Press, 1998.

———. "The Modern School of Nature-Study and Its Critics." *North America Review* 176 (May 1903): 687–696. Reprinted in *The Wild Animal Story*, edited by Ralph H. Lutts, 144–52. Philadelphia: Temple University Press, 1998.

———. Preface to *Northern Trails*. Boston: Ginn, 1905. Reprinted in *The Wild Animal Story*, edited by Ralph H. Lutts, 72–75. Philadelphia: Temple University Press, 1998.

Lott, Eric. "Blinded by Science." Review of *Fashionable Nonsense: Postmodern Intellectuals' Abuse of Science*, by Alan Sokal and Jean Bricmont. *Village Voice*. December 1998. Accessed June 26, 2007. http://www.villagevoice.com/specials/vls/159/lott.shtml.

———. *The Disappearing Liberal Intellectual*. New York: Basic Books, 2006.

———. *Love and Theft: Blackface Minstrelsy and the American Working Class*. New York: Oxford University Press, 1993.

———. "A Strange and Bitter Spectacle: James Allen's *Without Sanctuary: Lynching Photography in America*." *First of the Month: A Website of the Radical Imagination* June 2002. Accessed May 30, 2007. http://www.firstofthemonth.org/archives/2002/06/a_strange_and_b.html.

Lundblad, Michael. "Archaeology of a Humane Society: Animality, Savagery, Blackness." In *Species Matters: Humane Advocacy and Cultural Theory*, edited by Marianne DeKoven and Michael Lundblad, 75–102. New York: Columbia University Press, 2012.

———. "Emersonian Science Studies and the Fate of Ecocriticism." *ISLE: Interdisciplinary Studies in Literature and Environment* 10.2 (2003): 111–34.

———. "Epistemology of the Jungle: Progressive-Era Sexuality and the Nature of the Beast." *American Literature* 81.4 (2009): 747–73.

———. "From Animal to Animality Studies." *PMLA* 124.2 (2009): 496–502.

Luskin, Don. *The History of "Bull" and "Bear."* May 15, 2001. *TheStreet.com*. Accessed May 6, 2004. http://www.thestreet.com/comment/openbook/1428176.html.

Lutts, Ralph H. *The Nature Fakers: Wildlife, Science and Sentiment*. Charlottesville: University Press of Virginia, 2001.

———, ed. *The Wild Animal Story*. Philadelphia: Temple University Press, 1998.

Lye, Colleen. *America's Asia: Racial Form and American Literature, 1893–1945*. Princeton: Princeton University Press, 2005.

Maddox, Lucy, ed. *Locating American Studies: The Evolution of a Discipline*. Baltimore: Johns Hopkins University Press, 1999.

Magdoff, Henry. *Imperialism: From the Colonial Age to the Present*. New York: Monthly Review, 1978.

Malamud, Randy. *Reading Zoos: Representations of Animals and Captivity*. New York: New York University Press, 1998.

Manly, Alexander. "Mrs. Fellows's Speech." *Wilmington Daily Record*, August 18, 1898. Reprinted in *Lynching in America: A History in Documents*, edited by Christopher Waldrep, 146–47. New York: New York University Press, 2006.

Marx, Leo. *The Machine in the Garden: Technology and the Pastoral Ideal in America*. 2nd ed. Oxford: Oxford University Press, 2000.

Mason, Jennifer. *Civilized Creatures: Urban Animals, Sentimental Culture, and American Literature, 1850–1900*. Baltimore: Johns Hopkins University Press, 2005.

Massumi, Brian. "Translator's Foreword: Pleasures of Philosophy." In *A Thousand Plateaus: Capitalism and Schizophrenia*, by Gilles Deleuze and Felix Guattari, ix–xv. Minneapolis: University of Minnesota Press, 1987.

Mazel, David. "Performing 'Wilderness' in *The Last of the Mohicans*." In *Reading under the Sign of Nature: New Essays in Ecocriticism*, edited by John Tallmadge and Henry Harrington, 101–14. Salt Lake City: University of Utah Press, 2000.

McClintock, Anne. *Imperial Leather: Race, Gender, and Sexuality in the Colonial Conquest*. New York: Routledge, 1995.

McCrea, Roswell C. *The Humane Movement: A Descriptive Survey*. 1910. College Park, MD: McGrath, 1969.

Michaels, Walter Benn. *The Gold Standard and the Logic of Naturalism: American Literature at the Turn of the Century*. Berkeley: University of California Press, 1987.

Miller, Jonathan. "New Love Breaks up a 6-Year Relationship at the Zoo." *New York Times*, September 24, 2005. http://www.nytimes.com.

Mitman, Gregg. *Reel Nature: America's Romance with Wildlife on Film*. Cambridge: Harvard University Press, 1999.

Moran, Jeffrey P. *The Scopes Trial: A Brief History with Documents*. New York: Palgrave, 2002.

Morris, Errol, director. *Mr. Death*. Lions Gate, 1999.

"Negro Lynched with Torture." *New York Times*, October 31, 1895, 14.

Nelson, Barney. *The Wild and the Domestic: Animal Representation, Ecocriticism, and Western American Literature*. Reno: University of Nevada Press, 2000.

Norris, Frank. *The Octopus: A Story of California*. 1901. New York: Penguin, 1994.

Numbers, Ronald L. *Darwinism Comes to America*. Cambridge: Harvard University Press, 1999.

Offer, John. Introduction to *Political Writings*, by Herbert Spencer, vii–xxix. Cambridge: Cambridge University Press, 1994.

Oshinsky, David M. *"Worse Than Slavery": Parchman Farm and the Ordeal of Jim Crow Justice*. New York: Free Press, 1996.

Oxford English Dictionary. 2nd ed. Oxford: Oxford University Press, 1989. http://dictionary.oed.com/.

Palmer, T. S. *The Jack Rabbits of the United States*. Washington, DC: Government Printing Office, 1896.

Partridge, Eric. *Slang To-Day and Yesterday*. 3rd ed. New York: Macmillan, 1950.

Pearson, Susan J. *The Rights of the Defenseless: Protecting Animals and Children in Gilded Age America*. Chicago: University of Chicago Press, 2011.

Phillips, Dana. *The Truth of Ecology: Nature, Culture, and Literature in America*. New York: Oxford University Press, 2003.

Pickren, Wade, and Donald A. Dewsbury, eds. *Evolving Perspectives on the History of Psychology*. Washington, DC: American Psychological Association, 2002.

Pinker, Steven. *The Blank Slate: The Modern Denial of Human Nature*. New York: Viking, 2002.

Pizer, Donald, ed. *The Cambridge Companion to American Realism and Naturalism: Howells to London*. Cambridge: Cambridge University Press, 1995.

———, ed. *Documents of American Realism and Naturalism*. Carbondale: Southern Illinois University Press, 1998.

Price, Jennifer. *Flight Maps: Adventures with Nature in Modern America*. New York: Basic Books, 1999.

Reesman, Jeanne Campbell. *Jack London's Racial Lives: A Critical Biography*. Athens: University of Georgia Press, 2009.

Reverby, Susan M., ed. *Tuskegee's Truths: Rethinking the Tuskegee Syphilis Study*. Chapel Hill: University of North Carolina Press, 2000.

Ritvo, Harriet. *The Animal Estate: The English and Other Creatures in the Victorian Age*. Cambridge: Harvard University Press, 1987.

Ritvo, Lucille B. *Darwin's Influence on Freud: A Tale of Two Sciences*. New Haven: Yale University Press, 1990.

Roberts, Dorothy. *Killing the Black Body: Race, Reproduction, and the Meaning of Liberty*. New York: Pantheon, 1997.

Rolfe, John, and Peter Troob. *Monkey Business: Swinging through the Wall Street Jungle*. New York: Warner Books, 2000.

Roosevelt, Theodore. "'Nature Fakers.'" *Everybody's Magazine* 17 (September 1907): 427–30. Reprinted in *The Wild Animal Story*, edited by Ralph H. Lutts, 192–98. Philadelphia: Temple University Press, 1998.

Rosenzweig, Saul. *The Historic Expedition to America (1909): Freud, Jung, and Hall the King-Maker, with G. Stanley Hall as Host and William James as Guest*. 2nd, rev. ed. St. Louis: Rana House, 1994.

Ross, Andrew. *The Chicago Gangster Theory of Life: Nature's Debt to Society*. London: Verso, 1994.

Ross, Marlon B. *Manning the Race: Reforming Black Men in the Jim Crow Era*. New York: New York University Press, 2004.

Rothfels, Nigel, ed. *Representing Animals*. Bloomington: Indiana University Press, 2002.

———. *Savages and Beasts: The Birth of the Modern Zoo*. Baltimore: Johns Hopkins University Press, 2002.

Roughgarden, Joan. *Evolution's Rainbow: Diversity, Gender, and Sexuality in Nature and People*. Berkeley: University of California Press, 2004.

Russett, Cynthia Eagle. *Darwin in America: The Intellectual Response, 1865–1912*. San Francisco: W. H. Freeman, 1976.

Said, Edward W. *Culture and Imperialism*. New York: Knopf, 1993.

———. "Jungle Calling." In *Reflections on Exile and Other Essays*, 327–36. Cambridge: Harvard University Press, 2000.

Salt, Henry S. *Animals' Rights: Considered in Relation to Social Progress*. 1892. Clarks Summit, PA: Society for Animal Rights, 1980.

Scopes, John Thomas, William Jennings Bryan, and Tennessee. County Court (Rhea Co.). *The World's Most Famous Court Trial, State of Tennessee v. John Thomas Scopes; Complete Stenographic Report of the Court Test of the Tennessee Anti-Evolution Act at Dayton, July 10 to 21, 1925, Including Speeches and Arguments of Attorneys*. New York: Da Capo Press, 1971.

Sedgwick, Eve Kosofsky. *Between Men: English Literature and Male Homosocial Desire*. New York: Columbia University Press, 1985.

———. *Epistemology of the Closet*. Berkeley: University of California Press, 1990.

Seitler, Dana. *Atavistic Tendencies: The Culture of Science in American Modernity*. Minneapolis: University of Minnesota Press, 2008.

Seltzer, Mark. *Bodies and Machines*. New York: Routledge, 1992.

Shannon, Laurie. "The Eight Animals in Shakespeare; or, Before the Human." *PMLA* 124.2 (2009): 472–79.

"She Called for the Torch." *New York Times*, February 22, 1892, 5.

Shaw, Albert. *A Cartoon History of Roosevelt's Career*. New York: Review of Reviews Co., 1910.

Shukin, Nicole. *Animal Capital: Rendering Life in Biopolitical Times*. Minneapolis: University of Minnesota Press, 2009.

Sinclair, Andrew. *Jack: A Biography of Jack London*. New York: Harper and Row, 1977.

Sinclair, Upton. *The Autobiography of Upton Sinclair*. New York: Harcourt, Brace and World, 1962.

———. *The Jungle*. 1906. New York: Norton, 2003.

———. *The Lost First Edition of Upton Sinclair's the Jungle*. Edited by Gene De Gruson. Memphis: Peachtree, 1988.

———. "What Life Means to Me." *Cosmopolitan* 41.6 (October 1906): 591–95.

Singer, Peter. *Animal Liberation*. 1975. 3rd ed. New York: Random House, 2002.

Slater, Candace. "Amazonia as Edenic Narrative." In *Uncommon Ground: Rethinking the Human Place in Nature*, 2nd ed., edited by William Cronon, 114–31. New York: Norton, 1996.

Smith, Dinitia. "Love That Dare Not Squeak Its Name." *New York Times*, February 7, 2004, sec. Arts. http://www.nytimes.com.

Spencer, Herbert. *Political Writings*. Cambridge: Cambridge University Press, 1994.

Starr, Kevin. Introduction to *The Octopus: A Story of California*, by Frank Norris, vii–xxxi. New York: Penguin, 1986.

Stein, Edward. *The Mismeasure of Desire: The Science, Theory and Ethics of Sexual Orientation*. New York: Oxford University Press, 1999.

Stokes, Mason Boyd. *The Color of Sex: Whiteness, Heterosexuality, and the Fictions of White Supremacy*. Durham, NC: Duke University Press, 2001.

Stokes, Melvyn. *D. W. Griffith's The Birth of a Nation: A History of "The Most Controversial Motion Picture of All Time."* Oxford: Oxford University Press, 2007.

Stone, Geoffrey R., Louis M. Seidman, Cass R. Sunstein, and Mark V. Tushnet. *Constitutional Law*. 4th ed. New York: Aspen Law and Business, 2001.

Stromquist, Shelton, and Marvin Bergman. "Introduction: Unionizing the Jungles, Past and Present." In *Unionizing the Jungles: Labor and Community in the Twentieth-Century Meatpacking Industry*, edited by Shelton Stromquist and Marvin Bergman, 1–15. Iowa City: University of Iowa Press, 1997.

Terry, Jennifer. "'Unnatural Acts' in Nature: The Scientific Fascination with Queer Animals." *GLQ: A Journal of Lesbian and Gay Studies* 6.2 (2000): 151–93.

Tolnay, Stewart E., and E. M. Beck. *A Festival of Violence: An Analysis of Southern Lynchings, 1882–1930*. Urbana: University of Illinois Press, 1995.

Torgovnick, Marianna. *Gone Primitive: Savage Intellects, Modern Lives*. Chicago: University of Chicago Press, 1990.

Trachtenberg, Alan. *The Incorporation of America: Culture and Society in the Gilded Age*. New York: Hill and Wang, 1982.

Trindle, Carl. "The Missing Document: Or, Reviewing the Sokal Text." *Soundings* 82 (1999): 165–81.

Tucker, Robert C., ed. *The Marx-Engels Reader*. 2nd ed. New York: Norton, 1978.

United States Conference of Catholic Bishops. "Always Our Children: A Pastoral Message to Parents of Homosexual Children and Suggestions for Pastoral Ministers." June 24, 2003. *Committee for Family, Laity, Women and Youth*. Accessed February 20, 2004. http://www.usccb.org/laity/always.htm.

Waal, Frans B. M. de, and Frans Lanting. *Bonobo: The Forgotten Ape*. Berkeley: University of California Press, 1997.

Waal, Frans B. M. de, Robert Wright, Christine M. Korsgaard, Philip Kitcher, and Peter Singer. *Primates and Philosophers: How Morality Evolved*, edited by Stephen Macedo and Josiah Ober. Princeton: Princeton University Press, 2006.

Waldrep, Christopher, ed. *Lynching in America: A History in Documents*. New York: New York University Press, 2006.

Walker, Donald R. *Penology for Profit: A History of the Texas Prison System, 1867–1912*. College Station: Texas A&M University Press, 1988.

Webster, Noah, William Greenleaf Webster, and William Adolphus Wheeler. *A Dictionary of the English Language*. Academic ed. New York: Ivison Blakeman Taylor, 1878.

———. *Webster's New Standard Dictionary ... Based upon the Unabridged Dictionary of the English Language of Noah Webster*. New York: Syndicate, 1911.

Weeks, Jeffrey. "Remembering Foucault." *Journal of the History of Sexuality* 14.1/2 (2005): 186–201.

———. *Sexuality and Its Discontents: Meanings, Myths, and Modern Sexualities*. London: Routledge and Kegan Paul, 1985.

Wells, Ida B. "The Case Stated." In *A Red Record: Tabulated Statistics and Alleged Causes of Lynchings in the United States, 1892—1893—1894*. 1895. Reprinted in *Lynching in America: A History in Documents*, edited by Christopher Waldrep, 4–6. New York: New York University Press, 2006.

"Westinghouse Is Satisfied." *New York Times*, August 7, 1890, 2.

Wilson, Edward O. *Consilience: The Unity of Knowledge*. New York: Knopf, 1998.

———. "Foreword from the Scientific Side." In *The Literary Animal: Evolution and the Nature of Narrative*, edited by Jonathan Gottschall and David Sloan Wilson, vii–xi. Evanston, IL: Northwestern University Press, 2005.

Wolch, Jennifer R., and Jody Emel, eds. *Animal Geographies: Place, Politics and Identity in the Nature-Culture Borderlands*. London: Verso, 1998.

Wolfe, Cary. *Animal Rites: American Culture, the Discourse of Species, and Posthumanist Theory*. Chicago: University of Chicago Press, 2003.

———. *What Is Posthumanism?* Minneapolis: University of Minnesota Press, 2010.

———, ed. *Zoontologies: The Question of the Animal*. Minneapolis: University of Minnesota Press, 2003.

Worster, Donald. *Nature's Economy: A History of Ecological Ideas*. 2nd ed. Cambridge: Cambridge University Press, 1994.

Zimmerman, Francis. *The Jungle and the Aroma of Meats: An Ecological Theme in Hindu Medicine*. Berkeley: University of California Press, 1987.

Zinn, Howard. *A People's History of the United States: 1492–Present*. New York: HarperCollins, 1999.

Zuk, Marlene. *Sexual Selections: What We Can and Can't Learn about Sex from Animals*. Berkeley: University of California Press, 2002.

Index

Printed in the USA/Agawam, MA
March 14, 2014

586246.044